Offenbach

Drawing by Richard Cole

The Illustrated Lives of the Great Composers.

Offenbach

Peter Gammond.

Omnibus Press
London/New York/Sydney/Cologne

Cover design and art direction by Pearce Marchbank.
Cover photography by Gered Mankowitz, Rembrandt Bros.
Cover styled by Annie Hanson.

© Peter Gammond 1980.
First published by Midas Books in 1980.
This edition published in 1986 by Omnibus Press, a division of Book Sales Limited.

Order No. OP42431
UK ISBN 0.7119.0257.7

Exclusive Distributors:
Book Sales Limited,
78 Newman Street,
London W1P 3LA,
England.
Omnibus Press,
GPO Box 3304,
Sydney,
NSW 2001,
Australia.
To The Music Trade Only:
Music Sales Limited,
78 Newman Street,
London W1P 3LA,
England.

Acknowledgments

This book has been compiled with the help and encouragement of The Offenbach Society and its Committee under the chairmanship of Arthur F. Spencer-Bolland. I am particularly indebted to the very considerable help of Max Morris who made many valuable additions to the manuscript and to Geoffrey Wilson who kept a careful eye on the French material; also to Antoine Mitchell. I am also indebted to Richard Duployen for a very thorough vetting of details and many helpful suggestions, and to Andrew Lamb who put Offenbach information at my disposal. Photography by Roy Faulkner.

'To my Wife'

Dear Anna,

I use the words of Offenbach, not because I lack any of my own, as you well know, but because they say what I want to say with style and sincerity – 'I beg you will allow me to dedicate this volume to you, not for what it contains or for what it is worth, but because I love to manifest in every way my esteem and my affection for you'.

(From Offenbach's 'America and the Americans')

Contents

Introduction

I looked on with the greatest pleasure while all these people flew about in sheer delight to the music of my *Figaro* arranged for quadrilles and waltzes. For here they talk about nothing but *Figaro*. Nothing is played, sung or whistled but *Figaro*. No opera is drawing like *Figaro*. Nothing, nothing but *Figaro*. Certainly a great honour for me!

In such gratified terms did Wolfgang Amadeus Mozart write to his young pupil Baron Gottfried von Jacquin in a letter from Prague in 1787.

In those few words Mozart expressed all the delight of an artist that his creation had become the common property of the world. At this stage of history it signified a release from bondage that had confined and irritated musicians and painters for so long. They had good cause to be grateful for rich and noble patronage when there was no other sure way of earning a living; but it could become a tyranny which a good-natured man like Josef Haydn bore with fortitude, which Mozart found irksome and which Beethoven detested and fought against. A growing demand for public concerts helped, but it was the theatre that was gradually to offer the way of escape. It is all too easy to over-simplify a description of the process which took many decades, and whose circumstances varied from country to country and person to person, but the first half of the 19th century saw a remarkable change in the position of the artist and the gradual commercialisation of the arts.

In the first place it was a social change. As wealth gradually spread beyond the aristocracy and the rich upper middle-class traders, firstly to the large and increasingly well-educated middle class as a whole – though not to the working classes until almost the end of the century – composers and authors could depend more and more on the simple rule of commerce: Provide the goods that the general public wants and you can make a fortune. Today the commercial or 'popular' musical world is a totally different one from the academic or so-called 'serious'. Composers like Irving Berlin and Richard Rodgers would be disgruntled not to find people singing and whistling their works for they are written expressly for that purpose, and they, rather than the serious composers, who depend as greatly on official patronage to get their works produced as the early composers did on the nobility, are the real heirs to Mozart, Lully, Rossini, Donizetti and Offenbach.

Wolfgang Amadeus Mozart
(1756-1791)

What Mozart wrote in his letter was symptomatic of a growing, if not often openly expressed, belief that music, especially theatre music, was for 'everybody'. The divergence of music into two distinct streams, 'art for art's sake' and 'music for the people', was only hinted at in Mozart's time and for at least another sixty years composers were simply pulled toward such a situation because more and more people could afford to be entertained and so demanded material which suited their unacademic tastes. As the potential audience grew, so many new theatres were built and dance halls and ballrooms abounded. These created a further demand for works that could draw an audience in the face of growing competition and writers who could turn out the material quickly and efficiently. The advent of cheaper music printing, pioneered in England by Novello, likewise promoted a growing demand for music in the home.

The great opera houses of the world, La Scala, Milan, the Paris Opéra, Covent Garden, had been founded at the end of the 18th century and, in addition to the constant rebuilding forced on them by the prevalent fire hazard, so common in theatres in those candle and gaslit days, they were all enlarged and modernised during the early part of the 19th century. New theatres specifically intended for more popular forms of opera sprang up in profusion as the century proceeded. It is interesting to note that, by the time the working classes had added their demands in the latter half of the century, there were, by 1868, some two hundred premises devoted to an entertainment called 'music-hall' in London and another three hundred scattered throughout the rest of the British Isles.

The demands of 'the general public', a body hard to define categorically, can roughly be summed up as a good story coherently told (hence the growing tendency to supplant rambling recitatives with spoken dialogue and to keep the action moving), good melodies to hum, whistle and, in other forms, dance to (a tendency therefore toward isolated arias and choruses dramatically prepared for by the preceding dialogue), and plenty of spectacle. The Paris Opéra, for instance, which kept a large corps-de-ballet on its payroll, always demanded that operas staged there should have a built-in ballet, whether this assisted the plot or not. Eminent composers meekly obliged.

L'Opéra, Paris

Ferdinand Hérold
(1791-1833)

Adolphe Adam (1803-1856)

Following in the light-hearted and melodious tradition of *The Marriage of Figaro* came the great Italian composers of the golden age of opera – Gioacchino Rossini (1792-1868), whose *Barber of Seville* in 1816 soon established itself as one of the most popular works of all time, followed by many more transient pieces before the great final offering to l'Opéra (ballet and spectacle included), *William Tell*; Giuseppe Verdi (1813-1901) with such lasting triumphs as *Rigoletto* (1851), *Il Trovatore* and *La Traviata* of 1853; Vincenzo Bellini (1801-1835) and Gaetano Donizetti (1797-1848).

It was one particular work by Donizetti that suggests, in this context, a real turning point in the history of opera – *La Fille du Régiment* premièred at the Opéra-Comique in Paris in 1840. Rich in melody, with well-timed story and well-contrived ensembles, sparkling with good humour, it provided rich material for errand-boys, barrel-organs and the contrivers of polkas and quadrilles based on the operatic hits of the day. And, indeed, if we listen afresh to such arias as Maria's 'Chacun le sait, chacun le dit', extolling the virtues of *le régiment*, we are already quite firmly in the world of operetta. Its 'ra-ta-plans' and 'ta-ran-taras' and its satirical view of the military world are the basic material of a large part of the light operatic fare to come in the last decades of the 1800s.

If Paris appeared as the simmering pot of operatic revolution, it was not merely because the foreign composers found it a profitable market. French composers, likewise under the influence of Mozart, had gradually been building a substantial repertoire of their own particular brand of light opera under the general term of *opéra-comique*, the equivalent of the Italian *opera buffa*. Here also the trend was toward action in dialogue and isolated melodic arias, couplets and ensembles. Tuneful but essentially respectable conservatoire-trained composers like François Boïeldieu (1775-1834), Daniel Auber (1782-1871), Ferdinand Hérold (1791-1833) and Adolphe Adam (1803-1856), (following in the steps of Lully, Gluck, Grétry and Méhul) are now better remembered for their compact overtures than for what followed on the stage. These were the formidable rivals, along with the Italians and a few Germans such as Otto Nicolai (1810-1849), that an up-and-coming young composer of the 1850s would have to displace.

By 1850 it could have been clear to anyone able to soar above the complicated and animated musical scene, particularly in Paris, that music was all set to depart in two self-possessed ways. All that was needed was a dominant pioneering figure to give the final impetus; a leader, perhaps even a scapegoat. In view of all that had happened, as briefly sketched above, and of what was happening on all sides, it is probably not wise to give all the credit to one person. But if one person has to be singled out as the founding figure of true French opérette, it must be Jacques Offenbach, a young Jewish musician from Cologne, who found himself thrust into this competitive musical world in 1835 when he left the Conservatoire. In his adopted country of France he helped to make operetta a distinctive genre. It could probably have happened there without him. It was the unfavourable circumstances that pushed him into his historic rôle rather than favourable ones. But even more clearly he was the cause of much that was to happen in other countries – in England he inspired Gilbert and Sullivan; in Vienna Johann Strauss and, by a linked chain of reactions, all the turbulent and revolutionary things that were eventually to happen in America. Could we not even find echoes of Offenbach in the bright operetta strains of the modern Spanish zarzuela? There were other candidates for leadership such as Offenbach's close rival Hervé but it just happened that Offenbach was better at the game than anyone else, being both consistent and adventurous; so it was he who we must praise (or blame) for the clear emergence of the new, commercial, popular genre of theatrical entertainment that developed and thrived under such names as operetta, *opéra-bouffe*, light operetta and later musical comedy – or just plain 'musical'. Even today there are many people who would see this as a not unmixed blessing but, prejudice apart, there is no doubt that Offenbach played the major part in sparking off a musical revolution that had repercussions as great and far-reaching as any of its political or industrial equivalents.

Peter Gammond, Shepperton, 1979

1 Monsieur 'O' de Cologne

It is a fascinating paradox that the man behind the unmistakably French music of Les Bouffes-Parisiens – a music full of 'verve and reckless gaiety', as Constant Lambert described it, on the one hand, full of the elusive melancholy that we also find in Mozart, on the other – should turn out to be one of those enigmatic wandering Jews of the creative world who seem to have been responsible for nine-tenths of the best in popular music. It makes the chemistry of what happened to music in those eventful years of Parisian dominance interestingly devious.

There is no long family tree to examine. The first of Offenbach's ancestors to come to the attention of the public records was his grandfather Juda Eberst who had settled in Offenbach-am-Main, was the possessor of an excellent tenor voice and made a living by giving music lessons. Amongst his pupils were the offspring of the Rothschild family in the nearby town of Frankfurt of which Offenbach is now a suburb. A son, to be named Isaac Juda Eberst, was born on October 26th, 1779 and inherited his musical talent. At first Isaac was apprenticed to the safe and steady trade of bookbinding. This suited neither his inherited musical ambitions nor his wandering inclinations, so he left home at the age of twenty, earning a living as cantor in the synagogues of any towns he passed through by day and by playing his violin in taverns in the evenings. In 1802 he arrived in Deutz, a suburb of Cologne noted for a flourishing nightlife of gambling salons, inns and dance-halls. There were several itinerant Jewish bands in the area, offering ready and varied employment for a young bachelor musician, so Isaac Juda Eberst found himself lodgings and became a resident of Deutz. Known amongst his acquaintances as *der Offenbacher* he saw therein a better name for an ambitious musician than Eberst and began to call himself Offenbach. Under this name, in 1805, he married Marianne Rindskopf, the daughter of a respectable Deutz money-changer and lottery-promoter. During the ensuing years of the wars of liberation the entertainment business suffered many slumps and Isaac occasionally had to resort to his old trade of bookbinding in order to make a living. In 1816 the family moved into Cologne and found a small house in a courtyard off the Grossen Griechenmarkt which led to a school (all the buildings thereabouts disappeared in new housing developments sometime

Isaac Offenbach, the composer's father

Offenbach's Op. 1

after 1870). A youngster named Albert Wolff (later to become music critic of *Le Figaro* and to write an introduction for Offenbach's journal of his 1875 American trip) attended the school and knew the family well. He recollected:

The house in which Jacques was born was small. I see it still, on the right of the courtyard, at the farthest end of which my school was situated. The front door was low and narrow; the kitchen, clean and bright, was located under the hall; copper saucepans hanging on the walls in beautiful order; the mother busy at her range; on the right, after crossing the kitchen, a sitting-room looking out on the street. The father reclining in his big armchair near the window, when not giving music lessons; he had a good voice and played on the violin. Mr Offenbach was already an elderly man; I have preserved a two-fold remembrance of the good man; when, on leaving school, I made too much noise in the yard, he would come out and administer to me a gentle correction, and on holidays he would cram me with cakes, in the making of which Mother Offenbach had no rival in the town.

14

Isaac taught singing and violin, flute and guitar playing. He was an intelligent man who composed both for his own purposes and for the synagogue, wrote verse and occasional tracts on religion expressing strong beliefs mingled with rationalist ideas on Jewish emancipation. These included two publications which achieved some fame: *Hagyadah* (a story of the Israelites' flight from Egypt) and a Prayer Book for the use of the young. The other industry which Isaac and his wife engaged in with typical Jewish fervour, and in spite of a precarious income, was raising a family. The important event for the musical world came on June 20th, 1819 when the seventh child and second son arrived and was named Jakob. He grew up with his elder brother Julius and four surviving sisters, studying at the adjacent school and playing in the nearby streets lined with second-hand shops. At six he was taught by his father to play the violin and became his parents' special pride and joy when his exceptional musical talents began to emerge. At the age of eight he started to compose songs and dances. At the age of nine he revealed a special interest in the cello and as soon as he was big enough to cope with the instrument he was allowed to take it up and was given lessons by an eccentric professor in Cologne called Joseph Alexander. Albert Wolff also remembered him:

I used to see [him] sometimes in the street, wearing a threadbare coat with brass buttons, the tails of which reached down to his calves, a cane with an ivory handle, a brown wig, and one of those broad-brimmed hats then in fashion. Despite his comparatively comfortable income, Herr Alexander, the professor, was generally considered the greatest miser in the town. It was said that he had once exhibited great talent; and he was known in his own neighbourhood by the glorious name of 'the Artiste'. It was from him that Jacques took lessons at the rate of twenty-five cents each. The end of the month was generally a hard time for the Offenbach family; but they deprived themselves of many little comforts in order to save the price of the lessons, for Herr Alexander did not trifle with such matters; the twenty-five cents had to be spread on the table before the beginning of the lesson. No money, no music!

As the family continued to grow to a hungry brood of ten a certain amount of child-labour became essential. The three most musical, Jakob, Julius and sister Isabella were formed into a trio whose talents were hired out to local dance halls, cafés and taverns. They offered a repertoire of operatic arrangements and current dance music. Isaac had by now achieved the permanent post of Cantor to the Jewish faithful of Cologne and, with his modest stipend and what his hand-reared trio brought in, he kept to an unswerving determination to give them all the musical education they needed. Jakob was the star, billed as a prodigy, with a modest understatement of his true age. He was moved to a more progressive teacher, a cellist with a local reputation as a composer, named

Bernhard Breuer. Offenbach obviously enjoyed his time with Herr Breuer for he later dedicated his 'Op. 1' to him: *Divertimento über Schweizerlieder* for cello, two violins, viola and bass (J. M. Busch, Cologne, 1833). Offenbach's proletarian musical influences can only be hypothetically pieced together: a professional middle-brow mélange of Italian opera, café songs, Colognese carnival music, the popular dance tunes of the time. In distant Vienna young musicians like Josef Lanner (1801-1843), Johann Strauss (1804-1849), were already setting new trends in the dance halls; contemporaries such as Franz von Suppé (1819-1895) were learning their trade at the conservatoires; the younger Johann Strauss (1825-1899), in spite of parental discouragement, was, like Offenbach, fiddling in lowly taverns; in London Arthur Sullivan (1842-1900) was not even thought of.

Isaac Offenbach's ambition for his children was not bounded by the local world of music that he had, of necessity, brought them up in. The only place for a talented fourteen-year-old like Jakob (and his eighteen-year-old brother Julius) to learn and thrive was in Paris. At the Conservatoire, in the city where being Jewish or any other nationality didn't much matter, Jakob could become at least another Mendelssohn (already blossoming as conductor and composer) if not a Mozart or a Beethoven. Isaac and his sons took the long and arduous road to Paris in November 1833, leaving a weeping mother behind to imagine all the fearful things that could happen to them in such a wicked and avaricious place. They went straight to the formidable Luigi Cherubini, celebrated composer and director of the Conservatoire, with no doubt that such an infant prodigy as Jakob would be welcomed with open arms. Cherubini

Cologne, from an old print

Luigi Cherubini (1760-1842)

was a difficult man and he was backed by a rule that forbade foreign entrants to the Conservatoire. Even Liszt had been turned away on these grounds in 1823 and had found no way round the ruling of the intractable Cherubini. At fourteen, Offenbach was really too young to be officially admitted, but Cherubini was up against a practised preacher in the elder Offenbach who spoke with such eloquence and at such length that the stern professor consented to an audition. Jakob played his audition piece with such brilliance that, to the surprise of all, Cherubini stopped him halfway and said: 'Enough, young man, you are now a pupil of this Conservatoire.'

But it seems that the background of popular culture had already taken too strong a hold. Offenbach was never happy at the Conservatoire. The pages of his personal copy of one of Signor Cherubini's efficient but dull textbooks was well margined with disinterested doodles; even the cello lessons under M. Vaslin bore little fruit. In order to provide their keep and decent lodgings, the Offenbach boys earned a little by singing in a Paris synagogue choir. Isaac tried to find a permanent post in Paris but failed and eventually returned to Cologne, leaving his talented offspring to their fate. Julius passed dutifully through the Conservatoire, became a violin teacher, played for many years in his brother's orchestra at Les Bouffes-Parisiens and later conducted it, and died three days after his celebrated relative. He had maintained a frustrating rôle for an elder brother.

Jakob found the tyrannical discipline of Cherubini and his staff increasingly irksome and meanwhile dreamed of the theatre. Following one or two brushes with authority he left the Conservatoire, after only one year's incarceration, and, as *Grove* says: "without having distinguished himself or shown any taste for serious study". Cherubini once again tightened up his regulations

Fromental Halévy
(1799-1862)

18

about foreigners. So there was Offenbach in the battle-torn, rather desperate city of Paris, which he already instinctively felt to be his home and his stage, about to fend for himself. He was full of ambition and anxious not to disappoint his family, but he knew already that the world of academic music was not for him. The theatre and all its trappings, sights and sounds, attracted him most. He managed one or two temporary jobs in pit orchestras before getting a steady engagement at the Opéra-Comique. His friend at the time was the leading cellist in the band, a young man with a rather more successful career at the Conservatoire behind him, named Hippolyte Seligmann. They enjoyed themselves in the pit, their time mainly spent in annoying and deceiving the conductor. Seligmann was still studying his instrument under the celebrated cellist Norblin and Offenbach managed to afford the same luxury, obviously to his satisfaction as he was later to reward M. Norblin with the dedication of his *Introduction and Valse mélancolique* 'par son élève Jacques O.' Op. 14.

The great name in Paris opera just then was Fromental Halévy and Offenbach played in the pit for several of his works. On the strength of this he begged a free ticket from the composer for his new masterpiece at l'Opéra, *La Juive*. He had the honour of sitting with the composer and was so obviously appreciative that Halévy, then chorus-master at l'Opéra, agreed to give him lessons in composition and theatrical orchestration. Offenbach immediately put his new-found knowledge to good use at the Opéra-Comique where he was occasionally allowed to provide some pieces of incidental music. He was also able to help the young composer Friedrich von Flotow with his scores of *Martha* and *La Stradella*, which are said to bear his musical fingerprints; and he orchestrated *Le Naufrage de la Méduse*, a work arranged by a number of composers.

It was now the inevitable time of loneliness and frustration that the teenage creative artist passes through. The elation of being near the heart of the musical world offers only spasmodic relief from the sense of making no headway toward becoming one of its leading lights. The pride at being a man of the world in a worldly city gives way to frustration and loneliness. How often he must have wished that he could take flight and rush back to the bright little house in Cologne and the practical friendship of the large family that he loved and longed for. But he knew that he had to earn a living, at an age when most boys were still students. He later told how an old tune he knew in Cologne would insistently come back into his mind to remind him of his hard but happy childhood. Then, at other times, drinking and laughing with his friends and fellow-aspirants to fame, he would imagine that the world was only teasing him by keeping him waiting and that fame and fortune were just around the corner. The family back in Cologne, in turn, were heartened to

Louis Antoine Jullien
(1812-1860)

have a letter from Halévy to assure them that Jacques, as he was now known, was going to be a great composer.

The 'great' composer in the meantime had to content himself with writing a few dance-tunes in response to the constant demand for such passing trifles. The café-concerts, in the Parisian mode, half indoor and half outdoor, centres of eating, drinking, listening and dancing, were avid purchasers of the right material. The can-can was highly fashionable at this time but had such a low reputation that Offenbach as yet avoided making close acquaintance. He was due to elevate it to an art-form later when he could lend it respectability. Paris was full of great figures of the Lanner and Strauss stamp. There was Philippe Musard (1793-1859) who conducted the Opéra balls and was known as the 'King of Quadrilles'. He and Offenbach did not get on with each other so there was no casual free-lancing to come from that direction. The famous Tolbecque family were a waning influence by the 1830s when Musard took over and his great rival Louis Jullien was beginning to build a reputation at the Jardin Turc in the Boulevard du Temple. Jullien, handsome and conceited, later to become the legendary showman of conductors, white-gloved and be-cloaked, was about to conquer Europe and America. He was a prolific composer himself but, probably through the influence of Halévy, he accepted a number of waltz-suites from Offenbach and played them during the summer season of 1836. One of these, *Fleurs d'hiver*, became fairly popular and was played at the Opéra and Opéra-Comique balls later in the year. The work was praised in a Paris musical paper but the critic hastened to add a warning that young M. Offenbach should not start thinking that he was ready to supplant Messrs. Lanner and Strauss. Other waltz suites he wrote at this time were *Die Jungfrauen* and *Les Amazons*. The following year he supplied the Jardin-Turc with a waltz, *Rebecca*, which aroused some adverse criticism because it was based on 15th-century Jewish liturgical tunes. Offenbach replied that his father never hesitated to sing operatic tunes in the synagogue. Another waltz *Brunes et blondes* passed without comment.

No doubt Offenbach, had he really felt it his forte, could have dethroned them all with his special talent for gay and abandoned music. He could certainly have cornered the can-can market at any-

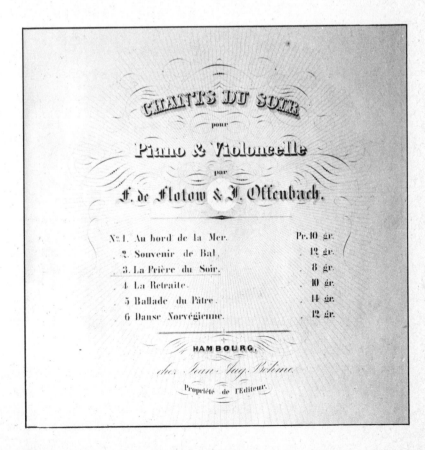

Cello pieces of 1839 by
Offenbach and Flotow

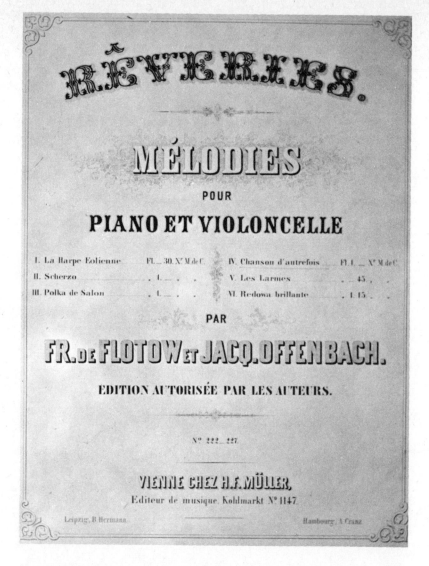

REVERIES.

MÉLODIES

POUR

PIANO ET VIOLONCELLE

I. La Harpe Eolienne. Fl. 30. N.^o M.de C. IV. Chanson d'autrefois Fl. 1. N.^o M.de C.
II. Scherzo . 1. . . V. Les Larmes . 45 .
III. Polka de Salon . 1. . . VI. Redowa brillante . 1.15.

PAR

FR.DE FLOTOW ET JACQ.OFFENBACH.

EDITION AUTORISÉE PAR LES AUTEURS.

N° 222–227.

VIENNE CHEZ H.F.MÜLLER,
Editeur de musique, Kohlmarkt N° 1147.

Leipzig, B Hermann Hambourg, A Cranz

Further collaborations by Offenbach and Flotow

time he wanted. But there was always one eye on the theatre and a feeling that this was the world to be conquered in spite of all setbacks. In 1839 he managed to get his name into a programme by writing the incidental music for the Anicet Bourgeois and Edouard Brisebarre comedy *Pascal et Chambord* which was produced at the Palais-Royal theatre. It was a fiasco from a musical viewpoint, and was made farcical by the clowning of its leading actor. It brought only meagre rewards. For the time being Offenbach relinquished his theatrical ambitions for a line that looked more profitable – that of virtuoso cellist. Friedrich von Flotow, already making his reputation as a composer in Paris, helped to introduce Offenbach to the fashionable salons. Between them they wrote two suites of cello pieces – *Chants du Soir* and *Rêveries*, which were soon published in Vienna on the strength of the growing reputation of the two young

One of the 'Chants du Soir',
the Offenbach style already
established

composers. Offenbach provided the melodies, which are curiously
prophetic of operetta talents to come; Flotow wrote some rather
awkward piano accompaniments to the quirkish tunes. They are
interesting in their foreshadowing of all the elements to be found in
the operettas. The flowing waltz of 'Au bord de la mer', the comic
3/4 of 'Souvenir de Bal' and the 'Redowa brillante' (in 3/8), the
folky simplicity of 'Danse Norvégienne', 'Scherzo' and 'Chanson
d'autrefois', the military nonsense of 'La Retraite', the gaiety of
'Polka de Salon'. They could now be enjoyably arranged into a
ballet score as Rossini's 'Sins of Old Age' have been. But these
would be the 'Follies of Youth'! These pieces the future composers
of *Martha* and *Orpheus in the Underworld* (works linked only by
their tunefulness) played together, the ink hardly dry on the hastily

23

written manuscripts, at a fashionable gathering at the house of the Countess Bertin de Vaux (the wife of an important newspaper owner and diplomat); and they went down very well. The skinny, six-and-a-half-stone, but attractive and loquacious Offenbach was, according to Flotow, a great success. He was invited back to the Countess's salon on many occasions and consequently to other fashionable evenings. So lucrative did the business become that he was soon able to give up his cello post with the Opéra-Comique to become a society entertainer. He also took the opportunity to provide further cello pieces and, in spite of the lavish competition around, turned out numerous ballads in the prevailing Italian opera style – lush melody over an arpeggio accompaniment – that served the Victorian drawing-rooms so well for so many years. His first professional appearance as a cellist was at Pape's Musical Emporium in January 1839 at which his 'romance dramatique', *Jalousie* (words by Aimée Gourdin), was also heard. Brother Jules took part in the same concert. Offenbach implemented his role of cello virtuoso with several works fully exploiting the instrument – *Fantasie über Themas polnischer Lieder* (republished in 1841 as *Fantaisie sur des Thèmes Russes*); and studies for two cellos – '*École de Violoncelle*'. The cello-playing took up more of his time, Jacques following his father's advice not to become too ambitious as a composer for the present but to make his way on the strength of his natural ability as a musician. He occasionally visited his home town, and enjoyed being a local celebrity. With Jules, he gave two concerts at the Cologne Assembly Rooms, with his proud family in attendance. Albert Wolff again remembers:

This earliest and most accurate impression which I have preserved of Jacques' youth, coincides with the first visit he paid his parents on returning from Paris. It was an event for all the friends of the family, where, for a long time past, nothing had been talked of except Jacques, who, it was currently reported, was coining millions in Paris by playing on the violoncello. Nobody in Cologne suspected that the father of Offenbach's son earned his scanty living with great difficulty on the banks of the Seine. Through the mere fact that he was listened to in Paris, the city of artists and rich people, no one ever doubted but what Jacques must be a millionaire. It was said in the town: 'Father Offenbach is a lucky man; it appears that his son is coming back with big diamonds instead of buttons in his waistcoat, and that his fortune is reckoned by hundreds of thousands of francs'. It was not this which drew me to the Offenbachs. In our youth we have but very vague idea of wealth; a ten-cent piece or the vaults of the Bank of France seem about alike; but if, in the evening, at the hour at which Jacques was expected, I found myself among the friends of the house, it was because on the morning of the same day I had smelt the savoury perfume of those famous cakes; I had been struck with astonishment at this extraordinary occurrence, for it was not the eve of a holiday. But, in reply to my eager inquiries, Mother Offenbach had replied: 'This is a fête-day for us all, my boy; my son Jacques comes back this evening from Paris. Come in by and by, and have some cakes; I can tell you that I have spared neither eggs, nor butter, nor sugar'.

When about sun-down I crossed the threshold of the house, in the Rue de la Cloche, Jacques, who was sitting on the sofa by the side of his father, whilst his mother was getting supper ready for the beloved son – Jacques, I repeat, was for me but an object of the greatest curiosity. But my heart beat faster as I caught sight of a bottle of Rhein-wine standing on the white table-cloth between two dishes filled with delicacies, the whole sparkling under the light of a small brass chandelier, which was only lighted on great occasions. At that moment there was not in the town a happier house than this. Relatives and friends came in one after another, to welcome Jacques; and each time a fresh visitor came in, the dishes were sent around, and each time I helped myself to some fresh delicacy, so that, as a natural consequence, a formidable fit of indigestion nailed me for a week to my bed.

But the next visit to Cologne at the end of the year was to be a sad occasion. The youngest member of the family, Michel, died of typhoid fever at the age of twelve and Offenbach and his brother stayed at the family home for a while when his mother became seriously ill. They gave another Cologne concert, which included Offenbach's *Grande scène espagnole* for string sextet (later orchestrated) which was highly praised in the local papers, and a *Grand Duo on themes by Auber* (written in collaboration with Julius). It was to be the last united family occasion. Offenbach's mother died a week later and on November 17th, 1840 he returned to Paris feeling that this must surely be the time for him to step out into the world and establish his name and his independence.

He took every opportunity to play in public, often for no payment. Although he made himself ill with overwork, he achieved his aim of becoming a fashionable virtuoso. Through this kind of fame, which was really of secondary importance to him, he knew that he could build opportunities to exploit his true calling as a composer. But it was to be as a very special sort of composer, a satirist, a popular entertainer, not as an exponent of the treacly drawing-room and salon material which he now had to play. More and more he was satirising the very stuff that gave him his reputation. In 1842 he had upset the critics by setting the *Fables* of La Fontaine to what they considered highly frivolous music, including a gay waltz. La Fontaine was later to supply the inspiration for several Offenbach operettas. In the Spring of 1843 he organised a concert at the Salle Herz which was made up entirely of his own music. It was a great success. One of the most popular items was a comic duet, 'Le Moine bourru', which had a clear flavour of similar duets in operettas to come – *Geneviève de Brabant* for instance. It satirised Victor Hugo and grand opera. It was a mild taste of Offenbach's destined artistic rampage. As a cellist he was now well-known, sufficiently so as to be caricatured in the papers with arms, legs and head growing out of a cello. His strange, bird-like appearance was a boon to artists and, without doubt, it did much to foster his public image. It is always a great help to look like a genius as well as being one. The next time he returned to Cologne he found the papers well briefed by his admiring father, and his reputation as a Parisian celebrity beyond question. He proved he was a serious composer by the performance of his *Grosse Concert-Phantasie*. This reputation was enhanced on his return to Paris by the writing of a song called 'À toi' (words Numa Armand) that soon became a best-seller. It was dedicated to a young lady called Herminie d'Alcain, the daughter of a rich hostess at whose soirées he had played. Published in English as 'Love Me' (Francis Bros. & Day), it was sung in the London production of Planquette's *Les Cloches de Corneville* in 1890 by Pattie Laverne. In April 1843 there was an important concert in Paris at which he played a brilliant fantasia on themes from Rossini's operas entitled *Hommage à Rossini* (which no doubt endeared him to the great composer for life) and his fine *Musette* for

Paroles de M: Numa Armand.

Musique de

JACQUES OFFENBACH

From the cover of the early song success 'A toi'

Gioacchino Rossini
(1792-1868), an Offenbach
admirer

cello and orchestra (described as an 'Air de ballet in 17th century style') which was to become a standard piece in the cello repertoire. At this point he became engaged to the charming Herminie. As final proof of his abilities and his desirability as a husband, he undertook a tour of France, then of Germany; and in 1844 he went overseas for the first time and arrived in the untried territory of the London musical world. He made his London début in the concert-room of Her Majesty's Theatre on May 15th in a 'grand morning concert' arranged by Madame Puzzi. His fellow artistes were Giulia Grisi, Fanny Persiani, Julie Dorus-Gras, the Lablaches and Joseph Staudigl – all famous virtuosi of the day. The accompanists were no less than Michael Costa and Julius Benedict, two of London's leading conductor composers. So Offenbach sailed into London in top-class company and the *Musical World* graciously remarked: 'Herr Offenbach, a violoncellist, made a highly favourable sensation and may be pronounced one of the masters of the instrument.' The *Dramatic and Musical Review* said 'He is on the violoncello what Paganini was on the Violin.' Another concert followed on June 10th and his odd appearance inspired one writer to describe him as 'the religious Offenbach'. Four days later he appeared with Anne Thillon, the young Joseph Joachim and Alfred Shaw with Louise Dulcken and F. Mendelssohn-Bartholdy at the pianos. It was entirely in keeping with the musical tastes of the day that Offenbach increasingly used his cello as a means of somewhat vulgar virtuoso display. Indeed one critic remarked that he made it sound like everything but a cello. He had a flair for imitation of other instruments and even animals. At a Melodists' Club concert he played his 'ancient dance tune of the (thirteenth) century' and 'introduced a capital imitation of the bagpipes which was loudly applauded and encored'. He became as popular in London as he had been in Paris, and would appear in public for nothing if the publicity was worth it; at the same time demanding high payment for private engagement. The general opinion was reflected in *The Musical World* of June 27th which commented:

He certainly is an artist of first-rate ability, and, we might add, agility on his instrument, and moreoever a man deserving the respect of every musician for his acquirements and of every gentleman for his deportment. Herr Offenbach has been heard at several of our most fashionable concerts, and has played with success at Court before Her Majesty and Prince Albert, from which illustrious personages he received, in addition to the highest marks of admiration, a valuable diamond ring.*

*(Although it was also reported in *The Times* and *Illustrated London News* that Offenbach had performed before Queen Victoria and her guests the Czar of Russia and the King of Saxony at Windsor Castle on June 6th, 1844 [works described as *Prière* and *Bolero for Piano and Cello*] a letter to the Registrar of the Royal Archives produced no official confirmation in the following reply:

Offenbach was always a favourite of the cartoonists (top) A German caricature (bottom) Offenbach portrayed in 1870

'The only records we have here in the Archives for the visit of the Czar of Russia and the King of Saxony in June 1844, give details of the dinners held in the Waterloo Chamber on 4th, 5th and 6th June, but do not mention the music played or the presence of Offenbach. On 6th June, 61 guests attended the dinner. In the Queen's account of the visit of the Czar she mentions the dinner of 6th June and that the Czar led her in and that "after dinner I talked to Lord Aberdeen". She then gives a brief summary of Lord Aberdeen's remarks on that occasion, ending with a note to the effect that: "Mr Parish-Alvars played beautifully on the harp". Her Journal account of the dinner also mentions Parish-Alvars playing but no one else'.)

In the comic press and elsewhere Offenbach continued to be the caricaturists' delight. When he played his cello he seemed to become part of the instrument and his eyes shone with a mad exhilaration to match the frenzy of his playing. In the Paganini tradition of eccentric musicianship, in league with the Devil, and so on – many considered that he had the evil eye. In fact, he rather alarmed some gentle souls. Some wit remarked that it was after he had come face to face with himself in the mirror that he made his hasty decision to get married. It was all good fodder for the legend that he was industriously building.

He now returned to Paris with a substantial bank balance and was able to marry Mademoiselle Herminie d'Alcain on August 14th, 1844. She was eighteen, he was twenty-five. The world seemed to become his oyster. His sights became even more firmly set on the other side of the footlights at the Opéra-Comique which must now surely welcome the natural successor of Auber, Adam, Thomas or, in other tongues, Nicolai, Rossini and Donizetti.

2 *Un compositeur à la porte*

So far Offenbach had mainly made his mark on the world as a performer. Certain of his cello pieces were being widely played, notably the *Musette*, very much a fashionable piece before 1850 and still going strong in the early years of the 20th century; a favourite piece in the repertoire of the popular cello virtuoso August van Biene (composer of *The Broken Melody*) and discussed in great detail in a series *Well-Known Violoncello Solos – How to Play Them* by E. van der Straeten as late as 1908. The song *A toi* had made its modest mark. The young composer, for so long a player of other composers' pieces in the orchestra pit of l'Opéra-Comique, already knew that his real ambition was to write for the theatre, but there were many frustrating years to go before he was to find a way to fulfil this ambition.

The Offenbachs now took up residence in a small house in the Passage Saulnier in Paris which became their campaign headquarters. Offenbach was fortunate in his marriage to Herminie. She was deeply devoted to him and though, in the first struggling years of their marriage, she went through many privations; she was always there to help, comfort and encourage. She rarely intruded on his public life and little is known about her, but she gave him a family life that was a reflection of the happy closely knit family that Jacques had once left in Cologne. When Offenbach died, one of his friends, Victorin de Joncières, said of Herminie that 'she gave him courage, shared his ordeals and comforted him always with tenderness and devotion'. The faithful Albert Wolff wrote in the preface to *Offenbach in America* (which he addressed to Herminie):

Whatever your husband writes, whether music or words, belongs to you by right. There is not a single one among your innumerable friends but is aware that you are not only the best of wives and the most excellent of mothers but that you have also had a part in the works produced by our illustrious composer . . . you have blessed this thoroughly Parisian artiste with a happy and genial home, where his heart has expanded at ease in the midst of a charming, joyful and spirited family.

To Herminie, Wolff credits the tender and romantic side of the composer's output which always contrasts so effectively with the champagne frivolity of those witty and dashing strains reflecting '*la vie parisienne*' by which the world is more inclined to remember

Music written for the Théâtre Français

Gaetano Donizetti
(1797-1848), an inspiration
to Offenbach

Offenbach's music. Offenbach hated to be parted from his family and when, in 1876, he went to America he left his wife and daughters in Paris so that the farewells at Le Havre would be less painful. They were never out of his thoughts till he returned a sadder and wiser man.

During the years in the orchestra of l'Opéra-Comique, then situated at La Salle des Nouveautés in the Place de la Bourse (it was to have many homes before settling in the present elegant edifice in 1882), Offenbach would have added his humble contribution to such important landmarks of opéra-comique as Adam's *Le Châlet* (1834), *Le Postillon de Longjumeau* (1836) and *Le Brasseur de Preston* (1838), Halévy's *L'Éclair* (1835), Clapisson's *Figurante* and Auber's *Le Domino Noir* (1837). He would have absorbed their stylish strains and would no doubt have spent his time imagining what he could do in similar vein given the opportunity. He could scarcely have escaped the enchanting *La Fille du Régiment* with music by Gaetano Donizetti which had arias in it that leaped forward magically into the true operetta vein. With its military theme and its 'ra-ta-plans' it provided operetta with one of its most fruitful settings and we can still feel its influence in later Offenbach master-pieces like *La Grande-Duchesse de Gérolstein*, *Geneviève de Brabant* and *La Fille du Tambour-Major*. Suddenly Offenbach was there on that turbulent evening of February 11th 1840 when Donizetti's delightfully naïve masterpiece first offended the sensibilities of the critic who wrote: 'Le tambour, le trombone, la trompette, les timbales y dominent de la manière la plus affligeante pour les oreilles'. He would have enjoyed all this and taken the work to his heart, perhaps even vowing to cause an equal stir. At the time its *vulgarité*, the not entirely successful début of Marie Borghese who sang the leading role, and its novelty failed to please and it was condemned by many writers – among them Berlioz. Eight years later *La Fille du Régiment* returned to l'Opéra-Comique and became

Le Théâtre Italien, later
l'Opéra-Comique, Paris

Daniel François Auber
(1782-1871)

a firm favourite with the Paris audiences, having already been successful in Italy, Germany and England. A tradition of regularly performing it on Bastille Day was later established. Subsequently critics, with Offenbach and operetta well established, were able to say:

There is a careless gaiety amounting to merriment, there is a frankness, always military, never vulgar, in this music. One might fancy it to have been thrown off during some sunny period of high spirits, when the well-spring of melody was in a sparkling humour. It is slight, it is familiar, it is catching, it is everything that pedants find easy to condemn.

It was, in fact, all that Offenbach was later to stand for and he must have found particular pleasure and instruction in its saucy charms, as he did in the popular chansons that he would have heard in the Paris cafés (he was a great collector of casual airs to incorporate into his own works).

With his head full of such ideas and influences, Offenbach became increasingly impatient to hear his own works being performed on the prestigious stage of l'Opéra-Comique; it seemed the one-and-only place to launch his operatic career. There was a growing taste, too, for burlesque to which Offenbach's nature inclined. So he started a campaign. At the Countess of Vaux's fashionable salon he produced a burlesque of Félicien David's then popular symphonic ode *Le Désert*. The two hundred guests were highly amused at Offenbach's biting satire on this sentimental piece. Then at a concert on April 24th, 1846 he gathered together a collection of seven operatic snippets that he had written and invited the journalists to come along. Their favourable reactions were laid before the director of l'Opéra-Comique, Monsieur Edouard Basset. Weakened by Offenbach's continued assault on his attentions, M. Basset finally agreed to let him write the music for a one-act vaudeville, *L'Alcôve*, which had previously been produced at the Palais-Royal in 1833. Offenbach, delighted, set to work and in a few weeks was back with the required score. There now began a frustrating passage of time during which M. Basset did his best to avoid meeting Offenbach, producing one excuse after another for *L'Alcôve* not appearing on the illustrious stage. A contemporary writer imagines the scene:

C'était en 1846.
    Un jeune homme blond, pâle, nerveux et tenant à la main un rouleau de musique, entrait dans la loge du concièrge de l'Opéra-Comique.
    —Monsieur le directeur, s'il vous plaît? . . .
    —Je crois bien qu'il n'est pas à son cabinet, répondit le cerbère; mais, si c'est quelque chose qu'on puisse lui dire . . .
    —Vous n'allez pas, j'imagine, vous mettre à lui chanter mon opéra.
    —Ah! c'est pour une audition . . . M. le directeur n'y est pas.

Offenbach as a young man
in 1844

– Bien, je repasserai . . . Mais, dites-moi, à quelle heure puis-je le trouver?

– Ah! dame! pour le trouver, ce serait le matin . . . ou bien le soir; à moins que monsieur ne préfère revenir dans le milieu de la journée; il y aurait encore des chances . . .

– Cela suffit.

Le jeune homme blond sortit. Le lendemain, il revint et tint à peu près le langage ci-dessus. Mêmes réponses, même sortie, même retour le surlendemain, et ainsi de suite pendant des semaines et des années.

By the Spring of 1847 Offenbach had had enough of M. Basset and l'Opéra-Comique and impulsively decided to take the piece elsewhere. He financed a concert version which was produced on April 24th, 1847 in front of a fashionable audience at La Salle de la Tour d'Auvergne. In the military vein that Donizetti had introduced, it pleased the listeners and prompted one critic (or was he prompted?) to write: 'On leaving the hall everyone was humming the attractive tunes and wondering why the composer should be left to wait in vain outside the temple [l'Opéra-Comique] which has welcomed so many mediocre talents'. Moreover the work was highly praised by the well-established composer Adolphe Adam who was about to launch his own Théâtre Lyrique. On the strength of his admiration he commissioned Offenbach to write a comic opera for early production.

In January 1848 the Offenbach operetta was announced but a hindrance larger and more ominous than opera directors foiled the struggling composer once again. The Revolution came. It has been said that Offenbach added little to his personal credit at this stage. At the first hint of trouble he left the little house in the Passage Saulnier, packed his bags and found urgent family reasons for taking his wife and first-born daughter back to Cologne. They used all Herminie's savings to make the journey. More or less penniless, they managed to rent a furnished room in Cologne that contained very little beyond an ancient out-of-tune piano. Finding Cologne very little less inflamed by revolutionary passions than Paris, though not so violently manifested, Offenbach changed his christian name back to Jakob and tried to behave like a good Colognial German. He composed some patriotic German songs, of very little artistic value, for use at various political occasions and he played the cello (reviving his Rossini fantasia) at a concert given in celebration of Cologne Cathedral's six-hundredth anniversary. There was now an ageing father to support, so Offenbach, having produced a German version of *L'Alcôve* (as *Marielle* oder *Sergeant und Commandant*) with little success, and having heard that all was once again quiet in Paris, resumed the name of Jacques and went back to continue his own battle with the authorities at the Opéra-Comique. M. Basset had disappeared from the scene on May 1st,

Offenbach as conductor at the Théâtre Français

'Les Voix Mystérieuses'

1848 (perhaps he too lost his head) to be replaced by M. Émile Perrin who was to hold the fort until 1857 and for two short periods in 1862 and 1876.

M. Perrin was no more impressed by Offenbach's budding talents than M. Basset had been, but Offenbach was taken on the orchestral strength again as a cellist and was given occasional opportunities to conduct. It was a frustrating time, enlightened by one command performance at the Elysée where he received the praises of Prince Louis Napoleon, the future Emperor. Nothing was written during the next year and there was a sad event on April 26th, 1850 when his father died and the last links with Cologne were severed.

Soon after, one of those happy chances, that beset the creative artist like summer storms, took place. Sitting and brooding one morning at the Café Cardinal he was approached by a bearded gentleman called Arsène Houssaye who had recently been appointed the Director of the Comédie Française. He knew of Offenbach and admired his talents. It had occurred to him on the spur of the moment that Offenbach would be just the man to re-organise a new and badly needed orchestra for his theatre. He made a modest offer of 6,000 francs (about £240) a year which Offenbach gladly accepted. Offenbach now threw himself enérgetically into enlarging and improving the orchestral forces, lending tone at the performances by adopting the Jullienesque attire of tails and white gloves.

The musical standards improved and the *Directeur* was pleased but the dramatic personnel were not entirely delighted at the attention bestowed on the operatic selections that the orchestra played. They much preferred the music to be bad and the audience indifferent to what went on in the pit. One of the first productions in

An Offenbach score, part of
La Chanson de Fortunio
(1861)

1850 had been of Alfred de Musset's *Le Chandelier* for one of whose characters, Fortunio, played by one Delaunay, a song was required. One of Offenbach's obituarists remembered it well, writing:

all the world knows the *Belle Hélène* and the composer of so many operas in which the mythological Olympus was made the subject of charming lively music. But some of us remember Offenbach in those early days when he used to play violon-cello solos at concerts, and was glad enough to accept the post of chef d'orchestre at the Comédie-Française. It is many years ago since one of the plays of Alfred de Musset, *Le Chandelier*, was brought out at the Française. I was in the house at the time and can even now remember the thrill of delight and surprise which ran through the audience on hearing the melody of the song of Fortunio, 'si vous croyez que je vais dire', which has since become so hackneyed. That was Offenbach's start as a composer. It led him to fame and fortune.

Later in 1852, the song was published as one of a set of six dedicated to *son Altesse Impériale la Princesse Mathilde* under the collective title *Les Voix Mystérieuses*. Marked *avec simplicité* it has that naïve melancholy that we find later used with even more distinction in such a gem as the Letter Song from *La Périchole*. The 'Chanson de Fortunio' was immensely popular and *did* lead to other things; and Offenbach thriftily used it again when he wrote a one-act operetta, *La Chanson de Fortunio*, in 1861.

Offenbach was always an amenable character and gave in to the actors and director of the Comédie-Française, henceforth never allowing the music to obtrude. Quietly, though, he maintained high standards and managed to get his musicians better paid. He suffered a few rebuffs; as when Gounod was brought in to write the incidental music for Ponsard's *Ulysse*; but mainly it was sheer drudgery. He published a few songs and a handful of works for the cello including a Concerto in 1851 (which seems to have vanished), the *Harmonies du Soir* casually designated Op. 68, *Fantaisies faciles*, Ops. 69-74, based on themes by Grétry, Boieldieu, Rossini, Mozart, Bellini and Mompou, *Gaîtés champêtres*, Op. 75, and *Harmonies des Bois*, Op. 76. Of this last, one piece, a reverie 'Le Soir', is still in print in a Peters' Edition *Originalstücke*, together with some items from Op. 29. They all have the same pastoral character and elusive charm.

Another flank attack on the Opéra-Comique was launched in May 1853 when he planned a production of a one-act opéra-comique, *Le Trésor à Mathurin*, with book by Léon Battu, at the Salle Herz. For the evening he employed some of M. Perrin's Opéra-Comique singers; Monsieur Sainte-Foy and Mesdames Meillet, Lemercier and Théric (with Messieurs Roger and Herman-Léon and Mesdames Ugalde and Sabatier, playing other pieces by Offenbach)—but even this strategy failed and, in spite of the gentle charms of the music, the doors of the temple remained unbreached.

Façade of the Théâtre des Variétés

In 1857 the little opera was to be re-fashioned as the then universally popular *Le Mariage aux Lanternes*. What further persuasion could he try? The next one-act piece, *Pépito*, a shapely work with a Spanish setting and book by Léon Battu and Jules Moinaux, which included an amusing take-off of *Largo al factotum*, was dedicated with utmost tact and forgiveness to Mme Émile Perrin, wife of the erring Directeur. It was produced at the reputable Théâtre des Variétés and yet again a friendly critic dropped the hint that such gems ought to be seen at the Opéra-Comique. To no avail. Offenbach even tried a private performance at his own home, playing the main role himself, with the dedicatee and other influential people invited. Still no result! He wrote to his sister in 1854 with the despairing words: 'The golden future I have dreamed of gets no nearer'. A volume of dances for the piano, a modestly successful song 'Le songe d'une Nuit d'hiver' and a few items of incidental music and a one-act operetta *Luc et Lucette*, played at the Salle Herz on May 2nd, were the main products of 1854. There was yet another attempt to get an audition with M. Perrin for a piece tentatively called *Blanche*. On a fruitless journey through the corridors of the theatre, Offenbach met Auber and they talked of music and the difficulties of production. When Auber confided that it had taken him seven years to get his first piece staged at l'Opéra it seemed to close the door for ever.

Offenbach began to feel that the only possible outlet for him was to run his own theatre, as many had before him. Indeed one of his rivals of his own generation, Florimond Roger (better known under his brief stage name of Hervé), had done just this and moreover was turning out the kind of work (including an early can-can) that Offenbach would have liked to have written. Composer, librettist, actor and producer, Hervé had opened his own Folies Nouvelles in 1854 and had mainly filled it with his own creations. It must have been somewhat humbling for Offenbach to have to go to Hervé (who was younger than he was) to suggest that he might be able to write just the sort of thing Les Folies Nouvelles wanted. He flattered Hervé and offered him the score of a work entitled *Oyayaie* ou *La Reine des Îles* with a libretto by Jules Moinaux. It was a weird little work set on a cannibal isle, but a charming piece of nonsense, and Hervé accepted it for production on June 26th, 1855 and it went down well. This was at least encouraging and helped Offenbach to decide to take the plunge on his own account.

3 Les Bouffes-Parisiens

At last Offenbach was about to do the right thing at the right time. Perhaps more by luck, or by a whim of those powers that so capriciously decide our fates, than by considered judgement, for the year 1855 was to be a remarkable one for him and for French culture. At the end of 1852 the Second Empire had been established and Prince Louis-Napoleon was proclaimed Emperor. A new Court had been established and, as London had had such a tremendous *succès d'estime* with the Great Exhibition of 1851, it was deemed right that Paris, amongst a great new furore of reconstruction and re-planning, should have its own International Exhibition. In 1852 a permanent Exhibition site was planned near the Champs-Elysées and a large building, one of the first with an iron structure, was put up. The Exhibition was opened on May 15th, 1855 and was to close on November 15th. It was a modest affair compared with the next one in 1867, but it attracted thousands of visitors, made Paris a popular excursion centre and was visited many times by the Emperor and Empress who even had a special room there for private entertaining. Queen Victoria paid a State visit to Paris in 1855 and found herself not only 'delighted, enchanted,' but (for once) 'amused and interested'.

So what better time, with Paris in carnival mood and full of foreign visitors, for Offenbach to take the great plunge that he had long contemplated as a direct result of his frustrating battle with the Opéra-Comique. He wrote in a letter:

During this period I often thought of the possibility, although it always seemed impossible, of founding a theatre. I told myself that the Opéra-Comique was no longer the home of true comic opera, that really gay, bright, spirited music – in short, the music with real life in it – was being forgotten. Composers working for the Opéra-Comique were simply writing small 'grand' operas. I felt sure that something could be done for young composers like myself who were being kept waiting in idleness. In the Champs-Elysées, there was a little theatre to let, built for the physicist Lazaca but closed for many years. I knew that the Exhibition of 1855 would bring many people into this locality. By May, I had found twenty supporters and on June 15th I secured the lease. Twenty days later, I gathered my librettists and I opened the 'Théâtre des Bouffes-Parisiens'.

The theatre was so small, its seating capacity of fifty guaranteeing only 1,200 francs from a full house, that it was nicknamed the

Bonbonnière – the 'chocolate-box'. It was a wooden building, and the seats were so steeply raked that they were described as being like a ladder with people desperately clinging to the rungs. There was a row of boxes at the top that were so small that you had to open the door to be able to take your coat off. The foyer was simply an open terrace. And yet it seemed that the intimate conditions were an added attraction, for the theatre was soon doing brisk business. The adverts had said that it would open on July 5th and, with a desperate effort by all concerned, the promise was kept. The audience were given plenty to laugh at in the generously packed opening programme which included a prologue *Entrez, Messieurs, Mesdames* written by Ludovic Halévy (under the name of 'Servières') and François Joseph Méry; a 'bouffonnerie musicale' *Les Deux Aveugles* with book by Jules Moinaux, a one-act opéra-comique *La Nuit Blanche* (originally intended to be called *Contrabandista*) – a coy country idyll with book by Edouard Plouvier; and a ballet-bouffon, a sort of pantomime, *Arlequin Barbier* with the music of Rossini's *Il Barbiere di Siviglia* arranged by Offenbach under the name of Lange. With his *Oyayaie* still running at the Folies-Nouvelles, Offenbach was now what he had always wanted to be – a busy and fully employed composer and a successful one to boot. July 5th was truly an evening of musical history. Especially, it marked the beginning of a long and fruitful collaboration between Offenbach and the young Ludovic Halévy, nephew of the Fromental Halévy who had done so much to encourage Offenbach in his early struggling days. Employed as a government official, Halévy had the same kind of burning ambition as Offenbach, but as a playwright. He was delighted when Offenbach approached him, after having been let down by Méry who had only managed part of the Prologue and by Lambert Thiboust who had written only one song. It was pointed out to Halévy that the strange rules of the Parisian licensing authorities only allowed three speaking characters on the stage of a theatre of that size (Hervé was only allowed two) so as four characters were needed, one had to be dumb. The actors had already been engaged for two parts already decided as Fantasy and Bilboquet, with the famous mime Derudder to play Polichinelle. It didn't give Halévy much freedom of choice but he did his best and thus set a famous collaboration on its way. The real success of the evening was *Les Deux Aveugles*, a story of two street musicians who pretend to be blind in order to gain sympathy. Working at adjacent pitches they have a violent quarrel about a coin that has fallen on the pavement. They each try to frighten the other away by telling alarming stories about themselves, finally deciding to settle the matter by playing cards, at which they cheat outrageously. Only the approach of another potential customer silences their argument. Nobody expected much of this rather sordid tale but the two actors

Pradeau and Berthelier put so much into their roles that the audience were helpless with laughter – a much needed tonic in those days. It made them and the Bouffes-Parisiens famous. There was one song, a waltz based on his earlier cello piece *Boléro* (1840) which was soon whistled by everyone and was used as a popular dance item at the Jardin d'Hiver next door. The little work was put into various Parisian revues and was the first Offenbach piece to blazen his name abroad. It was to be played in Vienna as early as 1856 by a touring company from the Palais-Royal, later as *Zwei Arme Blinde* and *Die Beiden Blinden;* in London under its original title at the Hanover Rooms on June 27th, 1856 and later as *A Mere Blind.*

It was as auspicious a beginning to a career as any theatrical entrepreneur could wish for. Parisians and foreign visitors alike clamoured for the limited seats. Offenbach, with his suppressed flair for opportunism now in full flower, next wrote a piece called *La Rêve d'une Nuit d'été* with libretto by Étienne Trefeu in which the main characters were two Englishmen, as alike in their idiocy as Parisians always fondly imagine the English, both chasing the same mademoiselle and providing the French with a popular catch-phrase 'very good'. This was produced on July 30th together with another pantomime written by Offenbach under the name of Lange, *Pierrot Clown.* At this stage Offenbach was visited at his home by a twenty-two-year old singer who was desperately trying to make her way in the Paris theatre with little success. (Like most actresses her age was obscured by fiction. If she was 22 she would have been born around 1833, but 1835 and 1838 are also given in other sources. If the latter she would have been around sixteen or seventeen when first engaged by Offenbach.) She sang a few notes for Offenbach who then made yet another of his fortunate snap decisions. He persuaded her to give up her singing lessons and engaged her for his next piece at Les Bouffes-Parisiens at 200 francs a month. The girl was Hortense Schneider who was to play the leading rôle in most of his later triumphs and by August 31st she was on the minuscule stage in a piece called *Le Violoneux* which Offenbach dedicated to the Marquise de las Marismas. The book was by Mestépès and Chevalet. It was another chapter of immediate success. Hortense was highly praised for her grace and polish, so was Darcier as the old Breton village musician, so was Offenbach for the wit and feeling of his music. The space limitations of the theatre dictated, as did the licensing laws, that the new pieces should be simple one-acters. A further pantomime *Polichinelle dans le Monde* was added to the repertoire on September 19th, a one-act 'bouffonnerie' *Madame Papillon* on October 3rd, and *Paimpol et Périnette* on the 29th. The popular *Les Deux Aveugles* was repeated on numerous occasions (it was soon to achieve 400 performances)

Drawing of Offenbach by Cajat

39

The Halévy-Meilhac
partnership caricatured

and a command performance at the Tuileries was due early in 1856.

Offenbach gave up his conducting post at the Comédie Francaise at the end of 1855 to concentrate on writing these satirical pieces that were now in great demand. They were written hastily but each had at least one attractive song that the audience would remember. Halévy had supplied the book for *Madame Papillon* and he too was finding his feet as a writer. However, the winter was coming and the little wooden theatre was not as cosy as it had seemed in the summer. The exhibition had closed in November and the locality was no longer at the hub of Parisian life. It was time to find something a little better.

In fact, the Théâtre des Jeunes Elèves in the Passage Choiseul which Offenbach was now able to acquire was not all that much bigger than the original theatre. But it had been in regular use for ventriloquist shows and vaudeville and it lay in the centre of Paris near the Italian opera.

Working as usual in tremendous haste, Offenbach brought in the builders and decorators and had the little theatre freshly painted, the boxes gilded, new carpets, curtains and upholstery; all done in three weeks at a cost of some 80,000 francs. It opened on December 29th, 1855 with the most substantial and effective work so far, a 'chinoiserie musicale in 1 act' called *Ba-ta-clan* (or *Ba-ta-Klan*) with book by Ludovic Halévy. By this time they were allowed four characters. Awareness of the East had been growing as a result of the various international exhibitions. Halévy's story was of a king called Fe-ni-han who ruled over a distant kingdom with a total population of twenty-seven. Even with such a small band of subjects to rule there was considerable disenchantment mainly brought about by the king's imperfect command of the Chinese language – for he turns out to be a Parisian. Intending to have five of his citizens honoured, as a result of his imperfect Chinese (a splendid gibberish with traces of French and Italian invented by Halévy), they had been executed instead. This causes some unease amongst other members of the court notably Ké-ki-ka-ko and the female Fé-an-nich-ton, who also turn out to be ex-Parisians, one an erstwhile dandy, the other a retired music hall star, and they plan to flee back to Paris. Their plot is discovered and they are brought before the King. In the course of a long interview Fe-ni-han reveals his personal longing for Paris. In the end all three strike a bargain with the chief of the guard Ko-ko-ri-ko who allows them to escape on the understanding that he takes over the throne. This simple plot allows for a great deal of subtle mockery of court life and intrigue. On the musical side, Offenbach enjoyed many pointed digs at the Italian style opera prevalent at l'Opéra even taking passages from Meyerbeer's *Les Huguenots* and using them for absurd and parodying situations. It was all done most light-

40

heartedly, so that anyone who took offence would reveal his true colours, but the French audience got the message all right and much enjoyed the joke.

Gervase Hughes in *Composers of Operetta* has remarked how, from *Pépito* (1953) onwards Offenbach was gradually evolving an operetta stereotype with regular ingredients – the *tyrolienne* (i.e. *Ländler*), the dreamy waltz, the polka, the can-can, the military ensemble with a 'ra-ta-plan' refrain, etc. Fortunately, for few people can absorb the characteristics of stage work from its bare score, we have a French recording of *Ba-ta-clan* available and find it full of

La Rose de Saint-Flour
(1856)

such Offenbachian traits. Its most memorable song, a lovely 'Romance' sung by Fé-an-nich-ton, is unmistakably Offenbach, even to the delightful cello obligato which accompanies the vocal line; and in their Parisian memories the trio evoke every strain that Offenbach had absorbed from Parisian musical life. There are numerous portents of future masterpieces. The exuberance and the melodic grace of the piece caused the critic Jules Janin to hail Offenbach as a master. The audience 'laughed, clapped and shouted at the miracle' and the music of *Ba-ta-clan* was to be heard everywhere, particularly, as was the custom in those days, arranged as polkas or quadrilles to be danced at the Opéra balls. One café-concert adopted the name 'Ba-ta-clan', such was its drawing power.

Offenbach was growing in confidence and was already aware that he was creating a new genre of opera; the opérette, light and graceful in the style of the 18th century opéra-comique as opposed to the heavier, melodramatic trends of the pieces dominating l'Opéra-Comique which were deserting their true French heritage in favour of the pompous and artificial Italian style. He put thoughts on these lines into a tactful but pointed article which he wrote about this time. Meanwhile in his music he assimilated every kind of traditional and popular song so that his music was always close to the tastes of the ordinary French citizen. Still hampered by the licensing laws (not revoked until 1858) he was forced to gain his effects with four singers and an orchestra never exceeding thirty players. But he was always a genius at turning necessity into an asset.

Writing at incredible speed Offenbach used his regular and polished musical ingredients with constantly changing approach and effect. In 1856 no fewer than seven of these one-act pieces were written and performed. On February 9th: *Un Postillon en gage* (libretto by Edouard Plouvier and Jules Adenis); on April 3rd, *Tromb-al-Cazar* ou *Les Criminels dramatiques* (Charles Desiré Dupeuty and Ernest Bourget) which satirised the stock grand opera plot and centred around a gang of romantic and highly vocal bandits; on June 12th, *La Rose de Saint-Flour* (Michel Carré); on June 18th, *Les Dragées du Baptême* (Dupeuty and Bourget) which was written and produced to celebrate the birth of the Prince Imperial; on July 31st, *Le 66* (Pittaud de Forges and Aimé Laurencin [Paul Aimée Chapelle]) the prelude of which Gervase Hughes has compared favourably with Bizet (the '66' in question being the number of a lottery ticket); on September 23rd, *Le Financier et le Savetier* (Hector Crémieux) adapting the music he had written in 1842, based on La Fontaine's fables, with the writer as the chief character gifted with an unexpected financial turn of mind; and on October 14th *La Bonne d'Enfants* (Eugène Bercioux). In addition there was a ballet divertissement *Les Bergers de Watteau* written again under the name of Lange. All of these contain their memorable moments and though stage production of the majority (beyond those by amateur enthusiasts) would seem an unlikely proposition today, they would provide admirable material, like *Ba-ta-clan*, for recordings. Perhaps some day, when the current repertoire has been wrung dry, we may get a complete Offenbach on disc!

During 1856, Offenbach and his fellow directors devised a competition to give Les Bouffes-Parisiens a little extra publicity. They offered a prize of 1200 francs, a medal worth 300 francs and subsequent production at the theatre for a one-act operetta in Bouffes-Parisiens style. The competition was open to all French composers resident in France whose works had not been produced at the Opéra or the Opéra-Comique – as might be expected – or who had had more than two pieces played at the Théâtre-Lyrique. There was a most distinguished panel of judges consisting of Daniel Auber, Fromental Halévy, Ambroise Thomas, Eugène Scribe, Jules Vernoy de Saint-Georges, Mélesville (Anne Duveyrier), Aimé Laborne, Victor Massé, Charles Gounod, François-Auguste Gevaert and François Bazin – enough to alarm even the most hardened composer entrant. The competition was organised in two parts. First, an eliminating round in which the entrants were asked to produce, by August 25th,

1. A song with choir, accompanied by piano;
2. A song with orchestral accompaniment;
3. An orchestral piece fully scored.

As a result of this, six finalists would be chosen, and their names were announced on September 15th. The lucky aspirants were five Parisians: Georges Bizet, M. Demersemann, Camille Erlanger, Charles Lecocq and M. Limagne, and a gentleman from Lyon, M. Manniquet, who were chosen from a total entry of seventy-eight, of which sixty-five came from Paris and thirteen from the provinces. The six were then asked to provide a score for a libretto *Le Docteur Miracle*, provided by Ludovic Halévy and Léon Battu, as a result of which the jury decided to split the award between Charles Lecocq and Georges Bizet, both deemed worthy winners. There was some delay in paying the prize money and this, and some alterations made to his score, annoyed Lecocq who always maintained thereafter a rather cool and ungrateful attitude toward Offenbach. The works were supposed to be produced on February 15th and March 1st, 1857 but eventually were seen on April 8th and 9th; neither made much impression at the time. Bizet's charming overture is the only part of his music to prove durable. But at least we can be grateful that Les Bouffes-Parisiens generous but demanding gesture produced something of lasting value in that it picked out accurately two young men who were to make their future mark on the musical scene.

Ludovic Halévy

Offenbach and his theatre thrived and became immensely popular among discerning Parisians and visitors. His discoveries, Berthelier, Pradeau and Hortense Schneider became stars. Among those who regularly visited the theatre was Meyerbeer, not at all incensed at the parodies of his own work which only served to increase their popularity and fame. He had a regular box reserved at the second night of each new production where Offenbach would always visit him and compliments would be exchanged. During September 1856, William Makepeace Thackeray was one of the foreign visitors who saw *Le Savetier et le Financier* and he predicted a great future for the composer. Tolstoy visited the theatre a few months later and found the entertainment truly French, the comedy wholesome and spontaneous. Another firm admirer was Camille Saint-Saëns who later wrote:

In a corner of Paris there was a little theatre where one could laugh with waistcoat unbuttoned. It was all charming and the public found it a great joy . . . The facility of Offenbach and the rapidity of his production were incredible . . . Great fertility, melodic gift, harmony that was often distinguished, much wit and invention, great dramatic skill . . . everything and more that was necessary for success.

Offenbach, in turn, was full of regular praise for the collaborators who provided him with librettos in response to his incessant and pressing demands. He liked to work with a complete libretto, but as he worked so rapidly himself his writers were always having great difficulty in keeping up with him. 'Il me faut absolument – de suite, de suite – pourquoi ne vois ai-je pas vu aujourd'hui?' he wrote to Michel Carré, 'Sardanapale, va!'. He was aware too of the demands of the Parisian audience, particularly their critical appreciation of *les femmes*. Having asked one colleague to find him some actresses who were not only talented but young and pretty, he sent him a note saying: 'Your "young and pretty" singer is neither young nor pretty; just find me what I want, but for goodness' sake put your glasses on! In my theatre the audience is very close to the stage and I must have something more attractive than you sent me yesterday!'

The spate of one-acters continued during 1857; another seven in fact. On January 15th, *Les Trois Baisers du Diable* (Eugène Méstèpes) broke with the satirical tradition, and, described as an 'opérette-fantastique', had an effect which *Le Ménéstrel* described as 'horrible and uncanny' – an early foretaste of *Les Contes d'Hoffmann*. The public, unprepared, assumed it was meant to be funny, so Offenbach avoided that vein for a time. On February 2nd, *Croquefer* ou *Le Dernier des Paladins* (Adolphe Jaime and Étienne Tréfeu) – an incredibly vivacious satire on medieval romances, in which the hero, as in *Ba-ta-clan*, dreams of Parisian haunts and which ends with an almost terrifyingly thrilling galop; April 30th,

Dragonette (Jaime and Méstèpes)—a work clearly showing the influence of Donizetti's *La Fille du Régiment*; May 16th, *Vent-du-Soir* ou *L'Horrible Festin* (Philippe Gille); 27th July, *Une Demoiselle en Loterie* (Jaime and Crémieux)—at this time Hortense Schneider had departed for a while to Les Variétés, as Offenbach had refused to increase her salary, and this was the first piece in which a new star Lise Tautin appeared; 10th October, *Le Mariage aux Lanternes* (Carré and Battu)—one of the most popular one-act pieces, blessed and the first to be produced in English; on November 13th, *Les Deux Pêcheurs* (Dupeuty and Bourget). On November 19th, *Les Deux Pêcheurs* (Dupeuty and Bourget). On November 19th *Les Petits Prodiges* (Jaime and Tréfeu) had a score mainly by Émile Jonas with Offenbach merely contributing a 'Valse des animaux'. Indeed the boards of Les Bouffes-Parisiens were by no means exclusively dedicated to Offenbach's works. On April 29th, 1856, when Adolphe Adam had died, a tribute was paid by producing his *Les Pantins de Violette*. Soon after there was a production of Mozart's *Der Schauspieldirektor* (20th May) as *L'Impresario* with the score newly arranged by Offenbach. Rossini's *Il Signor Bruschino*, similarly arranged, as *Don Bruschino*, was revived after Venetian failure in December 1857. It was at this time that Rossini coined a lasting title for Offenbach when he declared himself pleased to be able to do anything for 'the Mozart of the Champs-Elysées'. With this piece the theatre was allowed to augment its acting complement to five. Beside those mentioned above, Les Bouffes had produced during 1855 *Une Pleine-Eau* (Osmond and Costé); *Le Duel de Benjamin* (Jonas); *Les Statues de l'Alcade* (Pilati); *Sur un Volcan* (l'Épine); in 1856 *Élodie* ou *Le Forfait Nocturne* (Léopold Amat); *Venant de Pontoise* (Dufrène); *Le Thé de Polichinelle* (Ferdinand Poise); *Venus au Moulin d'Ampiphros* (Destribaud); *Marinette et Gros-René* (Hecquet); *La Parade* (Emile Jonas); *Les Deux Vieilles Gardes* (Léo Delibes); *Le Guetteur de Nuit* (Blacquière); *Un Duo de Serpents* (Cottin); *Le Cuvier* (Hassenbut); *Six Demoiselles à Marier* (Delibes); *M'sieu Landry* (Duprato); *L'Orgue de Barbarie* (Alary); in 1857—*Après L'Orage* (Galibert); *Le Docteur Miracle* (Lecocq) (Bizet); *Le Roi Boit!* (Jonas); *L'Opéra aux Fenêtres* (Gastinel); *La Pomme de Turquie* (Pauline Thys); *La Momie de Roscoco* (Eugène Ortolan); *Au Clair de la Lune* (Vilbac); *Rompons!* (Vogel); *Le Troisième Larron* (Corcy); the list gives an idea both of the quality, quantity and variety of the theatre's productions and to what extent Offenbach honoured his avowed obligation to the young composers of France.

On February 18th, 1857 a short 'parable', with book by Méry and music by Offenbach *Aimons notre Prochain*, was put on at the Theater an der Wien in Vienna, an adaptation of the original Bouffes-Parisiens opening material. Now Offenbach was attracted by the idea that his works could have as great an appeal elsewhere as they did in Paris. Accordingly he began to make arrangements with foreign agents for some tours abroad. 'Un théâtre qui voyage! . . . voilà bien de ces miracles que sait faire la magicienne Locomotive'. In May 1857 he started an international tour by departing for London for what was to be a 'short but prosperous season' at the St James's Theatre. He took with him a troupe of fifty actors and musicians and a repertoire of some of the most successful pieces at Les Bouffes-Parisiens so far. These included *Ba-ta-clan; Les Deux Aveugles; Dragonette; Le Savetier et le Financier* and Gastinel's *L'Opéra aux Fenêtres*. Offenbach conducted most of the performance himself and could have been well pleased with their enthusiastic reception. It reminded London of the virtuoso they had once applauded, now turned composer, but the time was not yet ripe for the real Offenbach fever that was to infect London a decade or so later when he was taken up by popular theatres like the Gaiety. Offenbach enjoyed his trip and took the opportunity of visiting the London opera where he found the Italians in a state of dominance; but probably heard more suitable material for his own musical absorption at song-and-supper haunts in the Strand. On July 1st a benefit performance was arranged when *Croquefer* was produced for the first time and the maestro took on his earlier rôle by playing a cello solo. One diversion during the visit was an invitation to Claremont where Marie-Amélie, the widow of Louis-Philippe, was living. There was a performance of *Dragonette* whose patriotic story and cries of *Vive la France!* in the finale proved a

A sample of Offenbach's handwriting

46

moving experience for everyone. Offenbach found, as he wrote to his wife, that laughter was ever close to tears.

The London visit was followed by a season at the Grand-Théâtre in Lyons where *Croquefer, Ba-ta-clan, Les deux Aveugles* and *Le Savetier et le Financier* were among the pieces played, and at the end of the summer he arranged a charity fête in the seaside town of Etretat which was so full that the cast had a job to find accommodation. Offenbach gratefully returned to the bosom of his family, which he always left with deep regret, and resumed the light-hearted and extravagantly generous life that his increasing wealth now made possible. In 1855 the receipts at the Bouffes box-office had been over 334,000 francs of which 33,000 had been paid out to the various writers. The income had been rising steadily ever since. The Offenbachs now lived in a stylish but medium-sized house in the Rue Lafitte, near the Rothschilds' palace, and they were becoming the centre of theatrical and musical social life. It had become a tradition, during Offenbach's conducting days, for Friday evenings to be party night at their home. At the time of the regrettable demolition of No. 11, Rue Lafitte decades later, to make way for the extension of the Boulevard Haussmann, Offenbach's grandson, Jacques Brindejont-Offenbach told how:

Offenbach occupied the two top floors of this house for over twenty years, and there gave full rein to an extremely sociable temperament. He hated to be left alone, and could not compose unless talk and noise was going on around him. Nothing except singing was forbidden, and if he noticed that voices were being purposely subdued, he would look up and ask if anyone was dead. He had an extraordinary number of friends who were always dropping in promiscuously. His Friday evenings at home were wildly amusing. On one of these occasions, in 1857, everyone went in fancy dress. Georges Bizet, the composer, was dressed as a baby, and Léo Delibes as a soldier. A fantastic musical drama in five acts was followed by a 'poultry-yard symphony' in which Delibes gave a lifelike imitation of a dog who has had his paw trodden on. On another occasion Edouard Détaille, the painter, and other celebrities of the day sang *Faust* accompanied by a musical genius who operated simultaneously on the piano and a cornet.

Such activities were frowned on by the more academic members of Parisian musical society: 'Delibes – dancing a polka and writing trifling operettas for Les Bouffes-Parisiens when he should have been turning out a grand opera!' At the fancy dress ball noted above, the celebrated Gustave Doré walked on his hands; and in the musical drama, *L'Enfant Trouvère*, Offenbach took the leading rôle with Ludovic Halévy as a page while Bizet played the piano. But it was all part of the strange, vital world of Offenbach's operettas; a 'mutual insurance company for the defeat of boredom', as he liked to describe it. There were also 'les soupers de Jacques', parties which always took place at the house after each first night. Even at

Léo Delibes (1836-1891)

these he would be seen to find a sheet of manuscript paper and start jotting down some musical ideas in his microscopic manner – the notes so small as to be almost invisible, involving a very personal musical shorthand.

His daily life in Paris usually included a regular lunch at the Restaurant Peters, a ritual meal that inevitably ended with a cigar and a cup of coffee in which he dipped a cake. Here he enjoyed the company of musicians and journalists. The only time he deserted the Restaurant Peters was when the proprietor introduced a performing bear. Once the bear had been removed, Offenbach returned.

4 Le Mozart
des Champs-Elysées

Les Bouffes-Parisiens continued to draw full houses for every production but surprisingly the theatre was losing money. It was mainly Offenbach's fault; bad business sense and a tendency to idealism. Determined that the theatre should please the eye as well as the ear, as suited his vision of delight, he spent over-lavishly on the productions and would have the walls repainted or the seats reupholstered at the slightest hint of damage. He was always lavish in his entertaining and also in help given to less fortunate members of the theatrical profession. The result was an overall loss and a life spent trying to avoid meeting his creditors. 1858 had seen two moderate successes *Mesdames de la Halle* on March 3rd and *La Chatte Métamorphosée en Femme* on April 19th. There was a considerable gap, by Offenbach's standards, while he worked on the next operetta. He knew that it was something especially right from the beginning and all his hopes were centred on it, both to bring the theatre back out of the red and to establish his own world reputation. It wasn't easy, as he often had to work in hotel rooms rather than risk meeting the debt collectors at his own home. The idea for an operetta based on the story of Orpheus and the 'goings-on' amongst the gods of Olympus had been in his mind for some time. Ludovic Halévy and Hector Crémieux had, in fact, written a provisional libretto in 1856. The real stumbling block for a lavish operetta had been the ridiculous licensing law which only allowed him four characters on the stage. By the beginning of 1858, however, this restriction had fortunately been lifted and the general efficiency of the theatre won it an unrestrained hand in these matters from now on. *Mesdames de la Halle* was the first piece to gain this freedom. Offenbach, full of ideas as usual and absolutely delighted at the quality of the music that he was inspired to produce, had to weather a number of frustrations. Halévy, offered an important government post, felt unable to remain involved in such frivolities as Les Bouffes-Parisiens indulged in, and handed over the work mainly to Crémieux who was a slow worker. Offenbach begged Halévy to continue to help, which he agreed to do, provided his name was not used.

The Spring 1858 productions at Les Bouffes-Parisiens were *Simone* (Laforestière); *Mademoiselle Jeanne* (Cohen); *Monsieur de Chimpanzé* (Hignard); *Mesdames de la Halle* (Offenbach); *Maître*

Well-known Offenbach
cartoon

Baton (Dufrêne); *La Charmeuse* (Caspers); and *La Chatte
Métamorphosée en Femme* (Offenbach). The theatre closed for the
summer and from June 1st to September 18th the company went on
tour visiting Marseilles (Grand-Théâtre) and Berlin. In Berlin they
played for a month at the Kroll-Theater, with all their expenses
guaranteed; at the end of the month they transferred to the Viktoria
Theater where they had little success and they cut short the tour to
return to Paris on September 18th. Immediately *Orphée aux Enfers*
(his first two-act operetta) went into rehearsal, with Désiré as
Jupiter, Léonce as Pluto, Tayan as Orpheus, Lise Tautin as
Eurydice. During the course of the rehearsals Offenbach introduced an eccentric actor from the Comédie-Française named Bache,
a tall, thin melancholy person of most unpredictable behaviour and
erratic performance. A victim of hallucinations, he would vary the
delivery of his lines, either speaking at great speed or very slowly, as
imaginary voices that he heard tended to distract him. This in turn
had a disastrous effect on the other actors. He had a high-pitched
voice and looked so odd that it took the quirkish imagination of
Offenbach to see his potential and to write in a special part and an
optional song which has become one of the favourite items in the
opera – 'Couplets du Roi de Béotie' ('When I was King of Beotia').
The public greatly enjoyed M. Bache in his role of John Styx and

50

assumed his oddities to be the result of art rather than nature; amply supporting Offenbach's contested choice of such a liability. A Parisian magazine *Journal Amusant* published an account of the typical Bouffes-Parisiens chaos on the day of the first production of *Orphée*: the principal actress demanding a change of costume; some friends from Cologne arriving to solicit free seats; one of the musicians being taken ill; the arrival and placation of the inevitable bailiffs; a threatening letter; a burst gas main in the street outside; a list of cuts to be made in the text by order of the Minister of the Interior; and a character (straight out of a Marx Brothers film) who appeared in the midst of it all to ask Offenbach to act as his second in a duel. The maestro weathered all such distractions with the calm of one who knows he has a masterpiece on his hands. As so often happens with an adventurous new work of genius, the public enjoyed the first production on October 21st, 1858, but they were not able to grasp its whole meaning or to appreciate that a brand new genre of operetta was being handed to the world on this historical evening. They enjoyed Bache and the frivolous goings-on of the rest of the cast and they greatly admired the splendid scenery and costumes, partly designed by Gustave Doré, which had been produced, according to the usual Offenbach creed, without any consideration of expense or acknowledgment of the bailiffs waiting at the door. Public and critical opinion is always slow to throw over old prejudices and to accept something new, especially if there is a dangerous element of satire involved. *Orphée aux Enfers* pulled no punches. It lampooned a classical story of great antiquity. Anyone brought up on the treatment of the Orpheus and Eurydice story by such predecessors as Monteverdi and Gluck, would certainly have found Offenbach's irreverence a little disturbing, left unsure as to whether they should laugh or disapprove. The critics on the whole supported the notion that disapproval was the right reaction. They tended to find it all a piece of flagrant bad taste, especially the blasphemous use of Gluck's revered 'Che faró', and wondered how anyone could enjoy such a poor joke. The dangerous satire, not only on the gods but (by implication) on the establishment, was enjoyed but tactfully deplored. In spite of all these half fearful doubts, the public continued to attend performances and it looked as if the production might run for a couple of months or so – not a failure exactly, but not quite the success that was needed to put Les Bouffes-Parisiens beyond the clutches of the debt collectors. Yet in spite of the comments of the critics and academics, it was hardly likely that anyone could visit the show without coming away with their head full of the uninhibited melody of the can-can which Offenbach had at last made his own particular property – or the luring strains of the inevitable waltz song – or the poignant humour of the song of the ex-king of the Beotians. Today, when the satire

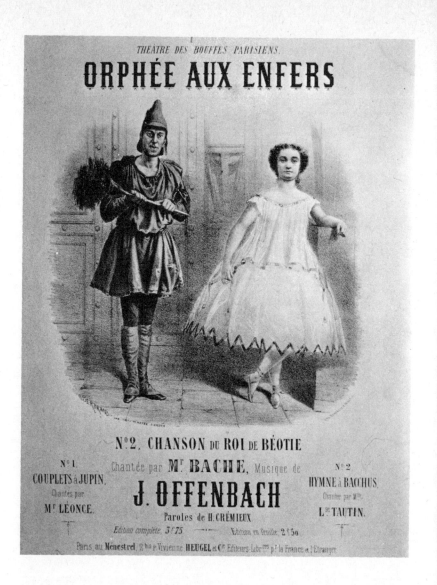

From the original production of *Orphée aux Enfers* (1858)

seems mild and we are conditioned to artistic irreverence, we can see *Orpheus in the Underworld*, in common with many operettas, as a light-hearted bit of nonsense skilfully handled. What matters now is Offenbach's splendid melodic score and our unabashed enjoyment of music like the famous can-can which has become one of the best-known compositions in the world. Even the overture, as later re-written, has become an orchestral favourite. Oh, for a seat in the stalls at that first night to measure our own uninitiated reaction! Would we have any real doubt as to the immortality of the piece? Maybe the production creaked a little – but surely the music must have been irresistible? The public continued to sneak in to the little theatre with a sidelong glance to see if anyone they knew had seen them. You didn't actually have to be a music lover to get a lot of pleasure there. As it was seen in retrospect in 1880:

The limits of vaudeville in these days was laxly fixed. The more wild hilarity there was in a comedietta the more it was liked and the new manager of the Bouffes-Parisiens conceived the idea of writing music as light and free in tone as the pieces it was to illustrate. He did not seek what was artistic, but what was amusing, and endeavoured to raise not admiration but unadulterated merriment. The proceeding was not altogether worthy of respect; but it paid. If it were hinted that the dresses were very short, the hint was taken and the dresses were cut shorter; if anyone said that the dancers were peculiarly free and unrestrained, it was not found that the result was to curtail that freedom. The first real hit was made in 1859 by *Orphée aux Enfers*, and the wild revelry of the famous galop, a measure than which none more irresistibly gay and dashing was ever written, may be called the apotheosis of opéra-bouffe. The melody was heard all over Paris within a week, and soon crossed the Channel, where, in spite of *Ba-ta-clan, Tromb-al-cazar*, and some half-dozen pieces of which extracts had been published, Offenbach was little known to the public. But his day was coming.

The writer of the above in Offenbach's *Times* obituary spoils his appreciation a little with his moral attitude and his further considered opinion that had Offenbach taken himself more seriously he might have been 'a second Adolphe Adam or a minor Ambroise Thomas'—but then he was still writing close to the composer and still in Victorian times. But even Offenbach recognised that the Bouffes entertainment was not exactly 'nice' and forbade any of his own four daughters to go there while they were still unmarried.

Undoubtedly *Orpheus* and Offenbach would gradually have won the day on the strength of the can-can alone, but matters were greatly, if unintentionally, helped by M. Jules Janin, highly respected critic of the *Journal des Débats* who revisited the Bouffes

Impressions of *Orphée aux Enfers* at the Théâtre de la Gaîté

some six weeks after the opening when, in fact, it looked as though the piece might be due for the customary replacement. Previously M. Janin had enjoyed the pastoral lightness and sly humour of some of the earlier productions, but *Orphée aux Enfers* deeply shocked him. He found the whole thing 'a profanation of holy and glorious antiquity', full of blasphemy and lascivious goings-on. He wrote in terms of high moral indignation. The attention actually amused Messrs Offenbach and Crémieux who replied vigorously and entertainingly in the pages of *Le Figaro*. They even wrote some of M. Janin's own words into the text of the play in a monologue for Pluto (sung in the 1874 version). Janin was historically on a poor wicket, for satire, far from being new, had been the favourite sport of intellectuals from Greek times onward. His moral indignation was based more on a protective instinct toward the establishment and this was hardly likely to impress a Parisian public who had lived through such unrighteous times. He lost the battle and merely made people curious to see the work, and to make their own judgements. Instead of *Orphée aux Enfers* being taken off, as it might well have been in the normal course of events, it now began to play to packed houses with clamorous queues at the box-office. Many pretended not to see the ridicule of their lords and masters and enjoyed it simply as a harmless romp. In their turn they took the infectious tunes onto the streets and into the dance-halls. From that week onward *Orphée aux Enfers* and Offenbach were artistically and musically made and, for a time at least, the financial troubles were solved. The music was heard everywhere from the most fashionable ballrooms to the lowest inns. In March 1859 the box-office receipts were averaging some 2,250 francs a night, attaining a total of 62,000 francs. By the time it had reached 228 performances the receipts were falling and the actors, although there had been numerous changes in the leading rôles, were totally exhausted; so a decision was made to take it out of the repertoire for a while. A crowning accolade was to come at the end of April 1860 when it was given a gala performance at the Italian Opera. In fact, *Orphée* was included in the programme at the express wish of the Emperor who said he would not otherwise attend. So Offenbach's masterpiece became the centre piece of the evening between a presentation by the artists from the Théâtre-Français and a scene involving some of the great composers of the past, *Le Musicien de l'Avenir*.

During the course of the operetta's run through 1858, 1859 and 1860 there were the usual parties to celebrate the 100th and 200th performances. To celebrate the 100th performance, the whole cast and orchestra raided Offenbach's house at 1 a.m. and struck up a rousing chorus in the courtyard, after which, headed by the orchestra playing vigorously, they marched upstairs and presented the composer with a gilded wreath. The first floor was occupied by

Henri Meilhac

an old lady who was known to be very ill, and she was asked beforehand if she objected. 'Not at all', she replied, 'I should not wonder if it prolongs my life.' There is no record of the other tenants' views. In December 1858 there had also been a very special celebration of three years of Les Bouffes-Parisiens. On December 18th the invitations went out:

Les Auteurs et Compositeurs joués aux Bouffes-Parisiens ont eu la pensée d'offrir un Banquet à J. Offenbach, pour fêter le troisième anniversaire de l'ouverture de son théâtre à la salle Choiseul.

Nous espérons vous être agréables en vous demandant de joindre votre adhésion à celles qui nous sont déjà parvenues.

Le banquet aura lieu le mercredi 29 Décembre à 6 heures et demi, chez Véfour, Palais-Royal. Le prix de la souscription est de 20 francs.

On souscrit jusqu'au 27, chez Véfour et chez M. C. du Locle, 5, rue de Hanovre.

	Les Commissaires:	
	J. DUFLOT	J. DUPRATO
	E. DE NAJAC	H. CASPERS
R.S.V.P.	C. DU LOCLE	L. DELIBES

The response was a tribute to the love and admiration felt for Offenbach by all those who had worked with him. 'Le bon Offenbach', 'l'illustre Offenbach'; it would be a great honour and pleasure to celebrate with him. There were many famous names amongst those who paid their 20 francs to attend the banquet. One reply on December 27th came in verse:

> *Au banquet d'Offenbach trop honoré convive,*
> *De coeur j'adresse mon écot;*
> *Mais comme au Figaro, si l'on criait: Qui vive!*
> *Il faudrait me souffler le mot.*

to which M. du Locle replied:

> *Au banquet d'Offenbach infortuné convive,*
> *J'ai grand peur de vous voir regretter votre écot*
> *Car vous n'y connaitrez peut-être âme qui vive*
> *Et je vous vois d'ici manger sans souffler mot.*

Coming as it did, during the triumph of *Orphée aux Enfers*, the banquet was a double success.

What was it in *Orpheus* that gave it such a fashionable, yet such a lasting impact? We have noted the timely shafts of its satire, but musically the meaningful elements are more difficult to pinpoint. A typical Bouffes-Parisiens audience would probably be fairly cultured but inclined to the middle-brow areas of music-making. They would be reasonably well-steeped in the classical operatic vein from Mozart to Rossini and would therefore appreciate the same clear, logical, rhythmical elements in Offenbach's music. They would sense that, although his work was far more frivolous in nature than the preceding vein of opéra-comique by French composers of note,

55

it did not otherwise deviate basically from an established style. But they would have enjoyed its novelties; the sweeping waltzes which blatantly proclaimed their nature with a rhythmical, lilting, *one*-two-three base, echoing but not copying the waltzes that were the vogue in Vienna with their one-*two-three* rhythm. They would have enjoyed the patter songs which were more or less an Offenbach innovation, though Donizetti had pointed the way—in *Don Pasquale*, for instance; and there are samples in Rossini. Above all, of course, the can-can which had led a naughty life in low places since the 1830s or thereabouts and now became a polite fashion, as uninhibited as ever, but at least made respectable by operatic clothing. The totally loose, relaxed feeling of the musical score must have made many half aware that a new spirit was abroad in the musical theatre.

Geneviève de Brabant (1859)

Les Bouffes-Parisiens continued its production for 1859 with *Frasquita* (De Rille); *Mesdames de Coeur-Volant* (Erlanger); *L'Omelette à la Follembuche* (Delibes); *L'Île d'Amour* (Délehelle); *Le Mari à la Porte* (Offenbach); *Les Vivandières de la Grande Armée* (Offenbach); *Le Fauteuil de mon Oncle* (Collinet); *Dans la Rue* (Caspers); *La Veuve Grapin* (Flotow); *Le Major Schlagmann* (Fétis); *La Polka des Sabots* (Varney) and *Geneviève de Brabant* (Offenbach) interspersed with regular performances of *Orphée aux Enfers* and other past successes. The first two Offenbach pieces were one-acters in the now traditional Offenbach vein. *Le Mari à la Porte* had one delectable tyrolean-style waltz song which was sung by Mlle Tautin with great success; *Les Vivandières de la Grand Armée* was quickly assembled and set in Italy to celebrate the marriage of Prince Napoleon to Princess Clotilde – the daughter of Victor-Emmanuel of Savoy – a political union which was anything but a love match.

In *Geneviève de Brabant*, a more substantial piece in two acts and seven tableaux, with the libretto by Adolphe Jaime and Étienne Tréfeu, Offenbach had hoped for a worthy successor to *Orphée*. Its comparative failure, a run of only fifty performances, was attributed to a rather weak libretto full of pointless music-hall jokes, although this was balanced by some sharpish satire on the goings-on at court. The music was enjoyed but the whole show lacked impact. For its 1867 revival for the 'Menus Plaisirs' Offenbach had the whole book revised in three-act form by Crémieux and Tréfeu and eventually *Geneviève* was to enjoy great success – particularly in England where the two gendarmes (originally 'men-at-arms') won tremendous popularity and proved a lasting source of inspiration to British operetta and music-hall.

1860 found Offenbach now occupying a position in the musical and entertainment world that he greatly liked; that of a successful man who was being successful on his own terms. He had always believed that Paris (and the world for that matter) needed music and entertainment that was light in spirit yet well-turned. Operetta was a personal 'holy grail' to him and now he was finding the world ready and eager to accept his vision. The box-office receipts for 1859 had reached a peak of almost 420,000 francs. Success bolstered his spirit and gave him the courage to be a bold satirist. On February 10th, Les Bouffes-Parisiens produced for the carnival season *Le Carnaval des Revues*. This kind of popular entertainment was very much in vogue in Paris and was usually of a very lowbrow nature. Even in this field Offenbach was able to add distinction and, with words supplied by Eugène Grangé, Philippe Gille and Ludovic Halévy, he provided an entertainment for his discerning clientèle that was several steps nearer to the intellectual 'little' revue of modern times. It provided a series of skits on Paris life, fashions

Offenbach parody of Wagner
in *La Revue des Bouffes*

and absurdities, with the melodies drawn from various popular Bouffes productions of the past few years. These included the 'Song of the violin' from *Le Violoneux*; the bourrée from *La Rose de Saint-Flour*; the boléro from *Les Deux Aveugles*; the 'airs de danse' from *Orphée aux Enfers*; the finale from *Vent du Soir*; the march and 'couplets de bébé' from *Geneviève de Brabant*; the 'choeur de table' from *Tromb-al-Cazar*; the valse from *Le Mari à la Porte*; the ballade from *Croquefer* and 'les miaulements' from *La Chatte Métamorphosée en Femme;* as one writer said: 'nous eussions donné son vrai nom a cette parade carnavalesque en l'appelant La Revue des Bouffes'. Its most sophisticated items were additionally *'La Symphonie de l'Avenir'* and *'La Tyrolienne de l'Avenir'* which were biting satires on the new music of Richard Wagner which had recently invaded Paris in a series of three concerts and had caused, as Wagner was to do for some time to come, a great deal of controversy amounting, on the one hand, to a degree of hysterical hostility. Offenbach was almost unaccountably vitriolic in his dislike of Wagner, probably feeling that this music was the opposite of everything he believed in. He had Wagner appear in a sketch in which he met Grétry, Weber, Mozart and Gluck and told them in no uncertain terms that their music was outmoded and useless, offering in its place two specimens of his own superior creation. The 'symphonie' was grotesquely overladen with leitmotives which Wagner carefully designated. The four virtuous composers naturally reacted indignantly to this and threw Herr Wagner out on his ear. The audience received all this with much delight and poor old Wagner was considered to have been given the boot. At this time Offenbach was not deeply experienced in Wagner's music, but this didn't deter him at all. He continued the attack in future years and in 1861, after the first performance of *Tannhäuser*, he was still dismissing Wagner's music as 'erudite and boring' and he got plenty of support from other masters of the old school like Auber. On the other hand, there were plenty of others to support the Wagnerian cause and, in the end, the controversy served as good publicity for the German master. Offenbach never relented and was still attacking Wagner to the end of his life. Wagner retaliated with feeling, penning the lines:

> *O wie süss und angenehm*
> *Und dabei für die Füsse so echt bequem!*
> *Krak! Krak! Krakerakrak!*
> *O herrlicher Jack von Offenbach!*

which, roughly translated, suggest that Offenbach's creations were mere sugary trifles to which one could only tap one's feet.

As a final accolade of acceptance, Les Bouffes-Parisiens was honoured in 1860 by the independent publication in Bourdilliat's *Libraire Nouvelle* of a small book *Histoire des Bouffes-Parisiens* by

Albert de Lasalle which perceptively begins with the words 'L'opérette a sa place marquée dans l'art Moderne' and the author, even at this date (its last entry is *Le Carnaval des Revues*) is aware that 'C'est M. Offenbach qui s'est avisé de cette restauration' to the sterling merits and standards of 'vieil opéra-comique'.

On March 27th there was a lightly pastoral piece, with book by Clairville (Louis François Nicolaie) and Jules Cordier, on the perennial theme of *Daphnis et Chloé*. The score was later utilised as the first act of a three-act opéra-comique *Les Bergers* produced in 1865. Still the Offenbach reputation soared and the bank balance became respectable. The money that he made from *Orpheus*, after settling all debts, allowed him to build himself a summer retreat at Etretat, as was the fashionable custom, and the 'Villa d'Orphée', as it was named, became yet another centre for lavish entertaining and hilarious parties. At the beginning of 1860 Offenbach became a

The 'Valse des Rayons' as used later at the Moulin Rouge

60

naturalised French citizen by Imperial decree and the following year he was made a Chevalier de la Légion d'Honneur for his services to French music. November 26th, 1860 was perhaps the most prestigious occasion so far when at last the erstwhile cellist and conductor, who had so long battered at the doors of the establishment, found his work being presented at l'Opéra. The work was the only full-length ballet that Offenbach ever wrote – *Le Papillon*. By a delightful quirk of fate it found itself, during a run of 42 performances in the same bill as *Tannhäuser*. More importantly, it was choreographed by the great Marie Taglioni, the bright star of the romantic dance era who had set the heyday of ballet in motion with her *La Sylphide* in 1832. Now mainly teaching, she was so excited by the talents of the up-and-coming Emma Livry, the star pupil of Mme Dominique, *maîtresse de ballet* at l'Opéra, who had lately shone in Taglioni's famous rôle in *La Sylphide,* that she took

Emma Livry – star of *Le Papillon*

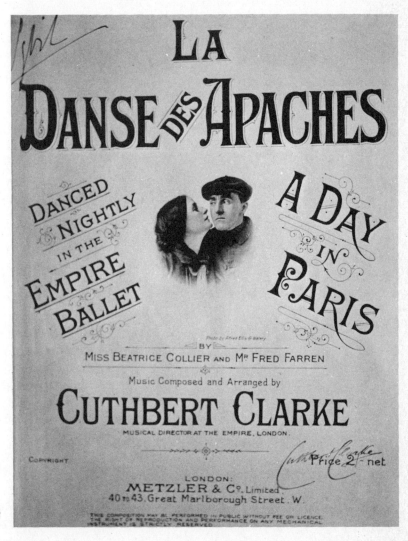

The 'Valse des Rayons' in its London guise

her on as her protégée and agreed to become involved in the production of a new rôle for her. The time had come to present Emma Livry in a full-scale ballet of her own. It is not clear how Offenbach came to be approached as the composer but it was probably through the influence of his patron and friend, the Comte de Morny, who had endorsed his application for French citizenship and, as a talented amateur, was actually to write a libretto for Offenbach the following year. The Chevalier St. Georges wrote the book based on an idea of Taglioni's who composed the choreography – her only effort of this nature. It was an enormous success. Offenbach's superb score was highly praised in the Press, its excellent orchestration being particularly noted, and it had the requisite memorable highlights – especially the 'Valse des Rayons' which was to become one of his most popular melodies. He was to use it again in the opera *Rheinnixen* which he wrote for Vienna and, although *Le Papillon* itself disappeared unaccountably from the repertoire, this captivating waltz has been added to many revivals of his operettas, notably *La Belle Hélène* in 1919 and *Madame l'Archiduc* in 1920. It even entered the repertoire of popular music when it was adapted by Charles Dubourg as *Valse Chaloupée* to which Max Dearly created the famous Apache Dance which he and Mistinguett performed in 1908 in the revue at Le Moulin Rouge. At that time it was played throughout Europe by every light orchestra and barrel organ. In London, as *La Danse des Apaches*, arranged by Cuthbert Clarke, musical director at the Empire, it was 'danced nightly' in the Empire ballet *A Day in Paris* by Beatrice Collier and Fred Farren, from October 19th, 1908. The score is full of delights, starting in unmistakably strutting Offenbach vein, and there is another little waltz at the beginning of Act 2 that sounds remarkably like the song 'The daring young man on the flying trapeze' which was written and popularised by George Leybourne shortly after. If he came across it in Paris it would make an interesting chain of musical influences particularly as Johann Strauss incorporated the song in one of his dance pieces soon after! Fortunately the ballet has been revived on record under the discerning baton of Richard Bonynge and it surely cannot be long before such a delightful score comes back into the regular repertoire. It was performed in America in 1969, and had its first British performance by the Sadler's Wells company in the centenary year of 1980, in a version arranged and orchestrated by John Lanchbery and its choreography much changed.

So Offenbach now found himself linked with a cultural success although there were voices raised in protest that the 'upstart from the Bouffes-Parisiens' should be elevated to the temple of Rossini, Meyerbeer and Halévy. The ballet made the reputation of Livry. Paul St Victor wrote in *La Presse:* 'It is an enchantment, a magic spell, to see her bound and rebound in the forest amid the playing light'. Paul Smith in *Revue et Gazette Musicale de Paris* wrote:

Did Mlle Livry not exist, the Butterfly would not be possible. For this role, so ethereal and diaphanous, an intangible artist is imperative, an artist with whom *ballon* is a natural gift and Mlle Livry has a *ballon* which has never been equalled . . . she bounds and leaps as no one else could do. She skims over the ground, the water and the flowers, apparently without touching them. She rises like a feather and falls like a snowflake.

Emma Livry was admirably supported by Louis Merante (choreographer of *Sylvia*) and Louise Marquet.

For Livry the triumph was to be followed by tragedy. As Taglioni was preparing a second ballet, *Zara*, for her, the dancer clashed with the authorities who, in accordance with new regulations, were demanding that all costumes should be dipped in a fireproof solution. It tended to make the costumes stiff and dull and Livry refused to use it, signing a document absolving the management from any subsequent responsibility. On November 15th, 1862 her skirt brushed a gas light and within seconds she was enveloped in flame. Two dancers attempted to save her and a soaking blanket was put around her. She was terribly burned and was heard praying as she tried to struggle to her feet. She survived in dreadful pain for eight months while the whole of the dancing world and its followers waited anxiously for news. She died on July 26th, 1863 and her passing seemed to symbolise the end of the great Romantic era of ballet.

Offenbach had been a part, at last, of a musical history beyond his own, quirkish, embattled world. Now, at last, the musical authorities had to accept him and, at last, l'Opéra-Comique felt that it ought to put its stage at his disposal. It was a mistake on both sides. Offenbach produced an opera that was not even of Bouffes-Parisiens standard. The libretto of *Barkouf*, by Eugène Scribe and Henri Boiseaux, had a dog as its centre of interest and Offenbach was tempted into dog imitations in his music. This enraged many of the critics, including Berlioz, who offered the ultimate insult by linking Offenbach's music with Wagner's as the product of the mad German mind. It was hissed at by the audience and lasted for only seven performances. *La Presse* said 'Ce n'est pas le chant du cygne, c'est le chant de l'oie'. Offenbach retreated from l'Opéra-Comique and found consolation at Les Bouffes-Parisiens by staging *La Chanson de Fortunio*, with book by the old faithful team of Hector Crémieux and Ludovic Halévy, on January 5th, 1861. This made telling use of the already popular song and other material that he had written in 1850 for De Musset's play. It was gratefully dedicated to De Musset. It turned the tables nicely, one critic observing that he would prefer 'un moineau volant comme Offen-

La Chanson de Fortunio
(1861)

bach' to 'un aigle empaillé comme Berlioz', and Meyerbeer added his praises to the general admiration for the piece. The next production on March 23rd was *Le Pont des Soupirs,* a two-act opéra-bouffe with its story, by Crémieux and Halévy, set in medieval Venice. It was successfully revived at Les Variétés in 1874. While this was running they were planning a piece of distinguished parentage, *Monsieur Choufleuri restera chez lui le . . .* (to which title the appropriate date was and subsequently could be added), whose book had been a 'secret' collaboration between Halévy and St Rémy – a pseudonym which hid the identity of no less a person than the Comte de Morny whose idea had sparked off the work. He took his collaboration seriously and attended all the rehearsals, his presence and the coach outside adding a distinguished air to the little theatre. The ducal touch was apparent when, on finding one of the characters using a cheap stage snuffbox, the Count thought such a trinket unsuitable for one playing an aristocratic part and gave him a solid gold snuffbox instead. The story of M. Choufleuri and his social climbing was naturally attended by the nobility and establishment of Paris when the identity of its author was tactfully revealed. The rôle of Mme Balandard was played in 'drag' by the actor Léonce. One elderly and wealthy member of the audience fell for Mme Balandard and sent flowers and an invitation to dinner. He was rather put out when a bespectacled gentleman turned up at the restaurant. This was the beginning of a new season and, for the first time, it found Offenbach able to concentrate wholly on composing as, at last, he had recognised his own failings as a business

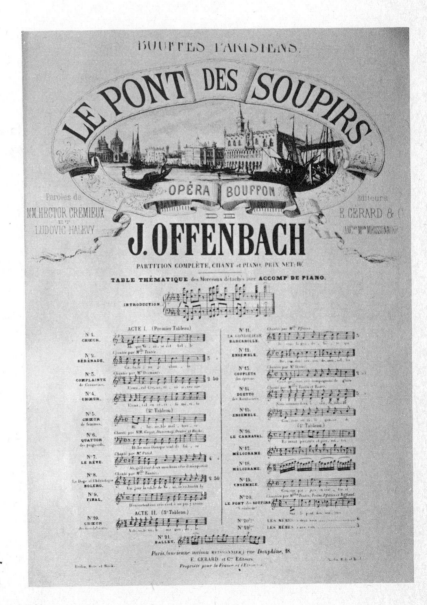

Le Pont des Soupirs (1861)

man and had handed over the management to M. Varney. If Offenbach had a failing it was his habitual extravagance. His favourite recreation was gambling and when the Offenbach home was not given over to parties the card-table would be the focus of his leisure hours – which, needless to say, were few. Away from home there was almost a daily luncheon party usually paid for by the composer. The same extravagance had flowed over into his running of the theatre where he had an obsessive dislike of anything shoddy. One day, offended by an impoverished-looking hat that one singer was wearing he told his secretary to order a new one. When he was told that there was not a penny in the kitty he gave the secretary his own gold watch with orders to pawn it and raise the necessary funds.

The final productions in 1861 were *Apothicaire et Perruquier*, with book by Elie Frébault, which was first staged on October 17th and *Le Roman Comique*, with book by Crémieux and Halévy, staged on December 10th. In between Offenbach's own creations, Les Bouffes-Parisiens continued its good work and avowed aims in providing a shop window for all composers of like mind whose works enhanced the true spirit of operetta. In 1860, in addition to the Offenbach pieces already mentioned, Les Bouffes staged *Le Nouveau Pourceaugnac* (Hignard); *Croquignole XXXVI* (L'Épine); *Madame de Bonne-Etoile* (Delibes); *C'était moi* (Debillemont); *Le Petit Cousin* (Gabrielli); *Titus et Berenice* (Gastinel); *Le sou de Lise* (Blagny); *L'Hôtel de la poste* (Dufrêne); and in 1861 *Le Mari sans le Savoir* (Saint-Rémy [De Morny]). *Les Musiciens de l'Orchestre* (Delibes, Erlanger and Hignard); *Les Deux Buveurs* (?); *La Servante à Nicolas* (Erlanger); and *La Baronne de San Francisco* (Caspers). Figures supplied by Albert de Lasalle indicate that, from its opening in 1855 to the beginning of 1860, the theatre had offered thirty pieces by Offenbach, four each by Delibes, Jonas and Lange [Offenbach], two each by Caspers, Dufrêne, Erlanger, Hignard and L'Épine, and amongst these, with a single production, were such established or up-and-coming composers as Adam, Bizet, Flotow, Lecocq, Mozart, Poise and Rossini.

5 Orphée à Vienne

Le 66 (1856)

If, by the end of 1861, Offenbach was wholeheartedly accepted as a focal point of Parisian music-making, his success as a composer of international importance had, of course, to be measured in other capitals. Musical history has always shown a marked reluctance for the English and French speaking worlds to accept each other's offerings. By the end of 1861 the following Offenbach works had been seen in London: *Pépito, Pascal et Chambord, Le Violoneux, Tromb-al-Cazar, Le Savetier et le Financier, La Bonne d'enfants, Croquefer, Les Deux Aveugles, Ba-ta-clan, La Rose de Saint-Flour, Le 66, Dragonette* and *Le Mariage aux Lanternes*. While there had been some appreciation amongst the discerning, it could hardly be said, as yet, that London was greatly aware of Offenbach's genius as a composer. There were already a few managerial noses twitching at the reports of the success of *Orphée aux Enfers*, but the Offenbach fever was still to come with the growing influence of forward looking managers like John Hollingshead and, later, George Edwardes, the opening of theatres like the Gaiety in 1868 and London's own Opéra-Comique in 1870; and the realisation by existing theatres that a new spirit was about. In America, so far, there was scarcely a twitch, for they were still following the fashions set by London, and French operetta was not to obtain a real foothold until 1866 with the building of the Théâtre Français in New York. The craze was really to start there with the début of Lucille Tosté in *La Grande-Duchesse de Gérolstein* in 1867.

In the summer of 1860 the Bouffes company had visited Amiens, Brussels and Lyons and then returned to Paris for further exploitation of *Orphée aux Enfers*. In May 1861 when the theatre closed for its summer recess, they made their first historical journey to Vienna and found that city wholeheartedly converted to Offenbachiana. In flourishing places of entertainment like the Theater an der Wien, Johann Nestroy (1801-1862) had already instilled the dual spirits of gaiety and satire very much in the Offenbach vein. Already Vienna was given over to the worship of the dance, especially the waltz, as exploited by Michael Pamer, Josef Lanner and the immortal Strauss family. The elder Johann Strauss had performed in Paris for sixteen weeks and helped to establish the lasting affinity between the two great musical centres of the time. Offenbach had absorbed the vein in his earlier attempts to write

Johann Strauss (1825-1899), friend and rival of Offenbach

similar dance music. The Theater an der Wien, built in 1801, was creating its own operetta tradition. But it was the Carltheater, then under Nestroy's management, that first wholly accepted Offenbach. Vienna's first taste of Offenbach had come, like London's, in 1856 when a company from the Palais-Royal had played *Les Deux Aveugles* at various concert halls. The Viennese critics and audiences had immediately fallen for the satirical humour and the lively music. The Carltheater now made a point of obtaining the latest Offenbach scores from Paris and such works as *Pépito* and *Bata-clan* began appearing under such strange guises as *Das Mädchen von Elizonde* and *Tschin-Tschin*. Usually only a piano score was obtainable and the Viennese management would make their own orchestral arrangements and generally tailor the piece to their own requirements. Quite early Offenbach had protested at this pirating but, as there was no established legal position in regard to such

68

things in those days and it would be too costly to take the matter to court, he became resigned to the state of affairs and decided it was all in the good cause of publicity. *Le Mariage aux Lanternes* was one such piece that established itself as a Viennese favourite, however remote from the original when it was put on at the Carltheater on October 16th, 1858. It also helped to establish the reputation of the comedian-singer Karl Treumann who was to appear in many later Offenbach productions both at the Carltheater and the Theater an der Wien. Offenbach must have been well pleased by the report in the *Theaterzeitung* which said: 'The music by Offenbach, whose work has been well received for years, is light and graceful, avoiding profundity and tonal effect, but full of lovely, singable melodies'. The house was nightly filled to the brim. The Carltheater became wholeheartedly Offenbachian, gave four more Offenbach productions – *Le Violoneux* (*Der Zaubergeige*), etc. – and started its 1859/60 season with *Le 66* (as *Die Savoyarden*) (24th November) and *Le Mari à la Porte* (as *Der Ehemann vor der Ture*) (28th December – only some six months after its Parisian première) – both with German book by Treumann. Again the critics found the music 'amusing, light and lively', the production 'fresh and gay'.

But the greatest success of all was, of course, *Orpheus in der Unterwelt* which, with German book by Johann Nestroy, opened at the Carltheater on March 17th, 1860. The music was slightly amended by Carl Binder with an extended pot-pourri overture (to replace Offenbach's slight, but effective, prelude) which has become the generally accepted orchestral version. The Viennese audience were, if anything, more cynical, in regard to the ways of government and court, than the Parisian. The critics, not wishing to offend the establishment by whole-heartedly praising its satire, cynicism and downright vulgarity (for the German version tended to overplay the latter aspect) wrote fairly coolly of the production. Some even went so far as to find its music inferior to earlier Offenbach productions. It was Paris all over again, for the more the critics and dictators of fashion condemned the work the more the public flocked to see it and remained to enjoy it. In all but critical terms, it was a tremendous success and whetted appetites for more masterpieces from the same source. Yet another theatre that encouraged operetta was the Franz-Josefs-Kai Theater, situated near one of the wharves on the Danube. They had also staged Offenbach from 1860 onward with considerable success.

So when Offenbach arrived with his Bouffes-Parisiens company in May 1861, to make his first personal appearance as conductor-composer, he was welcomed with open arms and a great deal of curious interest. *Le Mariage aux Lanternes* was produced in the genuine and original French at the Kai-Theater on June 21st and the reviewers, perhaps to show their familiarity with the true flavours of French art, seemed to have changed their tune somewhat since March for they now found Offenbach's works of a kind that appealed to 'cultured senses', showing 'a wealth of invention, graceful form and strict observance of style' that put him 'head and shoulders above most French composers of comic opera'. Nestroy, the favourite of the Viennese public, had himself been appearing in simultaneous German-speaking productions so that those who could not appreciate the luxury of the French language could enjoy them in the native tongue. On the 25th June the Bouffes-Parisiens company presented one of their latest productions *La Chanson de Fortunio* (which had been played in German only a couple of months previously) and the audience found new delight in one of Offenbach's most ingratiating songs and packed the theatre. It was said that the Viennese took to Offenbach as once before they had taken to Rossini. Offenbach once lightly referred to Vienna as his 'savings bank'. His works were performed everywhere and, for at least a decade to come, Vienna was Offenbach-mad. At a command performance before the Imperial court he even consented to play a cello solo once again.

After Vienna they went to Pest in Hungary and thence to Berlin. Here there was no repetition of the glittering Viennese welcome and hospitality. The company actually lost money and there was instilled in Offenbach a lasting prejudice that 'la Prusse ne ferait jamais le bonheur de nos nationaux'. They retreated from Berlin and went on to Brussels where a profitable stay recouped the losses made in Berlin. Then back to the familiar and beloved Bouffes-Parisiens to start off yet another productive season.

Le Voyage dans la Lune (1875)

In 1862 with M. Varney now in the hot seat – 'Pauvre Varney!' said one sympathising writer, 'Je le vois encore, mouillant son doigt et l'élévant en l'air pour savoir . . . *d'où vient le vent!*'. After *Le Roman Comique* had rounded off the end of 1861 with a modest run of 18 performances, there appeared, on 11th January, a charming little piece by Offenbach called *Monsieur et Madame Denis*, with libretto by Aimé Laurencin (Paul Aimé Chapelle) and Michel Delaporte. On March 23rd there was a rather feeble attempt to write another three-act success to a libretto by Paul Siraudin and Jules Moinaux – *Le Voyage de MM. Dunanan Père et Fils* which, nonetheless, had a considerable vogue in Vienna (there was even a Hungarian-speaking production there in 1866). The Bouffes also occupied its stage with *Une Fin de Bail* (Varney), *Un Premier Avril* (Debillemont), and *L'Homme Entre Deux Ages* (Cartier). During the Summer of 1862 there were further tours in Germany, Belgium and Holland under the harassed direction of M. Varney. One of the joys of 1862 was the birth of Offenbach's first son, Auguste (up to now Herminie had managed to produce four daughters), but poor

Offenbach with his son
Auguste-Jacques

Auguste was always a sickly child and was to die in 1883 at the age of 22, barely outliving his father.

There were still a good many Offenbach triumphs to come, in fact the major triumphs were still in the offing, but there were also many difficulties ahead. One of the main aggravations of his life was bad health. The results of overwork and over-indulgence were already beginning to show and the gourmet's traditional disease, gout, was causing him much suffering. Eventually it was to make him a complete invalid, but, at this stage when he had only just entered the troublesome forties, he liked to pretend that it was just a touch of rheumatism. Aware of the dangers to his career of letting his health deteriorate, he had started to go regularly each summer to the spa of Bad Ems, which, like Wiesbaden, Homburg and Baden-Baden, was then one of the fashionable resorts for the rich and ailing. It was not only the curative properties of famous springs that attracted Offenbach to this particular resort but also the fact that it was one of the few places where a licensed casino was operating at that time. And because the manager of the Kursaal there was a Parisian, visitors from that city felt particularly at home among their fellow citizens. Another attraction was a handsome little theatre where, in 1862, his reputation gone before him, Offenbach was asked to stage a work for the first time. The prestige involved was sufficient to induce him to write a work for first production at Bad Ems. It was one of his best integrated pieces so far, with a book by Charles Nuitter based on Cervantes' 1624 comedy *Los Habladores*, entitled *Les Bavards*. It had an excellent and adventurous libretto and the piece swung nicely between comedy and sentiment. The conductor Marcel Couraud (who has fortunately given us a recorded performance of *Les Bavards*) has written of the first act finale: 'l'ironie, l'éclat, la vivacité ne peuvent pas trouver de meilleur traduction musicale.' In the little Kursaal

Bad Ems

Theater, under the original title of *Bavard et Bavarde* the tuneful score and the light humour greatly pleased the elegant customers.

Offenbach returned, invigorated by the waters of Bad Ems, to Les Bouffes-Parisiens where he wrote a one-act piece *Jacqueline* with book by Crémieux and Halévy, under the pseudonym of Pol D'Arcy, and the music under the name of Lange once again. Why *Jacqueline* required such a modest approach is not quite clear. The operetta was produced on October 14th and was followed by L'Eveillé's *Monsieur Pygmalion et son Statue*. After further revivals, *Les Bavards*, turned by Nuitter into a two-act *opéra-bouffe* and further enhanced by the composer, was produced at Les Bouffes on February 20th, being sandwiched in the evening between Varney's *Une Fin de Bail* and *Apothicaire et Perruquier*; a sample of the good value the theatre offered its patrons. The production was a triumph for Delphine Ugalde who sang the male rôle of Roland, fresh from her success at l'Opéra-Comique in Victor Massé's *La Galatée*. She was well supported by some old stalwarts of the company, Pradeau and Desiré, and what seems to have been an exceptionally well-drilled team. The critic of *L'Entracte* wrote the next day: 'Tous les morceaux de la partition d'Offenbach ont été applaudis, tous se recommandant par la veine, le brio, la fraîcheur, le cachet particulier du compositeur'; and Saint-Saëns called it 'a masterpiece'. The score is not remembered by any particular tune but it all has a wonderful freshness and seems one long melody. As an example of the popularity of Offenbach's works of this period, and their promulgation throughout the world, it is interesting to note that *Les Bavards* was revived at Les Bouffes in 1864, after the re-opening, and in 1866 and 1872. It was produced in 1863 in Vienna and Berlin, in 1867 in Brussels and Moscow, in 1868 in New York, in 1871 in London and Rio de Janeiro, in 1872 in Madrid, in 1873 in Stockholm and in 1875 in Rome. As a final accolade it became a part of the repertoire of l'Opéra-Comique in 1924. And that was one of the lesser known pieces! The influence of *Orphée aux Enfers* can be judged when we survey the following selective list of its appearances: Breslau – Oct. 1859; Prague – Dec. 1859; Vienna – Mar. 1860; Berlin – June 1860; Brussels – June 1860; Stockholm – Sept. 1860; Copenhagen – Oct. 1860; New York – Mar. 1861; Warsaw – June 1861; St. Petersburg – Dec. 1861; Budapest – Dec. 1861; Zurich – May 1862; Amsterdam – June 1863; Madrid – Mar. 1864; Rio de Janeiro – Feb. 1865; Buenos Aires – Nov. 1866; Milan – May 1867; New York – Jan. 1867; Naples – Oct. 1868; Mexico City – May 1867; New York – Jan. 1867; Naples – Oct. 1868; Mexico City – June 1869; Valparaiso – June 1869; London – July 1869; and so on . . .

Les Bouffes-Parisiens closed on April 30th after *Les Bavards* had enjoyed 68 performances so that it could be entirely rebuilt and renovated, the old building now being considered unsafe and inadequate. It was almost the end of Offenbach's association with the theatre that he had founded. Poor M. Varney had proved an even less accomplished manager than Offenbach and brought the theatre to the verge of bankruptcy. His main default, at least in Offenbach's eyes, but probably from an objective viewpoint as well, was that the theatre was producing too many works by friends of Varney and not enough by Offenbach who was undoubtedly its main attraction. When Varney departed, his successor Hanappier was guilty of much the same faults. Offenbach took legal proceedings against the management to secure a financial settlement and he eventually won his case.

After the temporary closure of Les Bouffes, some of the principals went to perform *Les Pilules du Diable* at Porte-Saint-Martin; the rest with Offenbach set off to Ems again where he had a most enjoyable and fruitful time. The first production was *Il Signor Fagotto* which was a merciless parody of Berlioz. It picked on every device that imaginative and unkind writers had attributed to Berlioz, noises ranging from animal effects to the rattling of kitchen implements. It went down very well with the reactionary customers at Ems. Offenbach was given a banquet and a torchlight parade to honour his genius and life seemed very good. When he was challenged to write another operetta in a week, he accepted the challenge without a second thought and, within the week, *Lischen und Fritzchen* was written and rehearsed and had its production at the Kursaal Theater. There was an extra incentive in his discovery of a supremely attractive and supremely talented young actress and singer named Zulma Bouffar. She had been born in the South of France and had been brought up in a travelling theatre troupe. At twelve she had joined a troupe of German musicians in Lyons and went with them, by a curious coincidence, to Cologne, where she had appeared in one of the cafés where Offenbach himself had appeared as a young prodigy. She then toured Europe in various capacities, eventually settling in Brussels for three years before further travels. Her undoubted vocal capacities had led her to numerous operatic rôles including several appearances in works by Offenbach. He had followed her career with keen interest and now she was appearing in nearby Bad Homburg. Offenbach was enchanted by her talents and, it seems likely, by her charming appearance as well. She was persuaded to play the part of Lischen at Ems, a part calling for mime and the use of the Alsatian dialect – which she did to perfection. She was to play the part with tremendous success at Les Bouffes-Parisiens on January 5th, 1864 and her duet with Fritzchen 'Je suis alsacien, je suis alsacienne', with its 'disarming simplicity', became one of the popular hits of the season. *Lischen et Fritzchen* also had a great admirer in Rossini who always seemed to have found a special fascination in Offenbach's music. He visited Les Bouffes on several occasions during his last years in Paris and had *Lischen und Fritzchen* performed at one of the famous soirées at his own house. Offenbach was invited and Rossini applauded the work with tremendous

From *le Voyage dans la Lune*

enthusiasm and presented Offenbach with a signed score of his *Barber of Seville* which he inscribed:

au grand maître des petits chefs-d'oeuvre

While Offenbach was disporting himself at Ems, and enjoying the company of Bouffar, a pointer to the future was to be found in the appearance of Offenbach's work at the Palais-Royal where he had written the score for Meilhac and Halévy's one-act vaudeville, *Le Brésilien*, produced on May 9th, 1863. It had one good song 'Voulez-vous accepter mon bras' which Hortense Schneider sang with great success and profit. The Bouffes-Parisiens re-opened in January 1864 with *La Tradition* (Delibes), Offenbach's *Lischen et Fritzchen* (with Zulma Bouffar) and a one-act operetta *L'Amour Chanteur* which was the début rôle there of another Offenbach discovery, Mlle Irma Marie. On January 13th *Il Signor Fagotto* came to Les Bouffes; on March 16th *Les Georgiennes*, with book by Jules Moinaux and a striking chorus of large females proclaiming women's lib, was first seen at the Palais-Royal then came to the Bouffes on May 16th. That was more or less the end of Offenbach's new pieces for the theatre for a while. Meanwhile Offenbach was continuing and strengthening his fruitful association with Vienna and had become very much a cult figure there. On June 9th there was a sad event when the Franz-Josef-Kai Theater, which had seen so many Offenbach productions, was completely burnt out. Between November 1860 and June 1863 almost nine hundred pieces had been staged there. This number included no less than seventy-three French operettas; the rest of the productions being German repertoire. The Kai Theater had specialised in operetta with nearly 700 of its productions being in that vein, and twenty-five had their premières there. The actor-manager Karl Treumann found a new venue at the Carltheater, which had been temporarily out of use, and after opening it with Suppé's *Flötte Bursche* he staged several Offenbach pieces in quick succession.

Offenbach's influence on Vienna and Viennese operetta in particular was almost incalculable. At the end of 1863 he was asked by the famous journalists' club, the Concordia, to provide a waltz for their annual Concordiaball in the Sofiensaal on January 22nd, 1864. They had likewise approached Johann Strauss who also obliged. When Offenbach called his waltz *Abendblätter* (Evening papers), Strauss agreed to have his called *Morgenblätter* (Morning papers) and it was quite natural that their appearance at the same occasion should appear competitive. It seems that Offenbach's waltz, a pleasant piece in Offenbach's lightly melancholic vein (which ought to be revived) was found more immediately attractive; whereas Strauss's darker-hued piece, a composition of unusual depth and forerunner of many fine concert waltzes to come, may have seemed a bit heavy on first acquaintance. Strauss's piece has been vin-

Offenbach's waltz written to rival one by Johann Strauss

dicated by its continued survival, whereas Offenbach's has been unfairly forgotten. It was shortly after this that Strauss and Offenbach met for the first time in a Viennese café and were both delighted to make each other's acquaintance. There was a long and friendly conversation on music and the theatre in the course of which Offenbach suggested that Strauss's music had all the qualities in it that would make an ideal operetta score – why didn't he try his hand at operetta? Whether this remark carried the weight that has since been attributed to it is doubtful as Strauss did not get around to his first operetta production until 1871; but it might have sown the seed. Strauss, indeed, plunged into operetta reluctantly even then, largely through the machinations of his wife, and eventually was to write possibly the finest of them all – *Die Fledermaus* in

1874 – ten years after this historic conversation.

The Viennese writer probably most influenced by Offenbach's theatrical success and his musical style was Franz von Suppé, born in the Dalmatian port of Spalato [Split] in 1819. At the period of Offenbach's Viennese invasion he was conductor at both the Kai and Carl theatres and therefore most directly in line for insight into and influence by the witty Parisian imports. His first attempt at operetta *Das Pensionat* in 1860 is generally credited as the first true Viennese operetta, but, in fact, the boundary line is hard to define. There had been many works from the beginning of the 19th century which labelled themselves operetta and whose music was in that vein. Generally they were of the singspiel ilk with loosely written dialogue connecting a varied collection of songs. Offenbach gave shape and direction to the Viennese school and, when Suppé tried again with *Die Kartenschlägerin (The Fortune Teller)* in 1861, he was sharply rebuked, with Offenbach quoted as example – 'Herr Suppé must learn to remain within the realm of pure operetta, a rule strictly observed by Offenbach . . . his talent and ability are there yet his piece does not contain a single number worth mentioning . . . it was love's labour lost'. Suppé, who was, incidentally, the nephew of Donizetti, studied Offenbach further and learned his lessons well. Next year, 1862, his *Zehn Mädchen und kein Mann* was a tremendous success at the Theater an der Wien. Suppé was able to take over at the Carltheater in 1864 when Offenbach, in spite of past support from Karl Treumann at the Carl, signed an exclusive contract with the Theater an der Wien from 1864-7. In 1865 Suppé had a further success with *Die Schöne Galatea*, a lovely Offenbachian score, followed by *Leichte Kavalerie, Banditenstreiche* (there were twelve of his operettas performed at the Carl up to 1872), his first world-wide success *Fatinitza* in 1876, and his masterpiece *Boccaccio* in 1879. Suppé earned his title of 'Father of Viennese Operetta' while Strauss was still fiddling and waltzing. Perhaps he was lucky that Strauss did not stir himself earlier; but at least he had the foresight to see the future of the new music that Offenbach had brought to Vienna.

For Offenbach it was not all a tale of success. Once again he was tempted into the false path of grand opera when the Vienna Opera commissioned him to write a work for their exclusive use. Offenbach was delighted and asked Charles Nuitter to supply him with the text of a romantic opera; which he did, modelling it on the vein so well established at the Paris Opera by composers like Auber. It was called *Rheinnixen* (Rhine Water Sprites) and had a bemusing plot which mixed, with careless abandon, fairies and elves, soldiers and village maids, all gambolling amongst romantic ruins in the moonlight. It was put into German by Alfred von Wolzogen, a great Offenbach admirer. For its hastily written score Offenbach

Franz von Suppé
(1819-1895)

77

took the famous 'Valse des Rayons' from *Le Papillon* and also threw in *Das Vaterland*, originally composed for Cologne in 1848. It was premièred on February 8th, 1864, with the Imperial Court in attendance, but it only managed eight performances. There was one other tune, 'Goblins' song', which the critic Hanslick (as firm an ally of Offenbach as he, notoriously, was an enemy of Wagner) found 'lovely, luring and sensuous' (it was later to be used as the Barcarolle in *Les Contes d'Hoffmann)*, but the general consensus of opinion was that Offenbach was much happier in the realms of operetta. Only Wagner got much satisfaction out of the whole episode as he had been somewhat piqued to find the Vienna Opera commissioning a work from Offenbach after they had just rejected his.

This slight reversal of popular opinion did not worry Offenbach overmuch. He was still successful to the point of adulation, at least in Paris and Vienna: he had a happy home with a dutiful wife whose advice he obediently followed – if she didn't like anything he produced he re-wrote it – and he had no need to work at quite the same breakneck speed as required in the earlier days. The gout was not helpful but at least he could afford to drive about in a carriage wherever he went, and he had one fitted with a special work-table. However, it was time for another success. In the summer of 1864 he was again in the Ems where he noted a typical day's activities:

6.30 a.m. Offenbach va boire le verre d'eau obligatoire.

9 a.m. Il parcourt avec deux des interprètes la partition de *Jeanne qui pleure et Jean qui rit*.

10 a.m. Il se rend à la répétition générale de *La Chanson de Fortunio*.

11 a.m. Il déjeune, puisqu'il le faut.

12 a.m. Il répète un nouvel opéra-bouffe *Le soldat magicien*.

2.30 p.m. Il reçoit la visite de M. de Talleyrand, ambassadeur à Berlin qui desire le présenter à sa femme.

4 p.m. Il va prendre son bain obligatoire.

5 p.m. Il écrit a son épouse.

6.30 p.m. Il s'octroie le temps de dîner.

7.30 p.m. Il dirige chez lui, à son hôtel, une répétition d'ensemble des deux nouveaux opéras-bouffes.

It was indeed a pleasant summer with a production, on July 9th, of two one-act pieces that were to have a considerable success abroad – *Jeanne qui pleure et Jean qui rit* – book by Hector Crémieux and Philippe Gille, produced at Les Bouffes-Parisiens on December 16th, 1865; *Le Fifre enchanté* or *Le Soldat magicien* – book by Charles Nuitter and Étienne Tréfeu, produced at Les Bouffes on September 30th, 1868; and an enjoyable revival of *La Chanson de Fortunio*. In the midst of such pleasant activity it was inevitable that ideas should begin to flow. He had heard from Halévy who had agreed to collaborate with Meilhac on a follow-up to Orpheus that would likewise plunder and expose the 'establishment' of Greek mythology. The subject of Helen of Troy seemed ideal and all three agreed. Offenbach enthusiastically intruded on his librettists as usual, suggesting that Homer should be introduced as a war correspondent and putting forward various other fanciful ideas. As ever his old adversary Wagner lurked in the back of his mind and at one time it seemed likely that *La Belle Hélène* might turn out to be a parody of *Tannhäuser*. In September he was back in Vienna rehearsing *Les Georgiennes* for an October production at the Carl-theater, but *La Belle Hélène* was uppermost in his thoughts.

From *La Belle Hélène* (1864)

79

6 La Vie Parisienne

Back in Paris, *Hélène* was about to go into rehearsal and the vital
question was who was to be the leading lady. Offenbach had no
doubts at all – the great Hortense Schneider was the only possible
choice. She was approached and happened to be free; in fact, she
was about to make one of her regular 'retirements' from the stage
after a quarrel with the management of the Palais-Royal. But as it
was expected that *La Belle Hélène* was to be staged at the Palais-
Royal it then looked as though Schneider was probably not available after all. However when she heard some of the tunes that
Offenbach played for her at the piano she was sorely tempted. She
went home to her mother in Bordeaux still undecided, shortly to
receive a telegram from Messrs Offenbach, Meilhac and Halévy
with the news that they had managed to get the operetta accepted
by the management of the Variétés who had now been alerted to the
new vogue for musical shows. Schneider cabled back demanding
2,000 francs a month and by return the demand was accepted. All
was far from smooth-running at Les Variétés as the manager, M.
Cogniard, did not think on the same lavish lines as Offenbach,
while the ladies, Schneider and Silly, partook in elaborate quarrels,
with Hortense indulging in her regular walk-outs – in fact, it was
Orpheus all over again on a slightly grander scale. Meilhac was
always an irritable and nervous person at the best of times. At the
dress rehearsal the censor objected to the character of Calchas as an
effrontery to the Church, and to various lines as being of a politically
seditious nature. The help of the influential Duc de Morny once
again came in useful in quelling the censor's qualms. Dupuis, in the
part of Paris, found one of his songs unsuitable and this had to be
rewritten. As Rossini had so often done before him, Offenbach was
still writing the orchestration as the opening evening drew close;
working at home with great calm and equilibrium, undisturbed by
the noise of his children playing or by the endless flood of visitors.

Orpheus all over again! Even after the first night on December
17th, 1864. The critics once more raised their indignant hackles in
defence of desecrated antiquity; the old adversary Janin wading into
the attack yet again with cries of 'perfidious Meilhac, traitorous
Halévy and wretched Offenbach'. The editor of *Le Petit Journal*
leaped to the defence of Homer, and Prince Metternich said how
much he had regretted attending the première where he found

A letter concerning *La Belle Hélène* (from Bibliothèque de l'Opéra, Paris)

respectable people being so viciously lampooned. Indeed, *La Belle Hélène* was even sharper in implied satire than *Orpheus* was and the public as ever was perplexed, torn between the obvious pleasure of the piece and its dangerous frivolity. Like *Orpheus* it skated through the first perilous days when fortunately its advocates began to be heard. The theatre began to fill when Rochefort and Jules Valles, who happened to agree with the operetta's political implications, wrote appreciatively of the work. Soon it was as fashionable as *Orpheus* had been and Hortense Schneider again became the toast of Paris. Auber found her singing of the first order and there was no doubt that she had the sort of touch that stars like Marie Lloyd were to exploit later – the ability to make the most innocent remark sound loaded with innuendo. Her dressing room at the Variétés was nightly crowded with aristocratic and royal visitors. The Prince of Wales was a devoted follower, the Tsar of Russia another. Zola, in the first chapter of *Nana*, described her performance in *La Belle Hélène*. The songs from *Belle Hélène* were now heard everywhere and even a hot summer did not affect the box-office. There was the usual lavish supper to celebrate its hundredth performance.

The score of *La Belle Hélène* is refined and charming and shows the most Viennese influence. Perhaps it lacks 'hit' tunes but it is a cohesive and balanced score with excellent songs for Helen. When an English amateur acting edition was prepared in 1961, the editors thought it necessary to filch songs and choruses from other Offenbach operettas to keep the interest of the score alive. Many people find this outrageous and unnecessary. Being one of the most currently satirical of the librettos, the listener today has only the goings-on of the Greek characters to amuse him, which are not really all that daring by today's standards. We must simply imagine the impact of the work on the world of 1864. The result of Offenbach's contract with the Theater an der Wien was that Vienna

Scene from *Helen* (1932)

heard *Die schöne Helena* not so very long after it had delighted Paris, on March 17th, 1865. The German words were more than adequately supplied by F. Zell and Julius Hopp and, although they had to do without Hortense Schneider, there was an adequate replacement in Marie Geistinger who made her début in *Hélène* and became a star overnight and the toast of Vienna. She was a good actress and manageress as well as a singer and because there was a lack of such talent – soubrette was the fashionable word – Marie Geistinger became one of the best-known figures in the Viennese operetta of her day. The censors tried to object to certain passages that they considered 'offensive to morality and decency' but as it was, on the surface, a simple reflection of the morals of the figures of Greek mythology, it was difficult for them to make their point without openly pointing to the shortcomings of the aristocracy of the day — so they let things stand. Although *Hélène* was not considered quite the measure of *Orpheus*, it was still immensely popular and established Offenbach even more firmly as the favourite of the 1860s. His talent was no longer measured by trifling little one-act productions but by full-length operatic productions that could be lavishly presented at the Theater an der

ADELPHI THEATRE

Sole Proprietors : J. & R. GATTI   *Lessees :* MUSICAL PLAYS, LTD.

LICENSED BY THE LORD CHAMBERLAIN TO ... ... JAMES ERNEST SHARPE

EVERY EVENING at 8.20
Matinees : WEDNESDAY and SATURDAY at 2.30

EXTRA MATINEE EASTER MONDAY

"HELEN!"

Cast in order of appearance :

Calchas (Chief Augur in the Temple of Jupiter at Sparta)		W. H. BERRY
Philocomus (his Assistant)		W. E. C. JENKINS
Helen (Wife of Menelaus of Sparta)		EVELYN LAYE
Orestes (Son of Agamemnon)		DÉSIRÉE ELLINGER
Pylades (his Friend)		JOY SPRING
Leaena	His	SEPHA TREBLE
Parthenis	Girl Friends	IRIS BROWNE
Paris (Prince of Troy)		BRUCE CARFAX
Mercury (Messenger to the Gods)		HAY PETRIE
Juno		WINIFRED DAVIS
Minerva	Goddesses	SHIRLEY DALE
Venus		YETTA
Achilles (King of the Myrmidons)		ROY RUSSELL
Agamemnon (King of Mycenae)		LESLIE JONES
Ajax I. (King of Salamis)		W. E. C. JENKINS
Ajax II. (King of the Locrians)		JOHN GATRELL
Ulysses (King of Ithaca)		A. BLANDFORD
Nestor (King of Pylos)		CHARLES CORNFORD
Menelaus (King of Sparta)		GEORGE ROBEY
Bacchis (Helen's Maid)		MADELINE GIBSON
The Foreign Dancer		EVE
Dancer at Orgy		PEARL ARGYLE
Hector (Son of Priam, King of Troy)		VICTOR DILL
King Priam (King of Troy)		STRAFFORD MOSS
Captain of Galley		PAUL BASQUE

Greek Chorus, Worshippers, Citizens, Soldiers, Etc.—EDALA BROUGH, EVE LYND, DOROTHY COLETTE, BARBARA SILVERIUS, GRETA MAY, ANN ANGELA, DODO JAY, ELIZABETH ROMAINE, RUBY MacGILCHRIST, IRIS MAITLAND, MAUREEN MOORE, MARGARET WATSON, NANCY BROWN, MARJORIE RAYMONDE, MARJORIE VERNE.
HAROLD KELLEY, EVAN W. JONES, J. APPLETON, CLAUDE BRITTON-ELDRED, ROBERT ELLIOTT, J. FARLEIGH-PRICE, HECTOR THOMAS, SELWYN MORGAN, PAUL STANTON, HERBERT FRANCIS, JOHN LAURIE, BERTRAM PAYNE, ERNEST LUDLOW.

Mr. Cochran's Young Ladies.—MAISIE GREEN, SONIA HULLEY, JEAN BARNES, AIMÉE GILLESPIE, BUNTY PAIN, PEGGY BARTON, MARGARET NEESON, JACKIE MARCON, MOIRA TRACEY, BETTY WEDGWOOD, DOROTHY JACKSON, FLORITA FEY, MINA HILLMAN, PHYLLIS STICKLAND, JEAN GARMAN, CLEO NORDI, SHEILA WILSON.

Men Dancers.—CLAUDE NEWMAN, JACK SPURGEON, WALTER GORE, ROLLO GAMBLE, W. CHAPPELL, ROBERT STUART, GUY MASSEY, JEAN PERRIE, HARRY WEBSTER, IVOR BEDDOES, MARK FAWDRY, ROBERT LINDSAY, GEORGE BOWLER.

March 21

Cochran's famous
production of *Helen* (1932)

Wien. *La Belle Hélène* was pleasing Berlin audiences as well and by June 30th, 1866, it reached London as *Helen* or *Taken from the Greek* at the Adelphi. But, as intimated before, the English-speaking world's Offenbach craze was a delayed action affair. It was mainly a result of the dilettante attitude of British producers, directors and writers. The famous librettist J. R. Planché (author of *Oberon*) wrote in 1865:

In September this year I was applied to by Mr Buckstone to adapt for him Offenbach's opéra-bouffe, *Orphée aux Enfers*, with a view to the first appearance at the Haymarket of Miss Louise Keeley, who he promised should be adequately supported by vocalists he would engage expressly for the piece, there not being one in the company who professed to sing operatic music. It was necessary also that *Orpheus* should play the violin, and there were other difficulties to be got over. The good intentions of Mr Buckstone, however, only went the way of cartloads of similar excellent materials, to pave the regions we were about to lay the scene of in the Haymarket, and failed to induce any singers of celebrity to set their feet on them. I was so accustomed, however, to this sort of disappointment in an English theatre that it did not much disconcert me. I wrote the piece as well as I could, and got it acted as well as I could, William Farren, who had received a musical education, making a pleasant *Jupiter;* Mrs Chippendale, a splendid jealous *Juno;* Miss Helen Howard representing *Public Opinion* in a style calculated to obtain its favourable verdict; and an old favourite and true artist, Mr David Fisher, playing *Orpheus* with intelligence, and 'the fiddle like an angel'. Miss Louise Keeley was a charming *Eurydice*, and sang like a little nightingale; so with the addition of pretty scenery, pretty dresses, and some pretty faces, we pulled through pretty well. It was not Offenbach's opera; but the piece went merrily with the audience, and ran from Christmas to Easter. As far as I was concerned, the Press was most laudatory, and welcomed my reappearance as a writer of extravaganza, after a lapse of nine years, with a cordiality that was extremely gratifying to me, considering the change that in the meanwhile had come over the spirit of that class of entertainment.

The Duc de Morny passed away on March 10th, 1865 and the whole of France mourned him as well as his friends in the theatre. This great and cultured man, it had been said, might have saved the second Empire from the assault of the Republicans, but he died, worn out, at the age of fifty-six. Now the common people were beginning to dominate the Parisian night-life and the café-concerts flourished. All round the socialist forces were becoming more and more threatening. On July 24th Offenbach produced his regular piece for Ems, this time a two-act work called *Coscoletto* which got no further than the resort. For Les Bouffes-Parisiens he wrote a revue, *Les Refrains des Bouffes*, which on September 21st revived, as was now the established custom, some of the favourite items from previous shows. Next, on December 11th, *Les Bergers*, with book by Crémieux and Gille, an 18th century pastiche set in the time of Watteau. It proved too serious for Parisian—or at least,

Bouffes-Parisiens – tastes, and was one of the rare failures at this time. Albert Wolff considered it one of Offenbach's best scores, as did the composer, but the audience was unenthusiastic and there was such an uproar over a speech making fun of the 1789 Constitution that the police had to be called in.

Offenbach was, in spite of this setback, well and truly in his stride and the next three productions are a remarkable trio of works, each a full-length opera, each a considerable success. First came *Barbe-Bleue*, the follow-up to *La Belle Hélène*, with book by Meilhac and Halévy, produced at the Variétés on February 5th, 1866. Hortense Schneider played Boulotte, a peasant girl – 'with incomparable wit and talent' according to Halévy. The librettists were presented with the novel challenge of making a horror-story into a comedy and they did it well. Offenbach's score contains one or two excellent parts and one number at least, 'Qu'un bon courtesan s'incline', had a catchy tune that made it the hit of the season. But it was by no means his finest score and, when *Blaubart* was produced at the

Caricature by P. Cattelain, 1867

Theater an der Wien on September 21st, the critics, though fairly pleased with the piece, also noted a tendency in the score for Offenbach to borrow from his own compositions as well as liberally helping himself to other people's. The operetta also made a quick appearance in London as *Blue Beard Re-paired* at the Olympic Theatre on June 2nd, described as an operatic extravaganza in one-act, an adaptation with Nellie Farren and other stalwart burlesquers in the cast. The original version was not to be staged in London until 1869, when Schneider and Adolph Dupuis came with a Bouffes-Parisiens company.

Next came one of the truly great Offenbach operettas; the lightest and airiest of his three best pieces (the others I think are *La Grande-Duchesse de Gérolstein* and *La Périchole*) – the one that most nearly reflects Offenbach's own character – *La Vie Parisienne*. All the ingredients that had shone individually in earlier works seemed to

La Vie Parisienne quadrille, 1866

coalesce in *La Vie Parisienne* – it was his *Marriage of Figaro,* a work of exquisite rightness. Its most remarkable departure from the previous works was that, at last, here was something satirising modern times by means of contemporary characters and setting. *La Vie Parisienne* was nicely balanced between an affectionate tribute to Paris and sharp tilts at her pretensions. It was a splendid idea for an opera, this bringing together of all kinds of opportunities (with some nicely drawn characters from places like Sweden and Brazil) in the gay city of Paris. Meilhac and Halévy supplied a classic book almost worthy of Gilbert. Zulma Bouffar took the part of a delightful glove-maker called Gabrielle. And Offenbach's score was certainly his best so far. There was the can-can that almost rivalled the immortal one in *Orpheus;* there were unrivalled patter-songs like 'Je suis Brésilien'; there was a bold yet most haunting waltz, 'A minuit sonnant commence la fête', which used the simple but effective device of the cello following the vocal line; especially did

La Vie Parisienne (1866)

From the score of *La Vie Parisienne*

Offenbach excel at making into a catchy and delightful song the most utter nonsense – such as words to the effect that someone's clothes were splitting down the back – an ability that was to offer inspiration to two supreme writers of operetta in England within a few years. It opened in the original five-act version at the Palais-Royal on October 31st, 1866 and there was no doubting or trial period this time. Paris fell for it hook, line and sinker from the very first night. Conversely it had perhaps less success abroad simply because it was so very Parisian, so essentially French. It was seen in Vienna at the Kai-Theater in January of 1867 but Treumann did not take it into the Carltheater repertoire until 1871. A performance was planned at the St. James's Theatre in May 1868 but the licence was withdrawn and it was 1872 before it got to London. It was revised in four acts for production at the Variétés with the part of Alfred written in for Léonce. Meanwhile at Les Bouffes they were still playing *Orpheus* and, willing to try any novelty, the celebrated courtesan Cora Pearl made a brief and nervous two-night appearance in it as an anything but innocent Cupid.

Now came the greatest international success of them all. Just as Les Bouffes-Parisiens had opportunely founded its fortunes during the year of the Paris Exhibition of 1855, now the great World Exhibition of 1867 was to provide impetus for Offenbach's latest effort, *La Grande-Duchesse de Gérolstein.* The 1867 Exhibition was the apex of the Second Empire's cultural aspirations. In fact, like most manifestations of this nature, it was very much a political stratagem, a sop to the French nation now growing a little disconsolate at the lack of French triumphs, apprehensive at the constant threat of Franco-Prussian conflict, more than a little cynical about the dissolute ways of their lords and masters. Napoleon III thought that some lavish entertainment well spread around might drum up public support for him if things came to the crunch one way or another. The World Exhibition was to be the shopfront of the world and each nation was invited to exhibit its most significant traits. Victorian England demonstrated her worthy character with a pavilion filled with biblical tracts, agricultural instruments and a school – which may have seemed a bit dull to French tastes. But there were plenty of exotic exhibits from the Middle and Far East to counteract this. The British section was at least second only in size to the French and some of its trade exhibits – the pottery of Wedgwood, for example – showed solid good taste. The French, true to character, made a great display of food and wine.

Paris was full of visiting royalty – the King of Prussia came to see what was going on, bringing Count Bismarck with him, and the rich and affluent from every country were in the French capital. The exhibition was opened by the Emperor on April 1st and it closed on November 3rd. Nobody could deny that Offenbach's timing was good when he opened his most successful and most internationally popular show, *La Grande-Duchesse de Gérolstein*, on April 3rd, riding in on the full flood of initial enthusiasm for the Exhibition and a Paris full of well-heeled visitors.

As usual the rehearsals for an Offenbach piece, to be staged once again at the Variétés, were full of event. The main upset centred yet again round the now glittering figure of Hortense Schneider whose salary had risen to 4,500 francs a month. The general trend of the libretto was a quite deliberately pointed satire on war and the military mind; and a less definable satire on the Court. With the Austro-German War fresh in mind, Bismarck and the Prussians in their midst and a looming threat of the almost inevitable Franco-

From *La Grande-Duchesse de Gérolstein* (1867)

Prussian war in the air, the censor was a little touchy about the whole thing. It is always difficult to censor elusive satire, so he fixed his mind on things that could be materially altered. There was the ribbon of some imaginary grand order that Hortense Schneider as the Grande-Duchesse was to wear across her bosom – that must go. The lady exhibited all the standard tantrums and swore that she would leave the stage for ever. But then she remembered her star rating and the delights of Offenbach's score and resumed her place on the stage. There was no question that the first night was a roaring success. The audience rocked with laughter at the pompous humbug of General Boum, played by the comedian Couder, and encored Schneider's first song 'Ah, que j'aime les militaires'. The great hit of the show, 'Voici le sabre de mon père', brought the

Hortense Schneider as the
Grand Duchess

90

From *La Grande-Duchesse de Gérolstein*

house down. Halévy particularly admired the song 'Dîtes-lui qu'on l'a remarqué' which he described as 'a jewel'. There was a weak part in the second act which had to be altered so that by the third night all faults had been removed and the show was perfect in every respect. Hortense Schneider got most of the plaudits but there were still words to spare to praise Offenbach's splendid score. There was doubt expressed as to whether 1867 would be remembered as the year of the World Exhibition or the year of *La Grande-Duchesse de Gérolstein*. The whole thing confused the simple mind so much that when Hortense Schneider arrived in a carriage to drive round the Exhibition and was told that only royalty were allowed this privilege, she grandly said 'I am the Grande-Duchesse de Gérolstein' and was immediately admitted while the flunkeys bowed low as she swept by. The Prince of Wales paid a visit to Paris toward the end of May and found the theatre sold out. Schneider received him in her dressing-room. The Tsar of Russia, who arrived in Paris on June 1st took no chances by booking his seat well ahead. His visit to the Variétés was made only three hours after he had arrived in Paris. The King of Prussia went, and also Bismarck who had unwittingly contributed as much to the operetta's success as anyone. It confirmed his view that the French were decadent but he still greatly enjoyed it all. As far as the satire on the court was concerned, he couldn't agree more – 'C'est tout-a-fait ça', he said to one of his companions.

Practically unheeded amongst all the Offenbach worship, Johann Strauss was conducting Viennese waltzes in a restaurant near the Exhibition. He had come to Paris at the invitation of the Comte d'Osmont and with the encouragement of the Austrian ambassador to France and his wife, the Prince and Princess Richard Metternich. Strauss had left Vienna with something of a cloud hanging over his head. It is hard to believe now, but the first performance of the celebrated *Blue Danube* waltz had been marred by having inane and somewhat politically offensive words set to it by one Josef Weyl. Strauss shrugged off the failure – what was one waltz more or less to him? In Paris, Princess von Metternich invited him to play at a ball at the Austrian Embassy and he was a great success. *Le Figaro* took him up and in no time Strauss was a popular Parisian figure. So in his next concert at the World Fair he played them the waltz that Vienna had rejected, this time without words. The object of inviting Strauss to Paris had been politically slanted to endear the French to Austrian culture. The idea succeeded beyond all expectations when *The Blue Danube* swept the Parisians off their feet and became an immediate best-seller. Strauss had to play it time and time again and every orchestra took up the music that they called 'the waltz of waltzes'. Here was a turning of the tables indeed, with Strauss providing the musical motif of a Fair in Paris after Offenbach had outshone him in Vienna. The strains of *The Blue Danube* and selections from *La Grande-Duchesse de Gérolstein* rang out in fierce rivalry all over Paris — and, if anything, it must be admitted that probably *The Blue Danube* was the ultimate winner. It was one of the first pieces of music to sell over a million copies.

Unfortunately even the brilliant idea of the Fair, the distractions of Offenbach and the success of Strauss, in potent combination, failed to do what was required of them. All the dreams of a Franco-Austrian alliance faded when, on June 19th, Maximilian, the ex-Archduke of Austria, who had been persuaded by the French to accept the crown of Mexico so that he could protect Napoleonic interests there in return for military support, was condemned to

La Permission de Dix Heures (1873)

death by revolutionary forces led by the rebel Juarez. The sudden death of royalty was stunning news in those days but the murder of Emperor Franz Josef's brother also had such sinister political undertones. Empress Eugénie heard the news at the Fair and promptly fainted. All social functions were temporarily cancelled. As a result the tentative friendship between Austria and France faltered, Austria gradually drifted back into the German camp and Bismarck strengthened his hand. Things cooled off gradually but perceptibly. The Emperor Franz Josef visited Paris in October but he was in too sad and serious a mood even to book a seat for *La Grande-Duchesse* – which greatly piqued Hortense Schneider. Still the Exhibition had been visited by ten million people, including fifty-seven members of various royal families; and both Offenbach and Hortense Schneider were immeasurably wealthier for the opportunities taken.

Offenbach didn't wait in Paris to count the francs but took his usual holiday in Ems where he wrote and produced *La Permission de Dix Heures* and *La Lecon de Chant*. For the moment he no longer needed to write six or seven potboilers a year to keep the coffers filled. He was able to spend some of his time at Ems in writing another full-scale work for the Opéra-Comique. It was a three-act comic-opera, with book by Eugène Cormon and Hector Crémieux, based on Defoe's *Robinson Crusoe* – a free adaptation which threw in Crusoe's family and friends, a crew of pirates and a tribe of cannibals, to fill the operatic stage, and which bore little resemblance to the original beyond the title and the traditional Man Friday. Robinson Crusoe has a girl-friend in the opera named Edwige, a part that was taken by Mme Galli-Marie who, in 1875, was to be the original Carmen in Bizet's celebrated opera and was also the original Mignon. Edwige has a splendid waltz-song 'Conduisez-moi vers celui que j'adore' which lightly parodied typical operatic waltz-songs. It was not, as the Offenbachian opponents hoped, a total failure like *Barkouf*. It was quite favourably received and ran for thirty-two nights. On the other hand it was not quite the success that Offenbach expected. At this period Offenbach was in a poor state of health and suffering so much from gout that he had to be carried from his carriage to the rehearsals. Beyond this there is little question that 1867 was a triumphant year for Offenbach. In the December, to add to his glory, a revised version of *Geneviève de Brabant* was put on at the Théâtre des Menus Plaisirs and there were four revues running which included material from his recent successes. 1867 also saw the beginnings of his proper recognition in London. What H. C. Hibbert in *A Playgoer's Memories* has described as 'the first serious production of opéra bouffe in English' was *The Grand Duchess* at Covent Garden, produced by the elder Augustus Harris. That was in November, little more than six months after its Paris production. The title rôle was taken in succession by such eminent singers as Mrs Howard Paul, Julia Matthews and Emily Soldene.

Even Offenbach could not always maintain an unremitting flow of new, original and immortal material. *Le Château à Toto*, produced at the Palais-Royal, with book by Meilhac and Halévy, on May 6th, 1868 seemed, to some of the critics, to be simply a rehashing of old ideas to music that sounded vaguely familiar. Its satire of the nobility was even wearing a bit thin. The Bouffes-Parisiens were given a new one-act piece *L'Île de Tulipatan*, words by Chivot and Duru, with which to open its new season on September 30th, 1868 together with *Le Fifre Enchanté*, which had been originally written for Ems in 1864. The patrons of the Bouffes were well pleased with the continuation of the traditional Offenbach vein.

Satire is an art which has recurrent surges of vitality and vitriol which last for a year or two and then lose their fizz. We experienced such a period in the 1960s following on the heels of *Beyond the Fringe*, whose spirit was carried on in several TV shows, and history

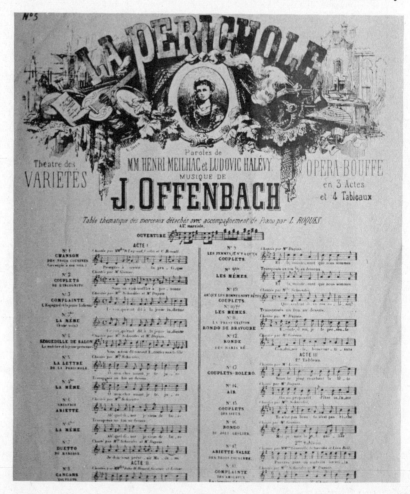

La Périchole (1874)

ETTRE DE LA PÉRICHOLE
(LA PÉRICHOLE)

Paroles de
MM. Henri MEILHAC
& Ludovic HALÉVY

Andante

O mon cher amant, je te

ju — re,Que je t'aime detout mon cœur, Mais, vrai,

avec l'Autorisation de M! C. JOUBERT
25, Rue d'Hauteville, Paris.
-37-

Tous droits de traduction
exécution, reproduction
réservés pour tous pays.

The famous letter song

is periodically dotted with such phases when great satirists have had their heyday. It is taking too golden a view of humanity to suggest that the victims mend their ways and consequently make the satire unnecessary. It is rather that we cease, after a time, to be able to distinguish between the true image and the reflection. The satire in the Offenbach burlesques began to lose its edge in 1868 and the need to move toward a romantic, less pointed story became obvious. The humour still relied on the absurdities of stock characters but the whiplash of unadorned wit was gradually lightened by more romantic human interest.

Offenbach's next substantial piece, *La Périchole*, clearly shows this trend which tended to suit middle-brow patrons but to displease the highbrows who still liked their satire. If operetta was to become similar to the opéra-comique and grand opera that it had previously lampooned, its purpose seemed, to some people, to be defeated. *La Périchole*, book by Meilhac and Halévy (with the name of the principal character, Piquillo, taken from Prosper Merimée's *Le Carosse du Saint Sacrement*, but otherwise only loosely connected with this generally attributed source), opened at the Variétés on October 6th and was very successful without quite having the scandalous lustre of some of its predecessors. It remains one of Offenbach's most delightful works and one of his very best scores. The charming love story of the street-singer Périchole and Piquille is encapsuled in what is possibly the finest aria that Offenbach ever wrote, the Letter Song 'O mon cher amant' which was rhyming version of Manon Lescaut's letter in Prévost's novel. It has an artful simplicity, a directness, a warmth that combine to make it almost Mozartian in its classical tenderness. The whole score is full of fine opportunities for good singers, the spicy couplets 'Ah! que les hommes sont bêtes', and the splendid ariette 'Ah! quel dîner je viens de faire' – to mention but two. However, there were critics around ready to wade into the attack, like Sarcey, who uncompromisingly declared that operetta was in decline and the public were beginning to tire of it. All that was fading was a certain kind of pioneering work; operetta, and its romantic offshoots, were, in fact, just beginning to blossom. The great golden age of operetta in France, Vienna, and subsequently England and America, had not even begun. Perhaps it was simply the ages-old confusion of terminology.

As usual the rehearsals were enlivened with the antics of Hortense Schneider, who had been delighting royalty and the general public in London in July in a production of *La Belle Hélène* at the St. James's Theatre. Her first stipulation for appearing was that her rival Mme Silly must never appear in the same show with her. At the rehearsals she refused to sing her words aloud and threw her score into the auditorium when Offenbach threatened to have

Marie Aimée as Périchole

her replaced. She announced that she was on her way to Italy but, as usual, peace was eventually made and Hortense was there on the opening night to give a superb performance and a particularly magical rendering of the Letter Song.

The substantial qualities of *La Périchole* are a clear indication that Offenbach was perfectly capable of writing a good comic opera, though why he should have so craved the badge of respectability that production at the Opéra-Comique gave is difficult to understand when popular success elsewhere was there for the asking. Difficult to understand in practical terms, at any rate; human nature is always a ready recipient of flattery, a willing victim of pride. The next work for the Opéra-Comique was *Vert-Vert*, a three-act piece with words by Meilhac and Nuitter, opening on March 10th. He was accused, in his setting of a girls' boarding-school, of tackling a subject more suited to Les Bouffes-Parisiens, but there was some delightful music and, if anything, it was a greater success than his previous production at the Opéra-Comique. It was something of a blow when the next production at Les Bouffes was an outright failure. *La Diva*, in which Meilhac and Halévy told the life story of Hortense Schneider, in fulfilment of an old promise, opened on March 22nd, 1869 and fell flat. This was not because Offenbach's work, or that of his librettists, was really in decline. Perhaps they relied too much on their old tricks, but it was simply one of the changes of fashion (that happens so abruptly and unreasoningly in the arts) that made the fickle public look for a new flavour. They found it in the musical farces of Hervé, Offenbach's old rival, who had tremendous success at about this time with such shows as *Chilpéric* and *L'Oeil Crevé*, and in the more romantic pieces by the new operetta composers like Lecocq who made his mark in 1868 with *Fleur-de-thé*. Suggestions that Offenbach was finished at this stage, when his maximum fame abroad was about to begin, would be an over-exaggeration. There was still no-one to surpass him musically. Who can remember anything that Hervé wrote? How many successful operettas did his younger rivals manage? An average of one apiece judging by the musical history books!

Offenbach was still affluent and now took the summer waters at Baden where he produced *La Princesse de Trébizonde* (Nuitter and Tréfeu) in July 1869 and was to be seen dressed in colourful and dandified clothes, still very much the centre of attraction and still applauded with warmth and affection. The operetta came to Les Bouffes on December 7th; and, on the 10th a substantial three-act opéra-bouffe, *Les Brigands* (Meilhac and Halévy), opened at Les Variétés. Again the veering toward the world of romantic comic-opera is increasingly obvious. It is a well-written score and indicated a desire by Offenbach to introduce a truly dramatic quality in his work. He wrote to Halévy during its creation: 'I would like to have more situations to put to music, not simply song upon song . . . my audience is tired of snippets and so am I!' *Les Brigands*, once a very popular piece, has not received the later attention that it deserves; for it is not only musically and dramatically sound, treading a firm path between opera and operetta, but immensely significant in many ways, looking both backward and forward in time. The story of a band of brigands is a familiar one in operetta. Offenbach and his collaborators adapted it to produce a devastating satire on the brigandry of the financial world – 'Il faut voler selon la position qu'on occupe dans la Société' – as one of the robbers remarks. But, perhaps, most interestingly of all, *Les Brigands* makes merciless fun of the gendarmes, far beyond the good-humoured nonsense in *Geneviève de Brabant*. The bandits, celebrating their latest success, are whooping it up when they hear the approaching footsteps of the law – 'ce sont les bottes, les bottes, les bottes des caribiniers' they sing alternately loudly and brashly and softly and fearfully, hiding themselves behind trees. The gendarmerie arrive and express, with utmost duplicity, their regret that they have arrived too late to be able to tackle the robbers. Offenbach has great fun with this idea, alternately suggesting the potential menace of the police and their incompetence at never being in the right spot at the right time, their over-sized boots setting up a recurring rhythm. That all this should be, musically, verbally and dramatically, so uncannily close to a famous scene in *The Pirates of Penzance*, first produced just ten years later in 1879, asks for some interesting explanation – especially when we note that the translator of the libretto of *Les Brigands*, when it was produced for the third time in English in London in 1889, was none other than W. S. Gilbert. In fact the plot thickens when we find that Gilbert's original translation was published (and later withdrawn) in 1871; presumably intended for the first English production at the Globe that year. The translation used was actually provided by Henry S. Leigh. *Les Brigands* had been seen in London, in French, in 1871 and 1873 and in English in 1871 (as *Falsacappa*) and in 1875 (as *The Brigands*) so there can be little doubt that both Gilbert and Sullivan were both well acquainted with the score. Most Gilbert and Sullivan commentators and historians make light of the potential connection between their operas and Offenbach's; but the possibilities of a work of detection and comparison would be endless and fascinating. The connections between Gilbert and Meilhac and Halévy have been interestingly discussed in an American paper by George McElroy of Indiana University, but the matter probably goes even deeper and further. Besides *Les Brigands* the only other new work to appear in 1869 was *La Romance de la Rose* at the Bouffes-Parisiens on December 11th.

Les Brigands (1869), Gilbertian source

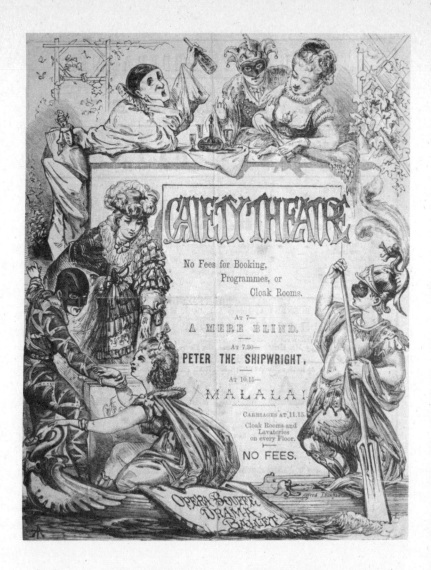

Gaiety programme for *A Mere Blind* and *Malala!*

A glance at a chronological listing of Offenbach's output reveals an untypical gap in 1870 and indeed there was to be no new Offenbach operetta for two years until *Boule de Neige* opened at the Bouffes on December 14th, 1871. The silence was not, of course, entirely Offenbach's fault for the Franco-Prussian war was occupying many people's thoughts. He was in a restless frame of mind and passed the time thinking of a truly grand opera in spite of all that was happening in the troubled world. Meanwhile there was a charity performance of *La Grande-Duchesse* for the Nice Carnival. Hortense Schneider appeared in it and Offenbach, postponing a trip to Vienna, conducted, thin and pale, 'une fantôme de carnaval'. He waved his baton without any noticeable enthusiasm. By now the English Offenbach craze was well under way. Mr John Hollingshead had opened his Gaiety Theatre in the Strand, a 2,000-seater shrine to operetta, beginning, in the prescribed Bouffes-Parisiens manner, with a triple bill on December 21st, 1868. There was an operetta in one act, *The Two Harlequins,* with music by Emile Jonas and English book by Gilbert A'Beckett, a comedy-drama in three acts, *On the Cards,* adapted from the French and an operatic extravaganza, *Robert the Devil,* with score arranged by the musical director M. Kettenus from various sources and book by W. S. Gilbert. There was still little hope of filling the theatres with English musicals so Hollingshead, cashing in on a growing fashion for French fare, was a regular visitor to Paris to see what could be brought back and adapted for English usage – and generally badly mauled in the process. In his net there were naturally a number of Offenbach pieces hot from Les Bouffes-Parisiens and elsewhere. The first Offenbach piece at the Gaiety was *Lischen et Fritzchen* on July 26th, 1869, followed by *The Rose of Auvergne* on November 8th, a typical Bouffes piece with three characters taken by Miss Tremaine, Mr C. Lyall and Mr Perrini. For Christmas, starting on December 20th there was a triple bill which included *The Rose of Auvergne, Uncle Dick's Darling* a new drama by H. J. Byron and a new operatic extravaganza *Wat Tyler M.P.* the burlesque book by George Augustus Sala, his first piece on the London stage, and music by Herr Meyer Lutz.

For the following season John Hollingshead decided that he must have a full-scale Offenbach production. He wrote in his *Gaiety Chronicles:*

The work of Offenbach that I decided to produce was *The Princess of Trébizonde,* an amusing and perfectly inoffensive comic opera in three acts then being performed at the Bouffes Parisiens in Paris in the winter of 1868-70 – the last days of the pleasant Second Empire. I had seen the piece once and went over to see it again, knowing that I should have some little difficulty in casting it musically with my existing company. On my second visit I was provided with an order for two seats from M. Offenbach the composer. The secretary of the theatre was evidently depressed by such an application, and when a French official is depressed he shows it visibly. Depressed or not, he could hardly avoid honouring M. Offenbach's order – one of the *droits d'auteur* in France – but he had his revenge. He gave me two seats but demanded the *droits des pauvres* – a tax of ten per cent on the face value of the ticket. I paid the money, and thought that England, in spite of the great butcher Napoleon's opinion, was not the only nation of shopkeepers.

The Princess of Trébizonde opened at the Gaiety on April 16th, 1870 with the celebrated comedian Mr J. L. Toole as Ciabriolo (the showman played in Paris by Desiré), Miss Hughes (Mrs Gaston Murray) as Manola, Constance Loseby as Prince Raphael, etc., while 'the most effective part in the piece, Regina, the daughter of the showman, was reserved for Miss Farren, who had much of the peculiar and fascinating spirit of the original, the incomparable

Mlle Celine Chaumont.' It was Nellie Farren's first appearance in opéra-bouffe and 'she faced the ordeal triumphantly'. Mr Toole 'worked up his part in good low comedian style, adding much to the words'. The dresses were 'thoroughly French' and the production and scenery 'far surpassed in artistic delicacy the original production in Paris. The pages (girls of course) were better looking and better dressed, and Herr Meyer Lutz, the clever and indefatigable conductor, turned them into well-drilled chorus singers'. The English press was visibly warming to Offenbach. 'On none of his operas', said *The Times*, 'has Offenbach lavished gayer or more obviously melodic music.' *The Daily Telegraph* was equally enthusiastic: 'The music that Offenbach has woven on this fantastic canvas is as gracefully piquante, and melodious as any that he has ever written.'

Offenbach came over to see the production, all expenses paid but with his usual reluctance to travel overseas. Wrote Mr Hollingshead:

M. Offenbach was a quiet, modest man, evidently in delicate health: a very different man from Hervé or Emile Jonas. He stayed about a week, and passed his evenings chiefly at the few music-halls which London could boast of at the time. He saw much, so he said, which he could utilize in his pieces on Paris. In particular he picked out two singers and dancers, named Brian and Conolly (both now dead); and his judgement was shown to be right, as they afterwards became popular at the Théâtre des Variétés in Paris, where Charles Mathews and E. A. Sothern made only a partial success, although Mathews played in good French. Offenbach was a careful eater, and particular about his food, and he begged not to be sent to what he called an English parody of a French café, but to some thoroughly English tavern, where he could get the best food cooked in the plain English style. He was sent, of course, to 'Simpson's in the Strand', where he ate his saddle of mutton and his boiled potatoes quite like a perfidious Albionite.

Thereafter Offenbach was regular fare at the Gaiety and the productions included *Tromb-al-cazar* and *Bluebeard* (1870); for the first ever matinée at the Gaiety *The Princess of Trébizonde* was revived (1871) followed by *Malala!*, a 'new African Musical Extravaganza', writers uncredited in the programme, utilising Offenbach's music, *A Mere Blind (Les Deux Aveugles), The Grand Duchess of Gérolstein, La Chanson de Fortunio, Les Bavards, La Belle Hélène, Le Mariage aux Lanternes* – all produced in 1871; *Les Deux Aveugles, Psychic Force* (an adaptation of Offenbach's music), *Geneviève de Brabant, The Two Blinds* (yet another version of the ever popular *Les Deux Aveugles*) and *The Magic Fife* (all 1872); and so on. Offenbach productions were to continue at the Gaiety till around 1885.

While Offenbach was enjoyably utilising the tramp of marching feet in *Les Brigands* and otherwise leading his blameless, if

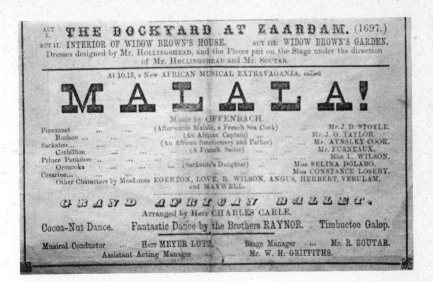

Malala! an Offenbach compilation in London

epicurean, life, more ominous feet were beginning to tramp over Europe. Once again the *Marseillaise* was a popular song and patriotic fervour spread throughout France. It all rather went into a minor key as France began to realise that she was being beaten by the forces that Bismarck had united against her. The theatres began to close and the Variétés, where *Les Brigands* was running, was turned into a military hospital. France was officially defeated at the Battle of Sedan on September 2nd, 1870. The Emperor surrendered and was held prisoner by the Prussians. On September 4th, France was once more declared a republic and the glorious, frivolous, Second Empire was no longer. Offenbach had returned from Ems at the start of the battle and suddenly found himself, with his German ancestry and his liking for aristocratic company, a rather unpopular figure. He sent his family off to San Sebastian and soon joined them. How soon a popular favourite can go out of popular favour was illustrated when a performance of *La Princesse de Trébizonde*, at Les Bouffes-Parisiens in February 1871, was deplored as the work of a 'Prussian'! Lecocq, the lifelong rival of Offenbach, gleefully prophesied his end. Paris was soon occupied by real Prussians and Offenbach dwelt in a state of physical illness and mental despair in Italy, not only fearing the end of his own world of light-hearted operetta, but sad for his beloved France overrun by the savages he had to acknowledge as his kinsfolk. He dwelt in Italy while the civil war now began in France between the government forces and the Socialist revolutionaries. The state of ferment that the population of France was in and the iron hold of the Commune for a brief period, when the middle-classes and aristocracy, like Offenbach and the Empress Eugénie, fled from the country, made it look as though there would never be a cultural life in Paris again. Eventually the government troops under Thiers managed to raise enough strength to rout the Commune. For days Paris was in flames and then it was all over. There were thoughts of restoring the monarchy once more but a commonsense compromise prevailed and France became a Republic.

Offenbach in the meantime was reviving his spirits by travelling around Europe and supervising productions of his operettas. In Vienna, in the summer of 1871, there was a production of *Les Brigands*. There was a brief visit to England as a guest of the Prince of Wales, which coincided with a season of French plays (1871/2) at the St. James's Theatre with Hortense Schneider starring in such pieces as *La Grande-Duchesse* and *La Périchole*. Eventually, as the smoke died down, and life returned to normal, he returned to Paris and the first thing was a rehearsal of *Les Brigands* at the Variétés,

Publishers' advert for London versions of Offenbach

La Petite Mademoiselle by
Charles Lecocq

now cleared of its war-wounded. He fussed around and interfered at the rehearsals with all his old enthusiasm.

Slowly the spirit of Paris revived; the elegant, frivolous spirit that had fostered the early Offenbach operettas. It could never be quite the same as during the Second Empire, but the differences were only material ones, not of the heart. Offenbach was no longer a leading figure in Parisian circles nor were the parties quite so frequent. In a rather more sober, working-class world there was no longer a place for new operettas in the old vein, although the old ones could comfortably be revived. For the moment he completed the score of *Le Roi Carotte*, a score left behind in his flight from Paris, and it was put on at the Gaîté Theatre in an unfashionable part of Paris. The Gaîté, a sort of Parisian Palladium, indulged in big productions and pantomimes, and put on a lavish production of *Le Roi Carotte* with Zulma Bouffar in the cast. Here was Offenbach writing for the people rather than an exclusive audience and some of his old supporters said that it was the Prussian element coming out in him. Then there was a rather boring work at the Opéra-Comique three days later – *Fantasio* which soon disappeared in spite of some worthy music. It was the last work of his to be produced at the Opéra-Comique during his lifetime.

For Vienna he wrote *Fleurette* which was produced at the Carl-theater on March 8th, 1872 without much success; and *Der schwarze Korsar* which was something of a disaster at the Theater an der Wien on September 21st. He made the unfortunate mistake of writing his own libretto and of making much capital out of imitations of an amateur orchestra that played out of tune. The production, which he supervised and attended, was so hastily put together that no-one quite knew whether the bad playing was intentional or merely unfortunate. One English critic wrote for his journal back home:

The Theater an der Wien has produced another operetta by Offenbach, *Der schwarze Korsar*, to which Offenbach (another Wagner) has written also the libretto. It is the worst of all his later works. This time more than ever he has sinned through his facility in writing; the experiment of making the libretto himself will, it is hoped, be the first and last one. The operetta nevertheless was richly mounted; the directrice, Frau Geistinger, and the tenor Swoboda sang in the best manner, and Frl Roeder showed a faultless figure – reason enough that the operetta filled the house, bad as it was.

So things were at a pretty low ebb and Offenbach was beginning to get those slighting reviews that often seem to have a longer historical echo than the generally good ones.

Still there was enough obstinate spirit in Offenbach to make him persevere. He saw a future in continuing, on the one hand, the

103

spectacular show like *Le Roi Carotte* and in pursuing the line of romantic operettas like *La Périchole*. The latter was certainly the more important, from the point of view of musical history, and had influenced a piece like Lecocq's *La Fille de Madame Angot* which, in turn, re-influenced Offenbach, mainly because it was such a roaring success. History repeated itself when he took over the management of the Théâtre de Gaîté on July 1st, 1873. Full of ambitious ideas, as ever, he took on two full troupes of actors, so that he could prepare both kinds of entertainment, and there was the usual extravagant rash of renovation and redecoration. Everything had to be of the best quality, as in the past, to present an Offenbach work. Unfortunately the youthful enthusiasm that produced the early Bouffes-Parisiens delights was no longer there. It was a tired Offenbach, an established but worn Offenbach, who tried to recapture the urge and spirit of his pioneering days. The first production at the Gaîté on September 2nd, 1874 was *Le Gascon*, a drama in three acts by Théodore Barrière to which Offenbach supplied the incidental music. It made very little impact and was soon taken off.

Rather desperate for a success, Offenbach now tried a revival of his world-famous *Orphée aux Enfers*. In a historical perspective he did what may now seem an unforgivable and tasteless thing. He made it into a sort of pantomime, getting Hector Crémieux and Ludovic Halévy to rewrite the libretto in four acts and twelve tableaux. They added numerous irrelevant characters and demanded scenes and effects that bore little relation to the original sharp and satirical story. Ballets were inserted at every possible point – 'Danse des élèves d'Orphée', 'Divertissement des heures dans l'Olympe', 'Ballet des Mouches en Enfer'. Offenbach betook himself to the South of France where he wrote the new music, an extended overture, new ballet music, some of it perhaps inferior to the original score, though the composer declared himself well satisfied. It was lavishly staged by Godin of the property department who had learned his art in some of London's more elaborate theatres. Dawn on Olympus was of breath-taking magnificence. The costumes were extravagant and there were one hundred and twenty in the chorus to be dressed and sixty-eight in the corps de ballet. After the first night on February 7th the critics, not unexpectedly, deplored the bastardisation of Offenbach's art and were unimpressed by the galaxies of chorus-girls in scanty costumes. But, as usual, the critics were a race apart from the public who loved it and kept the theatre packed for months on end. There was a gala 100th performance which Offenbach, although crippled by gout, conducted himself with a remarkable show of renewed vigour; and by then the box-office had already taken 1,800,000 francs and was making a nice profit. The spectacle was later seen at

London's Alhambra in 1877 on a similar scale. It is wise to remember, when today the National Opera at the Coliseum are criticised for making spectacles of the Offenbach shows which they stage, that they are only doing what Offenbach himself was perfectly prepared to do. Nevertheless his works are probably best seen and heard as pure operettas; the form in which, if they are to

Pomme d'Api (1873)

Royal Academy of Music
MARYLEBONE ROAD, LONDON NW1 5HT

———

OFFENBACH

LA JOLIE PARFUMEUSE

———

On Thursday, Friday, Monday and Tuesday
29th, 30th November, 3rd and 4th December 1973 at 7 p.m.

A modern performance of
La Jolie Parfumeuse in 1973

be successfully brought back to the world, they must be performed. Every true revival of an art-form has been at its most successful and potent (an example was the recently revival of genuine ragtime) when it is experienced in its original state and idiom, clearing away the trappings of subsequent commercialisation.

Offenbach was by no means unaware of his proper historical rôle. While his own company at the Gaîté made hard cash out of popularisation, he was busy, with undiminished zest, in not only supervising revivals of his works at various theatres but in writing new operettas. *Les Braconniers* had been put on at the Variétés on January 29th. Now, with *Orphée* keeping the Gaîté in business, he was able to produce the neatly written *Pomme d'Api*, (recently recorded in Russian) which starred Louise Théo at the Renaissance on September 4th; and an entirely successful opera *La Jolie Parfumeuse* at the same theatre on November 29th. Louise Theo was again the attractive lead and the show ran for over two hundred performances. The English-speaking markets were now reaching a peak of Offenbach appreciation and *La Jolie Parfumeuse* was in London by May 1874 as *The Pretty Perfumer*. London had not yet seen its own operetta boom in the shape of Gilbert and Sullivan, and America was still trailing. In Paris there was old rivalry in the shape of Hervé and new in the shape of Lecocq and other up-and-coming composers; while Vienna was offering a most formidable challenge from Johann Strauss, whom Offenbach had once nobly encouraged. He was adding new lustre and dimensions to the art of operetta with his *Die Fledermaus*, produced in April 1874, and setting in motion the golden age of Viennese operetta. Offenbach was still welcome at the Theater an der Wien, but there was less room to spare, and composers like Suppé, at the Carltheater, were dominating the other venues.

However, back in Paris, the success of *La Jolie Parfumeuse* at the Variétés led to an enlarged three-act version of *La Périchole* with the still magic name of Hortense Schneider to play the principal part. A new hazard that Offenbach now had to face was the breaking of his old writing partnership with Meilhac and Halévy. They were now taking more interest in the drama and disinclined to indulge in the frivolities of operetta. They reluctantly re-wrote *La Périchole* and were only just persuaded to produce a new libretto for *Madame l'Archiduc* which was produced at Les Bouffes-Parisiens on October 30th. The Bouffes had also produced a one-act operetta *Bagatelle* on May 21st. At this particular venue a return to the old style and subject seemed most in order, and *Madame l'Archiduc* had much of the old court satire in it, with the difference that it was now in retrospect and therefore seemed much milder. It made gentle fun of the military and of smart society and it all seemed very much like old times.

7 Voyage dans la Lune

If Offenbach had simply kept to his manuscript paper he might well have survived his last years on the strength of his old reputation and the not unsuccessful pieces that he still managed to write. As before, it was the strain of trying to run a theatre as well that was his undoing. By now he had made his erstwhile literary collaborator Etienne Tréfeu the business manager, and a very poor one he turned out to be, making continual errors of judgement which Offenbach himself had not the strength or acumen to counteract. In fact, he

Hortense Schneider's 1871-2 London season

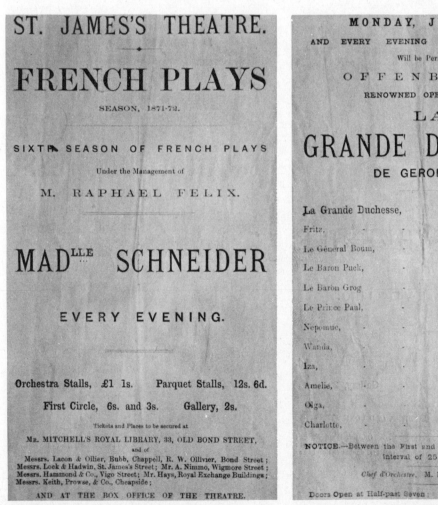

ST. JAMES'S THEATRE.

FRENCH PLAYS

SEASON, 1871-72.

SIXTH SEASON OF FRENCH PLAYS

Under the Management of

M. RAPHAEL FELIX.

MAD^{LLE} SCHNEIDER

EVERY EVENING.

Orchestra Stalls, £1 1s.   Parquet Stalls, 12s. 6d.

First Circle, 6s. and 3s.   Gallery, 2s.

Tickets and Places to be secured at

Mr. MITCHELL'S ROYAL LIBRARY, 33, OLD BOND STREET,
and of
Messrs. Lacon & Ollier, Bubb, Chappell, R. W. Ollivier, Bond Street ;
Messrs. Lock & Hadwin, St. James's Street ; Mr. A. Nimmo, Wigmore Street ;
Messrs. Hammond & Co., Vigo Street ; Mr. Hays, Royal Exchange Buildings ;
Messrs. Keith, Prowse, & Co., Cheapside ;

AND AT THE BOX OFFICE OF THE THEATRE.

MONDAY, JUNE 17th,
AND EVERY EVENING DURING THE WEEK,
Will be Performed,

OFFENBACH'S
RENOWNED OPERA BOUFFE,

LA
GRANDE DUCHESSE
DE GEROLSTEIN.

La Grande Duchesse,		Mlle. SCHNEIDER
Fritz,	-	MM. DUPLAN
Le Général Boum,	-	BECKERS
Le Baron Puck,	-	DESMONTS
Le Baron Grog	-	SCHEY
Le Prince Paul,	-	DESCHAMPS
Nepomuc,	-	LAPISSIDA
Wanda,	-	Mes. DESMONTS
Iza,	-	ESTHER BLOCH
Amelie,	-	GUERZY
Olga,	-	DAGUY
Charlotte,	-	FORAY

NOTICE.—Between the First and Second Acts there will be an interval of 25 Minutes.

Chef d'Orchestre, M. DE BILLEMONT.

Doors Open at Half-past Seven ;   Commence at Eight o'clock.

added to the wrong by making bad decisions himself. On December 3rd he agreed to stage an historical drama by Victorien Sardou, called *La Haine,* to which he supplied the incidental music. Apparently unable to conceive anything at the Gaîté as anything but spectacular, Offenbach and Tréfeu spent 36,000 francs on the production not only to find a comic fiasco on their hands but with the added misfortune of heavy snowstorms to keep the public away. Sardou indignantly withdrew his work and left Offenbach to foot the bill. There was some compensation in the fact that his pantomime *Dick Whittington* was doing very well at the Alhambra in London where it had been commissioned at a fee of 75,000 francs, opening in January 1875. But that was chicken feed compared with the funds that were needed to put the Gaîté on its feet and once again the frantic management resorted to dressing up an old Offenbach success in pantomime guise – and they chose *Geneviève de Brabant* for the treatment. It opened on February 25th, with new five-act libretto by Hector Crémieux, and special imported turns. This time the public did not respond. To add to his burdens, a well-turned and tuneful piece called *Les Hannetons* produced at Les Bouffes-Parisiens on April 22nd also failed. The final disaster came when Sardou once again persuaded Offenbach that the theatre could be saved by staging another gigantic spectacular, historical opéra-bouffe *féerie* based on *Don Quixote*. The wild dreams and fantasies that accompanied this project were fortunately never realised otherwise the ultimate disaster would have been even greater. The theatre went bankrupt and the company was liquidated at the end of May. Offenbach attempted to carry on alone for a short while but there was nothing he could do. He assembled

Carmen, Act 3 (British National Opera Company)

Madame Bourguignon as Carmen in an open-air performance in Paris (1925)

his staff and cast, an incredible eight hundred of them, and told them the irrevocable truth. He ended with the honourable promise that they would all be paid to the last farthing that he owed them. He then took to his bed with an accentuated attack of gout and gave himself up to deep despair. His ex-employees gave him a party at his house, with a firework display and speeches, but it didn't do much to alleviate the pain. He was left a broken man and with the prospect of spending his last years simply paying off his debts. He lost most of his belongings and property and had to promise to pay his creditors all the royalties he might earn for the next three years.

Further salt was rubbed into his wounds by the activities of his old colleagues. Meilhac and Halévy proved that they could help toward just the sort of work that Offenbach would have loved to have written by producing the libretto of *Carmen* with music by Georges Bizet, a composer whom Offenbach had once helped to set on his way. There was tragedy in that too for Bizet was to die believing *Carmen* to be a partial failure after a harsh reception. Soon after his death, it was on the way to becoming one of the world's favourite operas. There were more bitter pills to swallow. The Renaissance now put on Johann Strauss's *Indigo* with Offenbach's old star Zulma Bouffar and it was such a success that they immediately followed it with *Die Fledermaus* (as *La Tzigane*). Its libretto was based on a comedy, *La Reveillon*, by who else but Meilhac and Halévy. *Die Fledermaus* had suffered an initially poor reception in Vienna but Paris, reversing the honours that Vienna had once bestowed on Offenbach, took it to their hearts and went *Die Fledermaus*-mad. Where once the favours had been bestowed on *La Belle Hélène* or *La Grande-Duchesse* now it was *Die Fledermaus*, soon to return triumphant to its own city. Offenbach lay at home with the gout and heard reports about the new craze. His old friend Albert Wolff pointed out to anyone who would read and listen that it was all simply an extension of the art-form that Offenbach had created; but it was too near to the actual event for that to stand out as clearly as it does to us in the perspective of history. Even Wagner was becoming fashionable, and there could be no greater blow to Offenbach's pride than that!

He went off to stay in Etretat. Every now and then his natural gaiety and charm asserted themselves and all seemed right with the world. There were still parties and a few old friends to talk to. And there was still the happy family who adored and admired him, the faithful who believed that the good times would come again.

Over in America they now had a great and growing regard for Offenbach and they were just about to celebrate the centenary of American liberation. At the end of the spring of 1875 when Offenbach and family were staying in St. Germain, trying to sort out their many problems, watching their Parisian world crumble about them and trying to get the impetus for more work, the morning was disturbed by two visitors. First to come was Hortense Schneider. Offenbach had declared that no-one was to disturb his work but he admitted: 'I hadn't the heart to order the rules enforced against her; I have much friendship for the Grande-Duchesse de Gérolstein, and, when I meet her, it always seems to me as if I saw my successes walking about.' While he talked with the Duchesse 'of the great battles we had fought together before the footlights' he was handed the card of a second visitor whose name was unknown to him. Before he could tell the servant not to admit the stranger the gentleman followed his card and being a very respectable looking person Offenbach allowed him to make his introductions. He came to the point immediately and asked Offenbach if he would like to go to America. The object of the visit would be to make concert appearances at the Philadelphia Exhibition of 1876. In America Offenbach was considered a great French artist and his reception

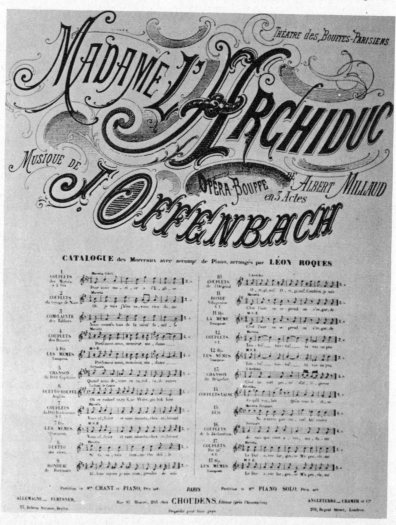

Madame L'Archiduc (1874)

La Boulangère (1875) in London

and his financial reward would both be considerable. In the current circumstances he could hardly turn down the offer. The prospect didn't please him, either leaving his family or travelling so far abroad, but he said he might consider it. The very next day he was visited by a M. Bacquero and a firm agreement was drawn up. The substantial fee on behalf of the American impresario Maurice Grau would be deposited in Offenbach's bank. He assured his family that it would all come to nothing. But on the appointed day the money was there, and Offenbach was committed to the trip.

In the meantime he tried to struggle back to his old position of eminence. Meilhac and Halévy repented their desertion and came back to help him write another piece for the Variétés. *La Boulangère a des Écus*, premièred on October 10th, 1875, produced the old pattern of theatrical jealousies. Hortense Schneider, engaged for the

111

lead, threw one of her accustomed tantrums and at a rehearsal, being displeased over some trifle, declared she was leaving. Arriving the next day she found she had been taken at her word and the part was now being played by Mlle Aimée. That would never have happened in the old days. This last joint work of Offenbach,

To be followed by a Novel and Original Comedy-Bouffe, founded upon the Opera Comique of the same name, entitled

THE CREOLE!

In One Act and Five Tableaux.

The Music by OFFENBACH.

The English Version by REECE & FARNIE.

Zoe	(Creole, Ward of the Commodore)	Miss KATHERINE MUNROE.
Rene	(Of the Mousquetaires Rouges, Nephew of the Commodore)	Miss NELLY BROMLEY.
Antoinette ...	(Commodore's daughter)	Miss VIOLET CAMERON.
The Commodore Patatras	(Of the Frigate " La Blague")	Mr. JOHN HOWSON.
Frontignac ...	(A Briefless Advocate) ...	Mr. DUDLEY THOMAS.
Gargotte	Notaries and Confidential Advisers	Mr. BEDFORD.
Babillard	of the Commodore	Mr. CHARLES ASHFORD.
Sabord	(Bo'sun and body servant of the Commodore)	Mr. F. MITCHELL.
Tribord	Quartermasters of	Mr. CHARLES LASCELLES.
Beret	" La Blague "	Mr. CLAVERING POWER.
Paul ...	(Cabin Boy of " La Blague ") ...	Miss JOSIE CORRI.
Yvonne	Maids to Antoinette	Miss JULIA EVANS.
Jacquelme		Miss ADELAIDE BARTON.
Lolotte	Maids in the Estaminet	Miss IMMS.
Berthe	" Aux Pecheurs Fideles "	Miss ANGEL.
Yagarita ...	(Zoe's Attendant) ...	Miss KATE POLETTI.
Casserole	(Cook at the Admiral's Villa)	Miss CLARA GRAHAME.
Jeanne, Pierre	(Peasants of the District)	Mr. LOPRESTI, Mr. ANDRINI.

Fishermen, Fisher Girls, Peasants, Sailors, the Crew of " La Blague " by Messrs. H. W. Cushing, Clavering Power, F. Andrini, A. J. Lopresti, Marshall, Parris; Mesdames Louie Cadogan, Ethel Barrington, Amy Barrington, Kate Grahame, Lucy Lee, Jessie Bailie, Rose St. George, Kate Leeson, Daisy Angel, Florence Lavender, Ethel Montaigne, Alice Poletti, Mary Douglas &c.

Conductor - - - - - Mr. FITZ-GERALD.

FOR LIST OF MUSIC SEE NEXT PAGE.

La Créole (1875) in London

112

ROYAL
HAMBRA ＊＊ THEATRE
LEICESTER SQUARE
ed by the Lord Chamberlain to Mr F. Leades, 27, Leicester Square.

At 7.15, Farce,

WARNING TO PARENTS

At 8,

VOYAGE DANS LA LUNE

rand Opera Bouffe, in Four Acts, and Fifteen Tableaux.

Original Libretto by

LETERRIER, A. VANLOO, and A. MORTIER.

The English Version by

HENRY S. LEIGH Esq.

Music by

OFFENBACH.

rand Ballets Composed and produced under the personal
direction of

Mons. JUSTAMANT

cenery by Mr A. CALCOT and Assistants. Costumes by
. GERVAISE (of Paris,) Miss FISHER and Mr MAY, after
s by Mons. Gasvin, (of Paris). The Properties by W.
BUCKLEY, and the Machinery by J. SLOMAN & SON.

Manager   Mr GEO. ROBERTS

ise-en-Scene and the Opera produced under the direction of

Mr G. JACOBI.

Musical Director.

Le Voyage dans la Lune
(1875) in London

Meilhac and Halévy enjoyed a moderate success. Offenbach, determined to pay off his creditors as soon as possible, had another piece on the stocks at the same time. The libretto to *La Créole* was the work of Meilhac in collaboration with Albert Millaud. It had a mild success at Les Bouffes with Mme Judic; but it went down very well in London in 1877 and was later revived with even greater acclaim as *The Commodore* at the Avenue Theatre. 1875 saw a London production of *Les Georgiennes* which prophetically shared the programme with a short musical piece by Sullivan called *The Zoo;* while the even more important *Trial by Jury* was being used as support to Offenbach's *La Périchole* at the Royalty Theatre. He rounded off the year with *Le Voyage dans la Lune* which was staged at the Gaîté, now managed by M. Vizentini, in the old spectacular style, on October 26th, 1875. It was based on Jules Verne's novel *De la Terre à la Lune* and it outdid all other spectaculars in its space-age prophecies. The second act was on the moon where the travellers had arrived in a rocket shot from a tremendous gun. In the fourth act there was a volcano that threatened to devour the theatre. And yet behind all this spectacular nonsense there was a good score and some pleasant tunes (with Zulma Bouffar to sing them) and it had a very considerable success. The vast stage of the Alhambra in London was ready for it in the following season and it was simultaneously seen at the Theater an der Wien. Slowly Offenbach's fortunes were recuperating and 1875 ended with a slight piece described as a 'Valse en un acte' *Tarte à la Crème* (words by Albert Millaud) at Les Bouffes-Parisiens. It was greatly enjoyed by those who liked the grace and lightness of Offenbach's music for its own sake.

Now came the moment which he had come to dread; the time for his departure to America. Such a journey in those days seemed incredibly hazardous and America formidably distant and full of strange beings. He left Paris on the 21st April, regretfully leaving his wife and daughters at home, and travelled to Le Havre with his two sons-in-law, Charles Comte and Achille Tournal, two brothers-in-law, Gaston and Robert Mitchell, a few friends, including the faithful Albert Wolff, and his son Auguste. He boarded the *Canada*, 'a fine ship, spick and span new' making, like Offenbach, her first trip to America and his feelings were much as they had been when he first left the family home in Cologne.

The ship started; and, as she grazed the pier, and my eyes dwelt for the last time on my young boy, I felt a pang within me such as none but a father can understand. While the ship was steaming away, my eyes were rivetted upon that little group, in the midst of which stood my dear child. The sun shining brightly on the brass buttons of his college uniform, enabled me for a long time to make out the exact spot where he stood, and which my heart would otherwise have guessed.

113

The touching departure irrevocably made, Offenbach's natural curiosity asserted itself and he enjoyed the company of his fellow travellers, finding the captain 'an excellent man and a charming talker', comforted by the fearless steward who had staunchly survived one shipwreck, and feeling pleasantly superior to the ship's doctor who was making his first Atlantic crossing and was seasick from the moment of departure. In his own party were Mlle Aimée, his orchestra leader M. Boulard and his young wife, the American Bacquero who had arranged the trip for him and Bacquero's secretary, one Arigotti, a *tenore robusto* who had lost his voice but played the piano well. There were also some charming ladies from Philadelphia and a few tradesmen and exhibitors on their way to the Exhibition. The first two days were fine, apart from one stoppage

Offenbach photographed in
Philadelphia

114

which drew Offenbach from his bed with palpitating heart. Trouble with the ship's propeller was eventually put right, but then came a tremendous storm which raged for three days and four nights. The captain's assertion that it was 'splendid just to see how the ship dashes right into the waves, only to come out magnificently a minute afterwards' left Offenbach unconvinced. He said that he would have enjoyed the spectacle more at a distance, rather as part of the audience than as one of the actors.

A pale and shaken Offenbach eventually reached New York where he was greeted by a boatload of reporters with whom he was soon on friendly terms. Another vessel decorated with flags and Venetian lanterns carried a military band of some sixty to eighty musicians who all became seasick and produced a performance which Offenbach compared to the last movement of Haydn's *Farewell* symphony as each musician quit his musical task and hastened to the side of the vessel. On the first day he visited two theatres and on returning to the hotel in the evening found it ablaze with light and a large inscription over the balcony proclaiming in large letters 'Welcome, Offenbach' while the recuperated musicians serenaded him with strains from *Orphée aux Enfers* and *La Grande-Duchesse de Gérolstein*. There were shouts of 'Hurrah for Offenbach' to which he politely replied 'Thank you, gentlemen'. If there was a basic trouble with Offenbach's visit it was simply that he did not live up to the expectations of the Americans. Robert Grau, brother of Maurice Grau the impresario, put it in these words:

The English edition (1876) of Offenbach's account of his American trip. Title-page by Faustin

My brother, Maurice, succeeded in enticing the famous composer to these shores. His idea was that the public would pay fabulous prices to gaze on the back of the man who had set people literally crazy with his entrancing melodies. Offenbach was accordingly engaged for thirty nights to conduct an orchestra of sixty musicians in programmes of his own compositions at Madison Square Garden, New York. He was to receive a fee of one thousand dollars a night – regarded at that time as unprecedented. In June 1876, the father of *opéra bouffe* arrived in New York amidst an excitement such as has never been equalled to this day. The people seemed to think that Offenbach would begin to dance the 'can-can' as soon as he set foot on our shores and crowds were at the steamship wharf to greet him.

On the night of his arrival he was serenaded at the Fifth Avenue Hotel by the Musicians' Union of New York. A crowd said to number fifty thousand people filled Madison Square and shouted a welcome to the composer until he appeared on the balcony of the hotel. Offenbach weighed just ninety pounds. He was perhaps the least imposing man in appearance one could possibly imagine. He spoke excellent English, thanking the people for his reception. He retired in less than one minute, and the crowd went home thoroughly disappointed because the man who wrote *Orphée aux Enfers* did not dance on the balcony.

At length the opening concert was given to an audience of six thousand persons. The garden was crowded, but the audience was not a distinctly musical one. The majority of the people had come to see how Offenbach would behave when he came to conduct the airs over which they had raved. At last Offenbach came into the orchestra pit. The orchestra gave him a fanfare. The audience rose at him as if he was a conqueror. The applause lasted two minutes and then silence prevailed. The absence of the voices of the opera singers, the lack of the *mise en scène*, seemed to cast a gloom over the night. After the first part was over one-third of the audience went home. When all seemed to be lost, my brother, with that ingenious foresight which characterised his business career, began to plead with Offenbach to meet the public clamour for a sensational conductor. 'What can I do? What will you have me do? I want to help you, but you can't get me to make a clown of myself', said Offenbach.

The only thing remaining was to induce Offenbach to conduct some performances with the hope of retrieving the great loss which the concerts had brought about. By producing 'La Jolie Parfumeuse' with Aimée in the cast, my brother succeeded in recovering his losses. Offenbach was, of course, the conductor, and the first seven performances brought 20,000 dollars. Despite the favourable financial outcome of this venture Offenbach was disgusted with America.

Offenbach remained in New York for several weeks and daily conducted selections of his music in the Gilmore Gardens, in a style reminiscent of Jullien in the Jardin Turc, among the waterfalls and tropical plant-life artificially induced. He then went to Philadelphia and his concerts in the Centennial Exhibition park were quite popular with the Philadelphians and the visitors. For a grand Sunday concert of Sacred Music he, in typical vein, planned to mingle, with Schubert's and Gounod's *Ave Maria*, items from his operettas carefully disguised with religious titles. But the Philadelphians were very strict about Sunday observance and severely censored his intentions. Although handbills had been printed the Sacred Concert never took place – much to Offenbach's regret. Otherwise his concerts at the Philadelphia Fair were a great success; and it is of great interest to note that the concert master of his orchestra was a young Washingtonian named John Philip Sousa.

He returned to New York and gave a grand banquet for his orchestra and the friends he had made during his visit and he made a witty speech. The final summary by one eminent journalist was that 'few European artists had been so highly honoured in New York'. In spite of the disappointment of the sensation seekers, the tour helped to establish his music in America even more than before and the strains of *La Belle Hélène*, *Orphée* and *La Grande-Duchesse* were played everywhere, in theatres, restaurants and parks for the next five years and more. Offenbach in his delightful book entitled in French *Offenbach en Amérique: notes d'un musicien en voyage,* and published simultaneously in America and England, proved himself as witty and entertaining a writer as he was a musician. He took a somewhat cynical but affectionate view of the American nation. He was delighted with the gadgetry of hotel and boarding-house life,

The 'Grand Sacred Concert'
that never materialised

the lavish shops, the rash of advertisements, the graceful American women (of course). But he did not much admire their worship of money and the standards promulgated by it. 'Offenbach must be a great musician' he heard someone say, 'he gets a thousand dollars an evening just for conducting!' He attended some American plays and some operas, including a performance of Meyerbeer's *L'Étoile du Nord* at Booth's Theatre where he found the chorus and orchestra in total conflict. It sounded to his ears like a mediocre performance of Wagner. At the Lyceum he found the management aping Bayreuth in having the orchestra covered in – with disastrous effect on their sound. The orchestra happily concealed took to puffing their pipes and cigars and filled the auditorium with smoke. Mainly he found the Americans hopelessly materialistic and forecast, wrongly, that they would never attract important European artists with the conditions they offered. The European artists, like Offenbach, were able to forgive most things for the lure of the dollar. Offenbach left America on July 8th, 1876.

The journey home in the good ship *Canada* was fortunately calm and Offenbach was able to meditate on his future in Republican France; not without trepidation. He concludes his book:

It was half-past eight when the *Canada*, under a radiant sun, and upon a sea whose surface was as smooth as a mirror, came in sight of the lovely hills of Normandy and entered the harbour of Havre. To complete my joy, my entire family and many of my friends had been waiting for me for hours, and all my children were waving their handkerchiefs excitedly as they caught sight of me on the deck.

My joy was great on again seeing my beloved family as my sorrow had been when I had left them. I wept with emotion, and could scarcely forbear throwing myself into the sea to put an end to this agony of seeing there all that was dearest to me in the world, and yet not being able to clasp them to my heart.

An hour later the ship was fast at the dock, and I had become once more Offenbach in France.

For an understanding of Offenbach's complex but very human nature it is essential to read his endearing and amusing account of his excursion. It was re-issued in 1957, in Germany, England and America as *Orpheus in America*. He knew now that his fame was well-established in America and he was reaping a steady income from his London productions. At the Alhambra theatre alone, during the 1870s there were lavish productions of *Blue Beard, Le Roi Carotte, La Belle Hélène, La Jolie Parfumeuse, Whittington, Le Voyage dans la Lune, Orphée aux Enfers, The Grand Duchess, Geneviève de Brabant, La Périchole, The Princess of Trébizonde* and *La Fille du Tambour-Major* – a new work of 1879. How the English-speaking world produced Offenbach and hedged their bets was perhaps beside the point but it offers an interesting sidelight on his position as a commercial proposition. Even allowing for the descent from 'the sublime totality to the ridiculous half-measure' which foreign opera in English presents, Emily Soldene's account of the 1871 production of *Geneviève de Brabant* at the Philharmonic in Islington provides diverting insight. Surviving the weeks of personality and production difficulties, the opening night looms near.

Our dress rehearsal was the sort of thing you can remember for a long time – a tale of woe, of disaster, of profane language, of offensive and personal remarks, of bursting buttons, and lost and misapplied and 'impossible to recollect' lines, of wrong notes in the band parts, generally in the double bass and clarinet. 'Good God, sir, here we've rehearsed for a fortnight, and now you find you've got a wrong note; pass over that part Jones; no, never mind'. And the conductor climbs over the musicians, and

Emily Soldene as Drogan in *Geneviève de Brabant*

The two gendarmes in the Islington production of *Geneviève de Brabant*

the music-stands shiver and totter on their uncertain bases, and all the parts (most of them loose sheets) fall to the ground. Then the scenery won't go right, but will go wrong, and Miss Somebody, in an access of nerves, forgets her cadenza. 'Cut it out,' roars Farnie, with sulphurous adjectives. 'But,' remonstrates the tearful girl. 'Cut it out,' and language unfit for Her Majesty's drawing-room dies away at the back of the pit.

Mr Morton sits in a front seat and severe judgment. At the end of the first act he pats his tidy little neck-tie several times, and confides to me, 'There's nothing in it, simply nothing in it; utter failure. And, as for your part, why, you do nothing.'

These frank expressions exactly reflect my own feelings, and no words can do justice to my depression.

The second act was even worse than the first. The band parts for my 'Sleep song' were not ready. The lime-light 'medium' was wrong, and converted my Rimmels complexion into a coat of many and unbecoming colours. Everything was too dreadful. The only satisfying ones were the gendarmes who seemed to have funny lines and, *mirabile dictu*, knew them too.

I had a sick headache, and Mr Morton and the distinguished adapter had a few words, after which Farnie and I adjourned to the theatre front doorstep, and he eased his mind by saying sultry and irreverent things about people in general and the management in particular. Then we two weary ones, partners in this great breakdown and unequalled frost, shook hands in dull and doleful and downcast commiseration with each other, and went our respective ways, chewing the cud of bitter and sorrowful reflections.

Next morning – it was on a Saturday, a memorable Saturday, the Saturday we expected the Prince of Wales would die – at ten o'clock there came a messenger in hot haste, with a letter from Mr Morton. A terrible thing had happened; Farnie had gone – fled – disappeared – packed his carpet-bag for parts unknown, leaving the disconsolate 'Geneviève' to her deserved and dreadful and disgraceful fate . . .

And so the disasters continued . . . but . . .

The success of that night was a record-breaker. The enthusiasm, the applause, the crowded house! The piece went with a snap and 'vim'. Everybody recollected every word and made every point. The gaiety of the audience was infectious. Every line, every topical allusion was given dash and received with shouts of laughter. How the Burgomaster blew his nose like the trumpet, 'too-ti-ti-too-ti-ti-too', and never got any further with his speech than 'In the year one'. How the gendarmes sang their 'We'll run 'em in' seventeen times. How everybody worked for the general good. How Mr Morton came on the stage and 'took it all back', and congratulated and thanked and treated everybody. How a certain gentleman, named Clement Scott, sat in the front and was good to us, and wrote a half-column notice, which appearing next morning in the *Observer* made a certain singer famous as Drogan, and grateful for ever . . .

On the Monday following the eventful and never-to-be-forgotten first night, Mr Farnie reappeared at the theatre. He had been to Brighton, he had read the papers. Of course he knew it would be a success, in spite of the wooden-headed management.

How Jacques Offenbach would have enjoyed all the hurly-burly and felt at home with all the trials and tribulations so much a pattern of the old Bouffes-Parisiens and Gaîté days! A year later *Geneviève* was still running to packed houses, the little Philharmonic was a fashionable resort and 'duchesses were glad to sit in the stalls

The Islington programme of
Geneviève de Brabant

Clara Vesey in the English production of *Geneviève de Brabant* (1871)

because there were no boxes for them'. H.R.H. The Prince of Wales, now recovered, paid an official visit and 'was treated with the greatest respect and consideration by her Majesty's lieges of Islington'. After the Franco-German war the famous actor Marius returned to London and had a special part written in for him, and among the bit players was one W. G. Ross who had once made himself famous by singing a 'dreadfully unpleasant and blasphemous ditty *Sam Hall*' at the song-and-supper rooms. The same people came, night after night.

It might be remarked, as a balancing footnote, at this point that Offenbach, often saddened by their quirkish moods, had, throughout his career, endured some malicious attacks from critics who attempted to be moralists as well. Things that would scarcely stir a whisker today were matters for righteous indignation then. Félix Clement, reviewing *Orphée:* 'These melodies might be considered charming and original if they were not associated with stage situations that were grotesque and even licentious'; the German critic Schluter in *Die allgemeine Geschichte der Musik* in 1863: 'Typical brothel-music'; Gustave Chouquet in *Histoire de la Musique Dramatique en France* in 1873: 'Often a charming melody is caricatured in a refrain of extreme vulgarity . . . our unfortunate country will plunge into ruin if she does not quickly recover her good sense and her good taste by throwing out once and for all these impudent corroders of the theatre.' These remarks were subsequently counterbalanced by the admirers of Offenbach's music who went to the other extreme and found him the Mozart of his day. Offenbach, as an artist must, rode on the crest of the waves but must often have dreaded the threatening troughs. As he did, we must choose our stance and stick to it. Probably the most balanced assessment of Offenbach in recent years comes in the three chapters devoted to him in Gervase Hughes' *Composers of Operetta* (1962).

8 Le Rideau

It was not so much financial matters, dreary and depressing as they were, nor lack of confidence that they could be overcome, that irked Offenbach most. It was the growing feeling, aggravated by the criticisms, that he had never written anything really worthy of his genius. We might now consider that *Orphée aux Enfers* and the other comic masterpieces were triumph enough, but all artists, especially, by tradition, all comedians, long to be seen in a more earnest light. It stems from the long-standing critical fallacy that only that which is serious and complex is qualified to be called great art. History proves the theory wrong time and time again, but it continues to be propounded and heeded.

The American trip seems to have unsettled Offenbach. Paris did its best to persuade him that his old craft was not unappreciated. The Variétés staged a superb production of *La Belle Hélène* in the autumn which even managed to put Offenbach's music back in favourite position after it had for so long been ousted by new favourites like Lecocq's *La Fille de Madame Angot*. It offered some encouragement to go on writing, not only to pay off his debts, but for its own sake. He wrote two more pieces for Les Bouffes-Parisiens – *Pierrette et Jacquot*, with book by Jules Noriac and Philippe Gille, which was produced on October 14th, 1876, and *La Boîte au Lait*, libretto by Eugène Grangé and Jules Noriac, produced on November 3rd.

At the beginning of 1877 his collaborators, Arnold Mortier and Philippe Gille, turned once again to Jules Verne for the story of *Le Docteur Ox* which was produced at Les Variétés in pantomime vein on January 26th. Dupuis and Judic managed to make quite a success out of it. On February 10th the Folies-Dramatiques staged *La Foire St. Laurent*, libretto by Hector Crémieux and Albert de Saint-Albin. But even the help of his old ally Crémieux didn't produce the kind of triumph that his spirits badly needed.

He was more than ever convinced that he must write a great serious work to gain the immortality that he felt might slip away if his reputation depended entirely on the frivolous. A play *Les Contes Fantastiques d'Hoffmann* had been produced at the Odéon in 1851. The strange stories, dramatised by Jules Barbier and Michel Carré had, even then, seemed excellent material for an opera and Offenbach had toyed with the thought at the time. Now the idea came

ANDRÉ MARTINET

OFFENBACH

SA VIE & SON ŒUVRE

PARIS
DENTU ET Cⁱᴱ, ÉDITEURS
LIBRAIRES DE LA SOCIÉTÉ DES GENS DE LETTRES
PALAIS-ROYAL, 15-17-19, GALERIE D'ORLÉANS
ET 3, PLACE DE VALOIS.

1887
Droits de traduction et de reproduction réservés.

An early book on Offenbach
(1887) by André Martinet

back to him and *Les Contes d'Hoffmann* seemed just the inspiration he had been looking for. In fact a libretto for such an opera had already been written by Barbier and Carré; and Hector Salomon, the chorus-master at l'Opéra, had almost completed a score. Perhaps he was not entirely satisfied with his work, but Salomon, with utmost nobility and generosity, agreed to withdraw his rights and gave Offenbach complete access to the libretto. Offenbach must have been at his most persuasive. He started to negotiate for a production of the opera immediately and found a taker in the management of the Théâtre-Lyrique. Unfortunately they went bankrupt and plans were shelved for a time. Offenbach was an extremely sick man by now but the inspiration of his new pre-occupation seemed to bolster his spirits considerably. Perhaps he saw something of Hoffmann in himself. He put his whole being into its creation and found a new way of writing his old Second Empire vein into the first act. The fine barcarolle from *Rheinnixen* proved a source of inspiration in the second act set in Venice. He knew he was writing good music and a work that would satisfy his most self-critical demands.

Money still had to be made and he stepped aside from the score to produce *Maître Péronilla,* an excellent opéra-bouffe in three acts, book by himself in collaboration with Charles Nuitter and Paul Ferrier, at the Bouffes-Parisiens on March 13th, 1878. It was noted at the rehearsals how much calmer and benign he now seemed and at one rehearsal, in spite of his gout, he danced a fandango with the chorus. For the new World Exhibition in 1878 he wanted to pro-duce something special as he had on previous occasions. He asked Meilhac and Halévy for a libretto but they refused. He wrote to Halévy, deeply hurt, that the writers had deserted their old friend in favour of Lecocq, 'the Meyerbeer of the Renaissance' as he called him. Indeed Meilhac and Halévy were aleady committed to write *Le Petit Duc* for Lecocq, and Offenbach was left with no new pro-duction for the Exhibition season which opened on May 1st. Even the suggestion of a piece for the Opéra-Comique left Halévy unmoved.

The World Exhibition, in a now comparatively peaceful France, attracted 250,000 visitors and several writers at least mollified Offenbach by protesting that he was not represented by a new work. 'Quelle détresse, quelle amertume dût étreindre le Maître sur ses vieux jours', wrote Max Nordau; and even Zola, who had merci-lessly attacked Offenbach for his frivolities in the past, was moved to sympathise. Heralding a new age there was a shop near Les Bouffes-Parisiens advertising the new phonograph of Monsieur Edison.

Most people, of course, did not know that the old master was busy producing his masterpiece and there was some consolation to hand when Weinschenck, the director of the Gaîté, decided that it was time to have a revival of *Orphée aux Enfers,* the old favourite which had now been staged nearly a thousand times. Offenbach became sufficiently interested in the project to ask his old rival Hervé if he would play the part of Jupiter. Hervé gallantly accepted on the condition that Offenbach would personally conduct. So the two veterans found themselves re-united. The production opened on August 4th with Hervé as Jupiter and Offenbach conducting the

Madame Favart (1878) in
London

second act (all that he had the strength for) and it had the desired effect of renewing public interest in Offenbach and in giving fresh hope for the future. A new production of *La Grande-Duchesse* was now planned at Les Bouffes-Parisiens. Offenbach, Meilhac and Halévy all implored Hortense Schneider to come out of retirement, where she had lurked since an unsuccessful production by Hervé of *La Belle Hélène*. She remained unmoved this time and the rôle was given to Paola Marie. Schneider did appear at the first night in a box and attracted almost as much attention as her successor on the stage. In the meantime Offenbach, with the help of Alfred Duru and Henri Chivot, had written a substantial new piece called *Madame Favart*. This was an old subject, dear to Parisian hearts, for Madame Favart, in reality Marie Justine Benoiste Duronceray, had been a celebrated singer, actress and dancer, born in 1727, and the subject of a play by Charles Moreau and Henri Dumolard as far back as 1806. As Mme Chantilly she had appeared, billed as '*Première danseuse* of the King of Poland' at the Opéra-Comique in 1744, and the following year she married the assistant manager of the theatre, Charles Simon Favart. She had become a favourite of Marshal Saxe, accompanying him on his expeditions to Flanders. He attempted to woo her and she suffered many adventures, including imprisonment, before she was re-united with M. Favart. She died in 1772 and her husband in 1792. The story had become a theatrical legend which Offenbach and his collaborators neatly encapsuled. It had meant a lot of hard work, as the management had hurriedly asked for a longer score, but Offenbach enjoyed being back in demand again. At the same time he was also expanding the score of *Les Brigands* for a new production at the Gaîté – so it was all rather like old times. His gout was constant and extremely painful but he hurried back from Nice, where he was trying to recuperate, hoping to work on a new piece called *La Marocaine*. He rushed back to Paris where he put his shoulder to the wheel once more and seemed full of life and energy. *Madame Favart* was well received at l'Opéra-Comique and had a moderate *succès d'estime* when it was produced on December 28th. Almost immediately he was involved in *La Marocaine*, with book by Ernst Blum, Eduard Blau and Raoul Toche, which was produced at Les Bouffes-Parisiens on January 13th, 1879. It had a spectacular production which was well received and *Les Brigands* enjoyed a substantial revival.

The year 1879 therefore loomed not too unpleasantly for the sick and frustrated old gentleman. There was still the consolation of his dear wife and family and his welcome home; and on August 14th he celebrated his silver wedding with a wonderful fête at the villa in Etretat. Family and old friends surrounded him and offered more than a grain of comfort for his declining years. On May 18th there

125

126

was a private performance of the parts of *Les Contes d'Hoffmann* so far completed at his house in the Boulevard des Capucines. Léon Carvalho, director of l'Opéra-Comique, was there and so was Herr Jauner of the Ringtheater in Vienna amongst quite a large invited audience. Both wanted the rights to the work but Offenbach promptly decided in favour of the French theatre perhaps simply for the possible satisfaction of having his last success at the old fortress that he had often attacked but never completely won. So that matter was at least settled and he could work towards the opera's completion and production. He now travelled to Germany and took the cure at Wildbad. He wrote a song about the dreams of youth and he visited his old haunts in Cologne, sadly finding the old house gone and most of his old friends departed. He even found the strength to write a scathing article on Wagner for *Le Paris-Mercure*. He returned to Etretat where he finally succumbed to the old persistent disease and became bed-ridden. In constant pain he worked on what was, paradoxically, one of the gayest and best operettas he had written for many years – *La Fille du Tambour-Major*, with book by Henri Chivot and Alfred Duru, which has been described (rather unfairly) as an inversion of *La Fille du Régiment*. It was produced at the Folies-Dramatiques on December 13th, 1879 and was a tremendous success. This was the old Offenbach spirit, the spirit that he had imbibed from Donizetti's motivating masterpiece way back in 1845. There was much 'ta-ran-ta-ra-ing', military colour, a splendid waltz-tune and a galop that almost rivalled the can-can of *Orphée*. Nobody could carp at *this* friendly glorification of French military life or the gentle humour. In the old days it would have been spiced with satire, but this was a mellow work. It was justified by its tunes which were hummed everywhere and once again Offenbach was top of the tree. He had been carried from his bed in a cold winter to supervise the rehearsals. He had driven the cast to achieve perfection and the management had respected his wishes that it should all be done tastefully without unreasoning spectacle. He knew what he wanted, he got it, and the audience commended him. Moreover it led to a delightful bonus in a commission from the management of the Renaissance Theatre – the stronghold of his old rival Lecocq. In March he was able to attend the customary gala dinner to celebrate the 100th performance of *La Fille du Tambour-Major* and when they played a pot-pourri of his old songs he was amused to find that he had difficulty in remembering which of his hundred or so works they came from.

He went in the spring to St. Germain to write the piece for the Renaissance – *La Belle Lurette* with book supplied by his old partner Ludovic Halévy and Paul Ferrier; of which was later written in *The Theatre*, May 1, 1883:

Les Contes d'Hoffmann in 'Le Théâtre Illustré, 1881

127

From beginning to end the music of 'Lurette' is pretty and taking, in Jacques Offenbach's latest and best manner. Its melodies are possibly not remarkable for originality—indeed, one or two of them are obviously 'borrowed' from Johann Strauss *avec intention*—but they are well put together and easy, as well as pleasant, to remember. If the orchestral accompaniments are a thought slenderly constructed, it must at least be admitted that their instrumentation is delightful. One of the numbers (Couplets: 'In London Town'), which obtains a double encore every evening, is simply a new version of 'Die schoene blaue Donau'; and this is not the only familiar Austrian tune utilized by the composer, for a homely old Styrian Laendler crops up in one of Lurette's subsequent *soli*. The rondo and ensemble (act ii), 'Colette one day slipt out', sparkles with gleefulness of a very contagious kind, such as is well described by the French work *entraînant*. A romance, sung by Lurette upon discovering that her newly wedded husband has voluntarily forsaken her, is the gem, musically speaking, of the whole work, and is exceptionally rendered by Miss St. John. It is called, 'Would I could die', and is well qualified to achieve social success as a drawing-room song.

But most of his days at St. Germain were mainly occupied in work on the large score of *Les Contes d'Hoffmann,* now in the last stages of completion. Occasionally he relaxed by reading a life of Mozart—'Le pauvre Mozart' as he called him and wept as he read. Most of the family were at Etretat. Production of the opera was now his pre-occupation; 'Hurry up and stage my opera', he wrote to Carvalho, 'I haven't much time left and my only wish is to attend the opening night.' He was visited by old friends who found him in the heat of July lying in a fur-lined coat, thinner than ever, pale, tired and looking like a corpse already. His humour remained: 'What a lovely article Wolff will write about me when I'm dead' he remarked.

As ever the Opéra-Comique kept him waiting. Scenery and costumes caused delays, but production was promised at the first opportunity in the winter season. In September he was brought back to Paris and was taken to l'Opéra-Comique so that he could hear some of the rehearsals. One evening in October he played the score through to some of the actors. The next afternoon he was looking over the piano arrangement, now complete, his family around him, when he had a choking fit. Between bouts of unconsciousness he murmured: 'It will be all over by tonight.' On the morning of October 5th, 1880, at about half-past three, he died, of gout of the heart. His old comedian friend Léonce called in the morning to see how he was. 'M. Offenbach, died without knowing anything about it', he was told by the porter. 'He will be surprised when he finds out', said Léonce. And there *was* a lovely article by Albert Wolff in the pages of *Le Figaro.*

9 Post mortem

Being a Chevalier of the Legion of Honour, Offenbach was buried, two days after his death, with full military honours in the cemetery at Montmartre. Mountains of wreaths arrived from the house in the Boulevard des Capucines to be piled around the coffin at the Madeleine where the memorial service was held. They came from the theatrical and musical world and friends in every city of Europe, as well as Paris. There were so many spectators for the funeral procession, including many foreign visitors, that many of those invited, including several close associates like Halévy and Crémieux, found themselves unable to get into the main body of the church. There was an emotional moment when the 'Song of Fortunio' was played by the organist and Jean Talzac sang an aria from *Les Contes d'Hoffmann*. Beside Herminie, the mourners included his son Auguste, his brother Jules (who died suddenly only three days later), his daughters and their husbands and his brothers-in-law. The pall-bearers were Victorien Sardou, Auguste Maquet (President of the Society of Composers), Émile Perrin (Director of the Comedie-Francaise) and Olivier Halanzier (Director of l'Opéra).

Hortense Schneider followed the procession to the cemetery. A detour was made along the Boulevards so that it would pass the theatres where Offenbach's works had been performed. The rain fell unremittingly. At the graveside Victorien de Joncières, a fellow composer, delivered an adddress in which he said:

It was not given to Offenbach to see on the stage the work he was finishing when death overtook him. You have been able to judge by what you heard in the church the development in the master's style acquired during the latter years of his life. The great composer wished to prove that he could write other than light music, and that his imagination could reach higher regions of the ideal. Adieu, Jacques Offenbach! Adieu, indefatigable worker! You taste today your first and last repose.

The obituaries tended to move in this rather condescending direction. *The Times* concluded:

As a musician, perhaps, M. Offenbach has been underrated. The ring and jingle of many of his tunes have annoyed sensitive ears; his effects were often obtained by vulgar means, and – pursuing his early plan – in scoring his operas he frequently wrote rather what pleased the public than what satisfied himself. But his melodic fancy was inexhaustible. If he sometimes

129

Offenbach's burial place

repeated himself, at other times, considering the large number of his works, he was surprisingly fresh; and scattered throughout his scores are many passages which show taste and feeling, as well as a great command of orchestral resources.

The most sincere tribute probably came from Clement Scott who wrote a poem *In Memoriam* in the October 16th issue of *Punch*:

Lightly lie the turf upon him! Muse of Music he
*   possessed,*
He of melody was master, let us sing him to his rest.
Friend of long ago remembered, you were girl and I was
*   boy,*
When he took our hearts to Paris, and he sang to us of
*   Troy.*
Tell him — dites lui, remember! — we recall the storm and
*   stress*
Of the nights Napoleonic, and the jewelled Grande-
*   Duchesse;*
We behold, as in a vista, art supreme and fancy free,
Struck to song by golden Schneider, and to wit by
*   quaint Dupuis.*

Classic days of merry music on the memory remain
With Eurydice and Orpheus, with John Styx and Belle
*   Hélène.*
Gods in high Olympus revelled on the mimic stage in
*   France*
When King Jove let loose his thunder, and Queen Juno
*   led the dance.*
Magic charm was yours, my master, for we tripped at
*   your command*
Through the dreamy valse, the galop, and the maddened
*   saraband.*
Evoe! cried jovial Bacchus, little Cupid loosed his bow,
In the Paris of the Empire, in the days of long ago.

Ah! my merry gipsy maiden, Périchole with Spanish
*   eyes,*
Sing your letter song; then take us to the tender Bridge
*   of Sighs,*
Where romance was set to music. Ah; but sweeter let it
*   flow*
Chanson matchless of de Musset! song of young
*   Fortunio!*
With a repertoire exhaustless, classic fable, folly, fun,
Cruel Thanatos gave signal, and the overture was
*   done —*

Still he won in competition, but his equal where and
*   when?*
For his life's success was Paris – yes, La Vie Parisienne!

Drape the orchestra in mourning, wreathe the violin
*   and bow,*
Leave the baton where he placed it – 'tis the final beat,
*   you know;*
Gather up the parts, 'tis over, come, dismiss the band
*   you can,*
Death is now the Tambour Major, and he rolls his
*   rataplan.*
Stop the dancing for a moment, take your partner to
*   the stairs,*
And together, in a dreamland, hear his operatic airs.
Mirth has ended, and a spirit full of melody has fled
To a land of sweeter music – merry Offenbach is dead!

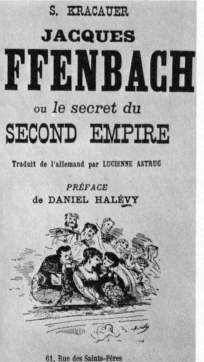

A well-known book on Offenbach by S. Kracauer (1937)

Well worth quoting to indicate how well they knew their Offenbach then and how much he was enjoyed and understood by those whose affection was based on sentiment and pure pleasure rather than the cool critical gaze with a glance over the shoulder toward academic opinion.

After Offenbach was in his coffin there was still much to make his ghostly presence felt. *La Belle Lurette*, with book by Paul Ferrier and Ludovic Halévy, the music orchestrated by Delibes, was duly produced at the Renaissance on October 30th. There was a sadness in its bubbling gaiety with the realisation that it was written by a man in great pain and aware of his imminent death. On November 18th the newspaper *Le Figaro*, no doubt persuaded by the faithful Albert Wolff, organised an 'occasion' at the Variétés. Many of his old actors, Léonce, Théo, Dupuis, Bouffar, among them, sang and recited excerpts from his works ranging from the joyful little one-acters turned out for the tiny Bouffes-Parisiens on the Champs-Elysées, through his triumphant masterpieces of the affluent years, to the rapidly growing immortal Barcarolle from the yet unseen *Tales of Hoffmann*. The Second Empire passed by once again in eventful retrospect. After the music was over Hortense Schneider, dressed as Périchole, stood by as a bust of Offenbach was unveiled and the actor Delaunay, who had first introduced the song of Fortunio recited some lines by one of his greatest librettists, Henri Meilhac:

Est-il un seul coin sur la terre
Ou son nom ne soit pas connu?
Dans l'un et dans l'autre hémisphère
Est il un village perdu,

131

The Carl Rosa Opera Co in
The Tales of Hoffmann

Une bourgade abandonnée
Ou, sur quelque vieux piano
On n'ait dit l'Evohé d'Orphée
Et l'amour de Fortunio?

Paris was again reminded of Offenbach when a revue *Les Parfums de Paris*, by Blum, Toche and Wolff was put on in December. Learning that one of the items was to be a potpourri of Offenbach songs, Hortense Schneider agreed to appear in it. Many old memories were brought to life as she sang the numbers she had helped to make immortal. It was her last stage appearance; and yet another chapter was closed.

At last, on February 10th, 1881, *Les Contes d'Hoffmann*, made its appearance on the stage of l'Opéra-Comique. The orchestration had been completed by Ernest Guiraud who nobly agreed to his own opera *La Galante Aventure* being postponed so that Offenbach's work should not be further delayed. It was not quite as Offenbach had conceived it. Carré, the director of the l'Opéra-Comique, and Guiraud had worked hard on the production but they had admittedly been left with many problems to solve and they made their own decisions. Offenbach had orchestrated the prologue and the first act; Guiraud tried nobly to keep the rest of the orchestration in Offenbach style – and, on the whole, succeeded. Offenbach had left much of the dialogue to be spoken, but Carré decided, with the operatic tradition behind him, to have it set as recitative. This then made the opera seem much too long so he decided to remove all the Giulietta or Venice scene. The setting of the Antonia scene was then changed from Munich to Venice which meant that the famous barcarolle (originally from *Rheinnixen*) which could not be lost, had to be added to the Antonia scene. A quartet in the Epilogue, which had been a great success at the earlier concert performance, was omitted and a duo for Stella and Hoffmann was put in its place.

There was still a fine and substantial work resulting which Offenbach would have relished hearing. As it was played on that first night, with Adèle Isaac in the principal rôles, attended by the prime-minister Jules Ferry and all the political bigwigs, many must have remembered Offenbach's words: 'I have one terrible, invincible vice, that of working all the time. I'm sorry for those people who do not like my music, for I shall certainly die with a tune on the tip of my pen.' As they heard in succession the assertive

Antonia and Dr Miracle in the Carl Rosa *Tales of Hoffmann*

133

Legend of Kleinzach in the prologue, the thrilling Doll Song of Olympia and, of course, the gorgeous Barcarolle, there was no question that Offenbach had died with many tunes to offer, and the audience applauded vociferously. If *The Tales of Hoffmann* is, in retrospect, not the heart and soul of Offenbach, it has gained and deserved critical acclaim and proved to the world that Offenbach could write an immortal opera that could stand by the world's masterpieces in the genre. And there was enough of the old Offenbach in it to confirm that he had not sold his soul to the academics. Herminie, unable to face the ordeal of a public appearance, heard at home that all was going well at the first night and was contented for her dear departed Jacques.

The opera ran for an initial hundred performances at l'Opéra-Comique and during the course of the run and thereafter there were many more alterations made to the score. At some time a mysterious septet was added to the Giulietta scene which is not in the published scores; nor does it seem to be in either Offenbach's or Guirard's style. The fascinating details of the many amendments are detailed by Richard Bonynge in an excellent introduction to the fine modern recording which he directed, with Joan Sutherland playing the three main female rôles (Decca SET545-7), in which he attempted to get as near to the original Offenbach conception as historical research and speculation could take him. Most other recordings and performances have been content with what he describes as the 'unidiomatic' versions.

There was yet another dramatic chapter in the history of the opera to come. Offenbach had decided that l'Opéra-Comique must be its first venue, but Vienna had also awaited eagerly to stage it. As it was, *Les Contes d'Hoffmann* was put on at the Ringtheater on December 7th, 1881 and had a successful first night. On the second evening the theatre was filled to capacity with an expectant audience. Just before the curtain went up a fire broke out and many members of the audience perished in the flames. The theatre being a hotbed of superstition, the opera was considered to have a jinx on it and further productions in Vienna were delayed for nearly two years. For the moment it broke the Offenbach links in the city that had always given him so much encouragement.

The only other 'new' work by Offenbach was *Mam'zelle Moucheron* at the Renaissance theatre on May 10th, 1881. His old colleague, Léo Delibes, completed a fragmentary score from Offenbach scraps and the book was supplied by Eugène Leterrier and Albert Vanloo. Of those nearest and dearest to Offenbach, brother Jules had already passed away and his son Auguste died in 1882 at the age of twenty-two. Herminie survived him by a well-catered-for seven years. Hortense Schneider became a religious and sparse-living recluse and lasted until 1920. Ludovic Halévy left the theatre but continued to encourage young writers until he died in 1908. Henri Meilhac died in 1897 and Hector Crémieux in 1892.

The works of Offenbach continued their vogue throughout the 1880s but by the following decade were gradually pushed aside by the new talents and new fashions that arose. In the days before copyright protection the music of Offenbach was unashamedly pilfered for numerous hotchpot entertainments and ballets, an occupation already much practised in his lifetime in works such as Alfred Thompson's *Columbus* in 1869 and *La Poule aux œufs d'or* at the Alhambra in 1879.

In later years more generally appreciative opportunists took music from his lesser-known works and wove them into new and often enjoyable tapestries. One of the more successful of these was *Der Goldschmied von Toledo*, a two-act opéra-comique first produced at Mannheim in 1919 and seen in London in 1922. Best-known of all, and doing full justice to Offenbach and his posthumous reputation was the ballet *Gaîté Parisienne* which was first produced at Monte Carlo by the Ballets Russes on April 5th, 1938. The music was arranged by Manuel Rosenthal with the help of Jacques Brindejont-Offenbach, grandson 'of the composer, and choreographed by Léonide Massine. It was entirely successful in capturing the wistful gaiety of Offenbach, as it indeed should, as its skilful arrangement incorporated music from *La Vie Parisienne, La Belle Hélène, La Périchole, Orphée aux Enfers* and *Les Contes d'Hoffmann* as well as lesser works. Mention should also be made of some ballets: *Bluebeard* produced by the Ballet Theatre in Mexico City on October 27th, 1941, music arranged by Antal Dorati from *Barbe-Bleu, Les Brigands, La Grande-Duchesse de Gérolstein* and other sources; and *Helen of Troy*, based by Dorati on *La Belle Hélène* and several other operettas, and produced by the Ballet Theatre in Detroit on November 29th, 1942. Offenbach's life has been portrayed in a film *Valse de Paris*, naturally romanticised but tastefully done on the whole and giving interesting glimpses of his lesser-known music. It was made in 1944 and starred Pierre Fresnay as Offenbach and Yvonne Printemps as Hortense Schneider.

The major Offenbach works have enjoyed frequent and regular revival. *Les Contes d'Hoffmann* has continued its career as a standard *opéra-comique* in France and elsewhere. It was a regular item in the Carl Rosa repertoire and was notably conducted by Beecham at Covent Garden in 1910 and 1936. He also directed the soundtrack when the opera was filmed in 1951 with Moira Shearer, Robert Helpmann, Léonide Massine, Frederick Ashton and other notable ballet stars miming the rôles with voices provided by such singers as Monica Sinclair and Owen Brannigan. The principal comedies were notably revived in English by the Sadler's Wells company in the 1960s; later less faithfully by the National Opera

La Poule – a London concoction

135

Company at the Coliseum where the larger stage forced the producers into those very excesses that had tempted Offenbach himself at the Gaîté. Like Rossini, Offenbach has survived musically through his captivating overtures, especially the expanded version of *Orpheus in the Underworld* of which orchestras and audiences never seem to tire. There is good reason to assume that the Can-can from *Orpheus* has remained one of the world's best known and most popular pieces, only rivalled in the Offenbach canon by the Barcarolle from *The Tales of Hoffmann.*

Offenbach has remained well-known, yet, as this book and others will prove, only half-known. Some of his pieces have become hackneyed through over-use, nine-tenths of his work has been lost to view, occasionally to be revived by the enthusiastic amateur or the small altruistic professional company. Sacheverell Sitwell neatly summarised his achievement on behalf of all Offenbach admirers in his book *La Vie Parisienne*:

This composer of more than a hundred operettas could achieve moments, like the 'letter song' [*La Vie Parisienne*], which have the purity, the clean jet of inspiration, of Mozart. This is no audacious comparison to anyone who knows enough Rossini to compare him with Mozart, and enough of Offenbach to think of him as close to the comic genius of Rossini. The *Contes d'Hoffmann* is in vindication of this coupling of their names. And it is more than probable that Mozart, himself, could we have seen it, would prefer this opera to a 'music-drama' that lasts for four evenings and has never a light or lyrical moment.

Reviewing the 1911 production of *Les Contes d'Hoffmann* at l'Opéra-Comique, Emile Vullermoz wrote:

Le maestro des Bouffes n'a pas paru en seul instant deplacé ni depaysé sur cette scène hostile aux arts mineurs. De plus, cette partition est instrumenté avec un tact et une discretion véritablement incomparables; c'est la formule du parfait orchestre d'accompagnement pour un opéra-comique de style: aucune parole ne fut perdue.

What greater praise could there be for any writer of opera?

Coda

. . . But before we can appreciate the elusive, mocking genius of a composer like Offenbach there is a whole cartload of misapprehensions and prejudices, delivered on our doorstep by the Victorian firm Musical Snobs Ltd., which has to be cleared away. If this daunting task is not coped with, in the first place, then a proper understanding of a very special and fascinating talent can never be reached.

Musical criticism has a bad habit of maintaining old prejudices and dogmas for decade after decade. What someone said, and probably said well, in ringing and certain tones, a century ago is still quoted as if it were an immortal truth that has remained unchanged through all the social, material and intellectual turmoil that has affected human life since that time. We may look back a hundred years and garner a grain of comfort from our Victorian ancestors; we may even look back at them with considerable envy and admire their cosy assurance; but we must realise that our minds work on entirely different wavelengths. After all they genuinely admired and were moved by the spirit and sentiments of a song like 'Come into the garden, Maud' (music by Balfe, words by Tennyson) while we, however hard and sincerely we try, cannot help finding it amusing. We have minds that now accept the music of, let us say, Bartók and Stravinsky, with equanimity and even 'old-fashioned' enjoyment; had a Victorian been suddenly exposed to *The Rite of Spring* the shock would surely have killed him.

The blight that affected the Victorian age was seriousness. This is not to say that they didn't have their own brand of humour; but, as a glimpse at the pages of *Punch* will show, even their humour was grave by our standards. Actual frivolity and high spirits were sincerely seen as elements that could not be exhibited by anyone who was to be admitted to the sanctified society of Art. In retrospect, one can understand this attitude in the Victorian mind and we have no right to sneer at it. But what is so astonishing is that these attitudes have remained so firmly entrenched in some thinking today—especially in regard to music. Part of the reason is that music is still something that most people do not understand. It exists on a slightly holier level than religion. Music is, for some reason, particularly prone to intellectual snobbery and much of its mystique remains intact. There is a middle-class pretence that being

137

conversant with what we still refer to as 'serious' music (a frightful and misleading term) is, like voting Conservative, a mark of respectability.

There are signs that the prejudices are at last beginning to crumble even though there are still strong pockets of resistance in the musical press and their followers. There are more people today who don't find it incongruous to like Beethoven alongside Gershwin, Bach alongside Joplin. The obscure, inherited instinct that insists that the 'Letter Song' from *La Périchole* is frivolous, while 'Non più andrai' from *The Marriage of Figaro* is 'serious', does not arise from any visible evidence in the written notes, but simply from association and old prejudice.

It is not that we should try to prove that Mozart and Offenbach have an equal capacity for great music-making – that would be absurd! It is simply that we must clear away a bias that leaves us in awe of Mozart and contemptuous of Offenbach. In the proper frame of mind we could take Mozart a little less seriously and Offenbach a little more seriously and vastly enhance our enjoyment of both.

The two composers, in the same line of business, who suffered mostly from Victorian sanctimoniousness were certainly Sullivan and Offenbach. Both had a tremendous talent for writing light-hearted and witty music and both were slighted because of it. The notorious slur on Sullivan made in the highly respectable pages of Grove's 'Dictionary of Music and Musicians' has been amended in later editions and yet its self-righteous message still has a curious hold on criticism and general appreciation today. Sullivan's meagre entry was rounded off with these apocalyptic words:

May we not fairly ask whether the ability so conspicuous in these operettas is always to be employed on works which from their very nature must be even more fugitive than comedy in general? Surely the time has come when so able and experienced a master of voice, orchestra and stage effect – master, too, of so much genuine sentiment – may apply his gifts to the production of a serious opera on some subject of abiding human or national interest.

At least we can now appreciate the fallacies embedded in that solemn statement – almost one in every loaded word. The frightful insinuation in the use of the words 'ability', 'these operettas' and 'employed' and the incredible suggestion that comedy is a fugitive art. The masterpieces that we would have to throw out of the window on the strength of their indulgence in comedy is beyond belief. Or did the writer simply mean comedy of the Gilbert and Sullivan kind that had the lack of taste to appeal to so wide a public? What would his reaction have been if he could see us today still flocking to hear and enjoy these 'fugitive' pieces? What was the

Sir Arthur Sullivan
(1842-1900)

'genuine' sentiment that he so admired – the ambitious *Golden Legend* or the lugubrious strains of *The Lost Chord*? Or the 'serious' opera *Ivanhoe* which nobody knows nowadays? We need hardly labour the point that 'abiding human or national interest' is firmly accorded to all those frivolous 'operettas' from *Trial by Jury* to *The Gondoliers*. They will never be forgotten and are the motivating reason for our justified re-awakening of interest in some of Sir Arthur's more 'serious' works.

If you realise how besmirched Sullivan's reputation was in those days, in academic circles, we can then realise how low Offenbach's reputation was when a storm of protest was aroused because Sullivan was once described by G. A. Macfarren as 'the English Offenbach'. The G. & S. champions (of which there were many in spite of what was said above) rose in unanimous condemnation of this 'absurd, ill-considered epithet' and Macfarren was verbally hung, drawn and quartered. One defendant wrote:

Offenbach's London obituary

That the learned Professor did not intend it as a compliment to his gifted British contemporary is obvious. By most of us it is accepted in the reverse sense; by many such facetious comparisons are resented as an affront, a slur on Sullivan's fame. There is an unmistakable savour of jealous spleen and ill-natured irony in the phrase 'The English Offenbach'. And it is much to be regretted that Macfarren should have handed the term down to posterity in the pages of the 'Encyclopaedia Britannica'. Musical savants in France have never, so far we know, returned the compliment by calling Offenbach 'The French Sullivan'. They are wiser and more polite across the Channel. Our French friends doubtless recognized the absurdity and questionable taste of linking together the names of two composers so distinct in their musical style and method. But then, it may be remarked, music-lovers in France have been far less prodigal in their praise of Sullivan than we English have been in our admiration of Offenbach. The comparison is entirely uncalled for!

What a tangled web of critical innuendo we face, and from what depths of musical wickedness do we have to salvage Offenbach's reputation. Fortunately, Offenbach's standing has not been irrevocably undermined. In the first place a considerable portion of his theatrical output is still accorded both personal and critical interest. Anyone will whistle for you the Can-can from *Orpheus in the Underworld* or the Barcarolle from *The Tales of Hoffmann*. The critics of today have sufficient appreciation of his talents to recognise that certain recent productions of his work have been tasteless and ill-judged, to recognise what is good Offenbach interpretation and what is not. Increasingly commentators on Sullivan and Johann Strauss acknowledge the debt that both English and Viennese operetta owes to Offenbach. It is likely that Sullivan would not have been quite so boldly entertaining had not the example of Offenbach been before him and there are numerous melodic and instrumental

139

debts to Offenbach in his music. Offenbach was unquestionably the key figure and the most powerful catalyst in the establishment of our popular musical theatre, boldly breaking away from, as well as building on, the operatic past.

As to his artistic abilities, we can fall back on various influential advocates, allowing that they too might be guilty of over-stating their case, as is anyone who writes in the cause of something which has given them lasting enjoyment and which others deride. The appraisal of Friedrich Nietzsche has often been quoted:

If by artistic genius we understand the most consummate freedom within the law, divine ease and facility in overcoming the greatest difficulties, then Offenbach has even more right to the title genius than Wagner has. Wagner is heavy and clumsy; nothing is more foreign to him than the moments of wanton perfection which this clown Offenbach achieves as many as five times, six times, in nearly every one of his buffooneries.

We may well wish that he had not dragged in such an explosive name as Wagner, but the point is well made. Rossini's tactful appraisal of Offenbach as 'the Mozart of the Champs-Elysées' we have to accept gratefully but carefully, as it was made just before Rossini had politely declined an invitation to attend the rehearsal of a French version of his *Il Signor Bruschino* which Offenbach had adapted for the Bouffes-Parisiens as *Don Bruschino*. He wrote: 'I have let you do what you wanted to do, but I have no intention of being your accomplice.' However, in granting permission for the adaption he had said, in a typical ironic vein, that he considered himself lucky to be able to oblige 'the Mozart of the Champs-Elysées'. Even Rossini had to be careful not to damage his artistic reputation, but sneaking regard for Offenbach was always, and not surprisingly, apparent. In a kindly spirit he wrote a delightful parody, a *Petit Caprice* (style of Offenbach) which is now familiar through its orchestrated use in *La Boutique Fantasque,* and another of his *Quelques Riens* is 'à la Offenbach'. He much admired *La Belle Hélène* and enjoyed a private performance of *Lischen et Fritzchen* at his own house. The affinity between the music of the two composers is obvious and Offenbach was plainly a disciple of Rossini; as early as 1848 he had composed a fantasia on the works of the Italian composer.

Equally predictable relations between Offenbach and Wagner were at the other extreme. There was no reason for Offenbach to feel any sympathy for the dark, highly-charged Wagnerian style so remote from his own and he took several opportunities to write mild satires on the German composer. With things being stirred up by such anti-Wagnerian critics as Alfred von Wolzogen and Nietzsche, and Offenbach holding the opinion that Wagner was 'a Gorgon's head which led young composers astray', it was not surprising that Wagner reacted rather sharply, in spite of his known ability to appreciate the works of Hervé and Strauss. A propos of *Orpheus* he declared that Offenbach's music was 'a dung-heap on which all the swine in Europe wallowed' and deplored his cosmopolitan tendencies. After Offenbach's death he relented sufficiently to write in a letter to Felix Motte on May 1st, 1882: 'He can do what the divine Mozart did . . . Offenbach could have been a Mozart.'

Well, how should we look at Offenbach one hundred years after his death with his music still around us hovering in an uneasy limbo between the 'serious' and the 'light'? The interesting, and justifiable, title to offer him is 'founder of operetta' (even though Hervé may deserve a part of the credit), a task which he achieved by having one ear bent to operatic developments from Mozart to Donizetti and one to the earthier music of the cafés and music-halls. Denied access to those temples of art, the opera-houses of Paris, through lacking the genteel refinement of the *opéra-comique* composers, he was forced to set himself up as a commercial enterprise. In coldly assessing terms, if we compare him with Sullivan, he was no less skilled as an orchestrator (Sullivan originally modelled his own orchestration on Offenbach's) but was perhaps more limited in his musical range. Nevertheless his racier creations had a vivacity that Sullivan aped for his finales and rousing choruses; and the patter song was clearly one of Offenbach's creations. Every Offenbach piece we hear seems to have some pre-echo of Sullivan in it somewhere. Oddly, Sullivan always seems less successful in his sentimental numbers where he falls back on the Italianate melodies of the Victorian drawing-room and is rather stiffly and self-consciously supplied with words by the un-romantic Gilbert. It is less widely recognised, under the dazzling influence of the can-cans and other manifestations of *la vie parisienne*, that Offenbach had a supreme ability to write long soaring melodies, particularly in waltz-time (which Sullivan rarely exploited fully), that have the true pathos and tenderness – an example, oft-quoted, is the exquisite Letter Song from *La Périchole*. Offenbach had a distinct disadvantage of working with so many various librettists – whose number may well create a record in the operatic field. His most frequent librettists were all well-established authors, but even Meilhac and Halévy never achieved quite the same literary memorability or unmistakable style of Sullivan's one consistent partner Gilbert, so that, even allowing for unfamiliarity with French, we have to remember Offenbach mainly by his tunes; though there are plenty of good lines and memorable quips in the Meilhac and Halévy librettos. No-one could say that Gilbert's librettos were examples of succinct drama and logic, or were particularly substantial, but they are memorably alive and have literary quality. Offenbach's librettos

A modern *La Périchole*
(1979-80)

are, as we might expect, full of wit (he was himself a tremendously witty man) but 'often shallow and occasionally vulgar'. Sullivan was fortunate in neither needing nor wanting to turn out an incessant flow of works although the cash that came in from the operettas was very useful in helping him keep up an extravagant life-style. His theatrical works might be summed up as eight sure-fire successes, four or five near-hits, and nine or ten misses. Offenbach had about the same number of near-hits and dozens of pot-boilers that remain temporarily forgotten. His achievement has been dissipated by the size of his output. It may not be too far-fetched a comparison to link his name with Mozart once again, in circumstance if not in actual stature, as we find Mozart's works, even those virtually unheard for years, coming back into circulation and establishing him as the most universal composer of all time; meanwhile others fade, apparently even Beethoven. With his instrumental works still completely overlooked and innumerable operettas, highly successful in their day, virtually neglected, apart from commendable attention from amateur enthusiasts, it will need a determined effort to get Offenbach fully back into perspective.

It is to be hoped that, after the tributes in the centenary of his death in 1980, this perspective will gradually be achieved. It was already a far cry from the *Times* obituary (quoted previously) to 1952 when we could take a random dip into a critical magazine and find, for example, a review of a newly released recording of *Orpheus in the Underworld* which starts off in apologetic and admissive vein:

After being wholly captivated by this recorded performance of *Orphée aux Enfers*, I turned up Martin Cooper's *French Music* and found with some relief that he judges *Hélène, La Vie Parisienne* and *The Grand Duchess* as having 'become classics'. Offenbach himself Cooper hits off neatly as 'the last of the court jesters'. Maybe it is the period of his humour and its innate Frenchness which have prevented the successes of the Bouffes-Parisiens Theatre from winning equal popularity here. The one revival of *Orpheus in the Underworld* during my time I missed on 'advice received'; having heard the music now, I regret that abstention, and only wonder why the wonderful score did not at once take London by storm. The fact remains that of Offenbach's works only *Tales of Hoffmann* survive on the stage today, and I feel we miss a great deal through that fact, for the music is not only gay, frothy, charming, and very neat-handed, it is also moving at times, quick in mood and remarkably well constructed. Deft scoring one would expect, though (unless it has been touched up!) the orchestral style is remarkable for its date (1858). Such free vocal line one did not expect, nor such imaginative use of parody and mocking quotation (*Che faro* is most affectionately laughed at!).

By now we have heard sufficient Offenbach, assisted by the gramo-phone as well as many productions, both amateur and professional; to be able to come straight to the point. Remarkably, the first draft of this book was finished the day after a visit to Sadler's Wells to hear *Robinson Crusoé* which has hardly been on a stage, French or otherwise, since its 1867 production. The critic of *The Times* was armed to plunge straight into a sharp (but mainly unfair) review of 'Offenbach's most charming work, halfway between *opéra-bouffe* and opera proper' with a certain knowledge of what was intended and with clear, if personal ideas, on by what margin its revivers had missed the mark.

With *La Belle Hélène* and the other popular operettas at the Coliseum, *Robinson Crusoé* and *Le Papillon* at Sadler's Wells and

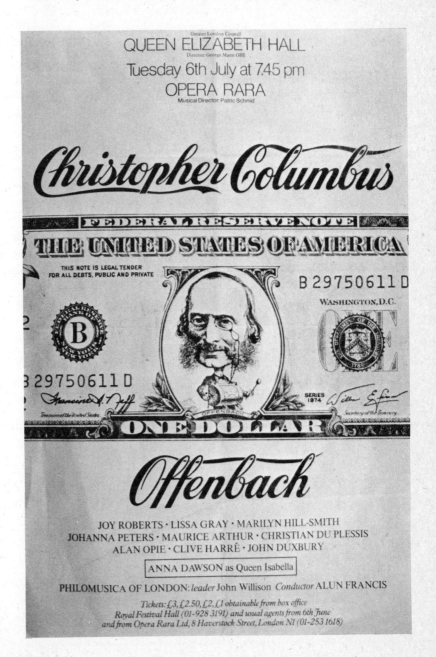

Christopher Columbus, an Offenbachian recreation

Hoffmann back at Covent Garden, there is no need to wonder if Offenbach has survived. All we need for a proper and full appreciation of Offenbach is an age that is not entirely taken up with admiration of the heavily romantic – and there is a trend away from that at the moment – but which enjoys and appreciates those attributes which Albert Wolff felt most conspicuous in Offenbach – namely Wit and Elegance. It is good to feel that musical taste is perceptibly beginning to move that way.

This book arose, as did a similar survey of Scott Joplin, from forty-odd years of devotion to the composer's music. I heard Offenbach whenever I could, after an early jubilant acquaintance with the inevitable can-can, playing his cello music as accompanist to my father and other cellists, and enthusiastically collecting and reading all that I could lay my hands on. If I now wish that I had written it earlier to prove my foresight, I also wish, as one always does, that I could get even nearer to Offenbach the man than any number of second-hand accounts will allow. Alas, Offenbach is one hundred years dead. But nothing will shake my belief that Offenbach's music with its magical mixture of vivacity and tenderness, is unique, unmistakable and undying. But it has still to be generally accepted on its own terms and in proper context. Let us end with some lines that neatly describe Offenbach's works, as Albert de Lasalle used them to preface his account of Les Bouffes-Parisiens:

> *Petit poisson deviendra grand,*
> *Pourvu que Dieu lui prête vie.*
>
> LA FONTAINE

Catalogue of works

(with principal early productions)

Abendwind see *Le Vent du Soir*.

Adventures of an Operatic Troupe, The see *Tromb-al-Cazar*.

Aimons Notre Prochain. Parable in 1 act. w. Méry. Vienna (Theater an der Wien) 18.2.1857. See *Entrez, Messieurs, Mesdames*.

Alcôve, L. Opéra-comique in 1 act. w. Philippe Auguste Alfred Pittaud de Forges & Adolphe de Leuven. Paris (Salle de la Tour d'Auvergne) 24.4.1847. Cologne, 9.1.1849 as *Marielle* oder *Sergeant und Commandant*. Ger. w. C. O. Sternau (Otto Inkermann).

Amour Chanteur, L'. Opérette in 1 act. w. Charles Nuitter & Ernest Lépine. Paris (Bouffes-Parisiens) 5.1.1864.

Apotheker und Der Friseur, Der see *Apothicaire et Perruquier*.

Apothicaire et Perruquier. Opérette in 1 act. w. Elie Frébault. Paris (Bouffes-Parisiens) 17.10.1861. Vienna (Carl) 6.3.1862 as *Der Apotheker und Der Friseur*. Vienna (Franz-Josefs-Kai) 28.6.1862 in French. London (Olympic) 18.12.1879 as *The Barber of Bath*, Eng. w. H. B. Farnie.

Arlequin Barbier. Ballet-Bouffon by Placet, m. Offenbach (as Lange), based on story and music of Rossini's *The Barber of Seville*. Paris (Bouffes-Parisiens) 5.7.1855.

Bagatelle. Opérette in 1 act. w. Hector Crémieux & Ernest Blum. Paris (Bouffes-Parisiens) 21.5.1874.

Banditen, Die see *Les Brigands*.

Barbe-Bleue. Opéra-Bouffe in 3 acts. w. Henri Meilhac & Ludovic Halévy. Paris (Variétés) 5.2.1866. London (Olympic) 2.6.1866 as *Blue Beard Repaired* (1 act version), Eng. w. Henry Bellingham. Vienna (Theater an der Wien) 21.9.1866 as *Blaubart*, Ger. w. Julius Hopp. New York (Francais) 13.7.1868. London (St. James's) 28.6.1869 in French. London (Gaiety) 29.8.1870 and 22.4.1871 as *Blue Beard*, Eng. w. Charles Lamb Kenney. New York (Grand Opera House) 21.12.1870. London (Alhambra) 15.5.1871 ditto. New York (Grand Opera) 19.8.1875 as *Boulette*. London (Avenue) 16.6.1883. London (Comedy) 16.1.1885. Vienna (Carl) 29.1.1887. Vienna (Jantsch) 14.3.1899. Berlin (Komische Oper) 24.9.1963 as *Ritter Blaubart*, Ger. w. Walter Felsenstein & Horst Seeger. p. Heugel, Paris.

Barber of Bath, The see *Apothicaire et Perruquier*.

Barkouf. Opéra-comique in 3 acts. w. Eugène Scribe & Henri Boiseaux. Paris (Opéra-Comique) 24.12.1860 (7).

Ba-ta-clan (originally *Ba-ta-klan*). Chinoiserie musicale in 1 act. w. Ludovic Halévy. Paris (Bouffes-Parisiens) 29.12.1855 (1st production at La Salle Choiseul). London (St. James's) 20.5.1857. Vienna (Carl) 13.10.1860 as *Tschin-Tschin*. Vienna (Franz-Josefs-Kai) 1.11.1860. London (Gallery of Illustration) 14.8.1865 as *Ching Chow Hi*, Eng. w. German Reed & William Brough.

Bavard et Bavarde see *Les Bavards*.

Bavards, Les. Opéra-Bouffe in 2 acts. w. Charles Nuitter, based on Cervantes' 'Los Habladores', Ems. 11.7.1862 as *Bavard et Bavarde*, Paris (Bouffes-Parisiens) 20.2.1863. London (Gaiety) 26.6.1871 in French. Vienna (Carl) 20.1.1896 as *Die Schwatzerin von Saragossa*, Ger. w. Carl Treumann. Paris (Opéra-Comique) 3.5.1924.

Beiden Blinden, Die see *Les Deux Aveugles*.

Belle Hélène, La. Opéra-bouffe in 3 acts. w. Henri Meilhac & Ludovic Halévy. Paris (Variétés) 17.12.1864. Berlin (Friedrich-Wilhelm) 1865. Vienna (Theater an der Wien) 17.3.1865 as *Die Schöne Helena*, Ger. w. F. Zell & Julius Hopp; London (Adelphi) 30.6.1866 as *Helen or Taken from the Greek*, Eng. w. F. C.

Burnand & M. Williams. New York (Francais) 26.3.1868. London (St. James's) 13.7.1868 in French. Vienna (Varietetheater) 4.8.1869 as *Die Schöne Helena*. London (Gaiety) 28.10.1871 as *La Belle Hélène*, Eng. w. Charles Lamb Kenney. London (St. James's) 12.8.1873. London (Alhambra) 16.8.1873, Eng. w. F. C. Burnand (109). Vienna (Carl) 20.4.1886 and 3.12.1893 in French. Paris (Variétés) 20.11.1886 and 9.4.1887. Viennese productions in 1899, 1901 and 1911. London (Adelphi) 30.1.1932 as *Helen*, m. arr. E. W. Korngold, Eng. w. A. P. Herbert. Vienna (Volksoper) 6.6.1932, Ger. w. Egon Freidell. New York (Alvin) 24.4.1944, modern version *Helen Goes to Troy*, m. arr. Erich Wolfgang Korngold. Vienna (Rextheater) 10.5.1946. London (Sadler's Wells) 1958.

Belle Lurette, La, Opéra-bouffe in 3 acts. w. Paul Ferrier & Ludovic Halévy. Paris (Renaissance) 30.10.1880, mus. orch. Léo Delibes. London (Gaiety) 9.7.1881 in French. London (Avenue) 24.3.1883 as *Lurette*, Eng. w. Frank Desprez & Alfred Murray, 1. Henry S. Leigh. [Review in 'The Theatre' May 1, 1883]. Vienna (Janscht) 3.5.1900 as *Die Schöne Lurette*, Ger. w. F. Heidrich & F. Meierfeld. p. Éditions Choudens, Paris.

Bergers, Les. Opéra-comique in 3 acts. w. Hector Crémieux & Philippe Gille. Paris (Bouffes-Parisiens) 11.12.1865. Vienna (Theater an der Wien) 17.2.1866 as *Die Schäfer*, Ger. w. Julius Hopp.

Bergers de Watteau, Les. Divertissement in 1 act by Mathieu & Placet. Paris (Bouffes-Parisiens) 24.6.1856.

Blaubart see *Barbe-Bleue.*

Blind Beggars, The see *Les Deux Aveugles.*

Blue Beard Repaired see *Barbe-Bleue.*

Bohemians, The see *Le Roman Comique.*

Boîte au Lait, La, Opéretta in 4 acts. Cavron w. Eugène Grangé & (Jules Noriac). Paris (Bouffes-Parisiens) 3.11.1876. p. Éditions Choudens, Paris.

Bonne d'Enfants, La. Opérette-Bouffe in 1 act. w. Eugène Bercioux. Paris (Bouffes-Parisiens) 14.10.1856. London (St. James's) 12.6.1857, in French. Vienna (Franz-Josefs-Kai) 1.6.1862 in French. London (Crystal Palace) 22.9.1874 as *Rouge et Noir*, in English. Vienna (Fursttheater) 31.8.1884 as *Die Kindergärtnerin.*

Boulangère a des Ecus, La. Opéra-bouffe in 3 acts. w. Henri Meilhac & Ludovic Halévy. Paris (Variétés) 19.10.1875. Vienna (Carl) 17.2.1877 as *Margot die Millionbäckerin von Paris.* London (Globe) 16.4.1881 as *La Boulangère*, Eng. w. H. B. Farnie. p. Éditions Choudens, Paris.

Boule-de-Neige. Opéra-bouffe in 3 acts. w. Charles Nuitter & Etienne Tréfeu (revised version of *Barkouf*). Paris (Bouffes-Parisiens) 14.12.1871. Vienna (Carl) 3.2.1871 as *Schneeball*, Ger. w. Julius Hopp.

Boulette see *Barbe-Bleue.*

Braconniers, Les. Opéra-bouffe in 3 acts. w. Henri Charles Chivot & Alfred Duru. Paris (Variétés) 29.1.1873. London (St. James's) 21.7.1873 in French. Vienna (Theater an der Wien) 22.11.1873 as *Die Wilderer*, Ger. w. F. Zell & Richard Genée. Berlin (Stadt) 6.11.1958 as *Die Listige Frau*, Ger. w. Jan Möhwald, m. arr, Giudo Masenetz. p. Éditions Choudens, Paris.

Breaking the Spell see *Le Violoneux.*

Brésilien, Le. Vaudeville in 1 act. w. Henri Meilhac & Ludovic Halévy. Paris (Palais-Royal) 9.5.1863. Berlin. 1863 as *Fürst Acapulco*. London (Princess's) May 1873.

Bridge of Sighs, The see *Le Pont des Soupirs.*

Brigands, Les. Opéra-bouffe in 3 acts. w. Henri Meilhac & Ludovic Halévy. Paris (Variétés) 10.12.1869. Vienna (Theater an der Wien) 12.3.1870 as *Die Banditen*, Ger. w. Ernst Dohm. New York (Grand Opera House) 1870/1 season. London (Globe) 22.4.1871 as *Falsacappa*, Eng. w. Henry S. Leigh. London (Lyceum) 1.7.1871 in French. London (St. James's) 1.7.1873 in French. London (Globe) 13.9.1875 as *The Brigands*, Eng. w. Henry S. Leigh. New York (Casino) 9.5.1889 as *The Brigands*, Eng. w. W. S. Gilbert (167). Plymouth (Theatre Royal) 2.9.1889 as *The Brigands*, Eng. W. S. Gilbert. London (Avenue) 16.9.1889, ditto. Paris (Gaité Lyrique) 10.12.1921. Paris (Opéra-Comique) 13.6.1931. p. Colombier, Paris.

146

Carnaval des Revues, Le. Revue. w. Eugène Grangé, Philippe Gille & Ludovic Halévy, Paris (Bouffes-Parisiens) 10.2.1860.

Chanson de Fortunio, La. Opérette in 1 act. w. Hector Crémieux & Ludovic Halévy. Paris (Bouffes-Parisiens) 5.1.1861. Vienna (Franz-Josefs-Kai) 25.6. 1861 in French. Vienna (Franz-Josefs-Kai) 25.4.1861 as *Meister Fortunio und sein Liebeslied*. Berlin (Friedrich-Wilhelmstädtisches) 1861 as *Fortunios Lied*, Ger. w. Ferdinand Gumbert. London (Gaiety) 1.7.1871 in French. Vienna (Carl) 20.7.1871 in French. Vienna (Theater an der Wien) 14.11.1881 in German. London (Royal Academy of Music) 11.12.1907 as *The Magic Melody* (originally intended for production in 1868), Eng. w. Louis H. F. du Terreaux. p. Heugel & Cie, Paris.

Chat du Diable, Le see *Dick Whittington*.

Château à Toto, Le. Opéra-bouffe in 3 acts. w. Henri Meilhac & Ludovic Halévy. Paris (Palais-Royal) 6.5.1868. Vienna (Carl) 1.2.1869 as *Toto*.

Chatte Métamorphosée en Femme, La. Opérette in 1 act. w. Eugène Scribe & Mélesville (Anne Honoré Joseph Duveyrier). Paris (Bouffes-Parisiens) 19.4.1858. Vienna (Franz-Josefs-Kai) 10.6.1861 in French. Vienna (Franz-Josefs-Kai) 25.9.1862 as *Die in Eine Frau Verwandelte Katze*. London (Drury Lane) 23.6.1866 as *La Chatte*.

Ching Chow Hi see *Ba-ta-clan*.

Christopher Columbus. Operetta in 4 acts. Eng. w. Don White. m. arr. from various Offenbach operettas. London (Queen Elizabeth Hall) 6.7.1976. Based on *La Boîte au Lait*.

Cigarette. Operetta. W. G. D'Arcy. London (Globe) 9.9.1876.

Commodore, The see *La Créole*.

Contes d'Hoffmann, Les. Opéra-fantastique in 4 acts. w. Jules Barbier & Michel Carré [credited in 1st edition only]. Score completed and orchestrated by Ernest Guiraud. Paris (Opéra-Comique) 10.2.1881. Vienna (Ringtheater) 7.12.1881 as *Hoffmanns Erzählungen*, Ger. w. Julius Hopp. New York (Fifth Avenue) 16.10.1882. Vienna (Theater an der Wien) 8.6.1883 as *Hoffmann Mesai* in Hungarian. Paris (Renaissance) 7.2.1893. Vienna (Theater an der Wien) 3.10.1901 as *Hoffmanns Erzählungen* (49). Vienna (K. K. Hoftheater) 11.11.1901. Berlin (Komische Oper) 15.11.1905. London (Adelphi) 17.4.1907 in German. Vienna (Kaiserjubiläums) 1.4.1907. London (His Majesty's) 12.5.1910 as *The Tales of Hoffmann*. London (Covent Garden) 5.10.1910. Paris (Salle Favart) 13.11.1911. New York (Metropolitan) 1913. Paris (Opéra-Comique) 2.3.1918. Paris (Opéra-Comique) 3.4.1948. London (Coliseum) 20.8.1970, Eng. w. Colin Graham & Edmund Tracey. p. Editions Choudens, Paris.

Corsaire Noire, Le see *Der Schwarze Korsar*.

Coscoletto ou Le Lazzarone. Opéra-comique in 2 acts. w. Charles Nuitter & Etienne Tréfeu. Ems 11.7.1865. (Theater an der Wien) 5.1.1866. Ger. w. Julius Hopp.

Créole, La. Opéra-comique in 3 acts. w. Albert Millaud, Henri Meilhac & Ludovic Halévy. Paris (Bouffes-Parisiens) 3.11.1875. Vienna (Theater an der Wien) 8.2.1876 as *Die Creolin*. Ger. w. Julius Hopp. Brighton (Theatre Royal) 3.9.1877 as *The Creole!*, Eng. w. Robert Reece & H. B. Farnie. London (Folly) 15.9.1877, ditto. London (Avenue) 10.5.1886 as *The Commodore*, Eng. w. Reece & Farnie. p. Éditions Choudens, Paris.

Creole, The see *La Créole*.

Creolin Die or *Die Kreolin* see *La Créole*.

Criminels Dramatiques, les see *Tromb-al-Cazar*.

Croquefer ou Le Dernier des Paladins. Opéra-bouffe in 1 act. w. Adolphe Jaime & Etienne Tréfeu. Paris (Bouffes-Parisiens) 12.2.1857. London (St. James's) 24.6.1857 in French. Vienna (Franz-Josefs-Kai) 1.6.1862 in French. Vienna (Theater an der Wien) 1.10.1864 in French. Vienna (Theater an der Wien) 1.10.1864 as *Ritter Eisenfrass, Der Letzte der Paladine*. London (Gallery of Illustration) 23.12.1868 as *The Last of the Paladins*, Eng. w. Robert Reece.

Damen von Strand, Die see *Mesdames de la Halle*.

Daphnis et Chloé. Opérette in 1 act. w. Clairville (Louis Francois Nicolaie) & Jules Cordier (E. de Vaulabelle). Paris (Bouffes-Parisiens) 27.3.1860. Vienna (Franz-

Josefs-Kai) 2.3.1861 as *Daphnis und Chloe.* Vienna (K. K. Hoftheater) 6.6.1862 in French. Vienna (Varietetheater) 13.8.1870. Vienna (Komische Oper) 8.12.1874. Vienna (Simpl) 1.7.1945 as *Daphnis und Chloe,* Ger. w. Otto Oegyn & Hans Pflanzer.

Demoiselle en Loterie, Une. Opérette-bouffe in 1 act. Adolphe Jaime & Hector Crémieux. Paris (Bouffes-Parisiens) 27.7.1857. Vienna (Franz-Josefs-Kai) 10.6.1861 as *Une Mademoiselle en Lotterie* and 7.6.1862 in French. Vienna (Theater an der Wien) 15.2.1864 as *Eine Kunstreiterin,* Ger. W. F. Zell. Vienna (Fursttheater) 28.6.1884, ditto.

Deux Aveugles, Les. Bouffonnêrie musicale in 1 act. 2. Jules Moineaux. Paris (Bouffes-Parisiens) 5.7.1855. London (Hanover Square Rooms) 27.6.1856 in French. Vienna (touring company) 1856. London (St. James's) 20.5.1857 in French. Paris (Opéra-Comique) 28.5.1858. Vienna (Franz-Josefs-Kai) 26.5.1863 as *Zwei Arme Blinde.* Vienna (Meidling) 23.9.1863 as *Zwei Arme Blinde.* Vienna (Varietetheater) 22.6.1869 as *Die Beiden Blinden.* As *A Mere Blind,* London (Gaiety) 15.4.1871, Eng. w. Edwin Villiers. London (Gaiety) 15.7.1872 as *The Blind Beggars,* Eng. w. H. B. Farnie. Vienna (Theater an der Wien) 25.12.1872 as *Zwei Arme Blinde.* Vienna (Carl) 11.3.1873 as *Zwei Arme Blinde.* London (Gaiety) 31.8.1874 as *A Mere Blind,* Eng. w. Arthur Clements. London (Opéra-Comique) 21.5.1877, ditto. Paris (Opéra-Comique) 6.11.1900. Vienna (Danzers Orpheum) 2.10.1902 as *Die Beiden Blinden.* London (Ambassadors) 11.5.1914 as *A Mere Blind.* Paris (Opéra-Comique) 12.12.1934 etc.

Deux Pêcheurs, Les. Bouffonérie musicale in 1 act. w. Charles Désiré Dupeuty & Ernest Bourget. Paris (Bouffes-Parisiens) 6.11.1857.

Dick Whittington (published as *Whittington*) Féerie (Ballet-pantomime) in 4 acts. w. Henry Brougham Farnie. London (Alhambra) 26.12.1874. Paris (Chatelet) 19.10.1893 as *Le Chat du Diable.* Fr. w. Charles Nuitter & Etienne Tréfeu.

Diva, La. Opéra-bouffe in 3 acts. w. Henri Meilhac & Ludovic Halévy. Paris (Bouffes-Parisiens) 22.3.1869. Vienna (Theater an der Wien) 21.12.1872 as *Die Theaterprinzessin* (23).

Docteur Ox, Le. Opéra-bouffe in 3 acts. 2. Arnold Mortier & Philippe Gille, based on Jules Verne. Paris (Variétés) 26.1.1877. Vienna (Theater an der Wien) 29.4.1882 as *Doktor Ox.*

Doktor Ox see *Le Docteur Ox.*

Don Quichotte (incomplete work).

Do-re-mi-fa see *La Leçon de Chant.*

Dorothéa see *Jacqueline.*

Dragées du Baptême, Les. Pièce d'occasion in 1 act. w. Charles Desiré Dupeuty & Ernest Bourget. Paris (Bouffes-Parisiens) 15.6.1856.

Dragonette. Opérette-bouffe in 1 act. w. Adolphe Jaime & Eugène Mestépès. Paris (Bouffes-Parisiens) 30.3.1857. London (St. James's) 17.6.1857 in French.

Dramatischen Verbrecher, Die see *Tromb-al-Cazar.*

Drei Küsse des Teufels, Die see *Les Trois Baisers du Diable.*

Dreimal Offenbach, collective title of three Offenbach revivals in 1947.

Drum-Major, The/Drum-Major's Daughter, The see *La Fille du Tambour-Major.*

Duchesse d'Alba, La. Opéra-comique, w. St. Georges (not produced).

Dunanan Apo és Fia ut Azása see *Le Voyage de MM. Dunanan Père et Fils.*

Ehemann vor der Türe, Der see *Le Mari à la Porte.*

Entrez, Messieurs, Mesdames. Prologue w. Francois Joseph Méry & Serviéres (Ludovic Halévy). Paris (Bouffes-Parisiens) 5.7.1855. Adapted as a parable in 1 act as *Aimons Notre Prochain,* Vienna (Theater an der Wien) 18.2.1857, w. Méry.

Eurydice see *Orphée aux Enfers.*

Fair Helen see *La Belle Hélène.*

Falsacappa see *Les Brigands.*

Fantasio. Opéra-comique in 3 acts. w. Paul de Musset, based on book by Alfred de Musset. Paris (Opéra-Comique) 18.1.1872. Vienna (Theater an der Wien) 21.1.1872 as *Fantasio (Der Narr des Herzogs),* Ger. w. Richard Genée & Eduard Mautner.

Farvartne see *Madame Favart.*

Ferj az Aito Elött see *Le Mari à la Porte.*

148

Fifre Enchanté, Le ou Le Soldat Magicien. Opérette in 1 act. w. Charles Nuitter & Etienne Tréfeu. Ems 12.7.1864 as *Le Soldat Magicien.* Paris (Bouffes-Parisiens) 30.9.1868 as *Le Fifre Enchanté.* Vienna (Carl) 4.2.1865 as *Der Regimentszauberer.* London (Gaiety) 25.1.1873 as *The Magic Fife.* Vienna (Redoutensal) 28.9.1947 as *Die Kleine Zauberflöte.*

Fille du Tambour-Major, La. Opéra-comique in 3 acts. w. Henri Charles Chivot & Alfred Duru. Paris (Folies-Dramatiques) 13.12.1879. Vienna (Theater an der Wien) 10.4.1880 as *Die Töchter des Tambours-Majors* or *Die Franzosen in Holland* (7). London (Alhambra) 19.4.1880 as *The Drum-Major's Daughter,* Eng. w. H. B. Farnie. New York (Grau's French Opera) 13.9.1880. London (Coronet) 1.10.1900 as *The Drum-Major,* Eng. w. Fred Bower & W. E. Sprange. London (Shaftesbury) 1.6.1908 in French. p. Éditions Choudens, Paris.

Financier et le Savetier, Le. Opérette-bouffe in 1 act. w. Hector Crémieux, based on La Fontaine. Paris (Bouffes-Parisiens) 23.9.1856. London (St. James's) 21.5.1857, in French. Vienna (Carl) 15.1.1859 as *Schuhflicker und Millionär.* Vienna (Franz-Josefs-Kai) 6.4.1861, ditto. Vienna (Carl) 4.7.1862, in French. [Often titled *Le Savetier et le Financier* as in the La Fontaine original]

Fleurette or *Näherin und Trompeter.* Opérette in 1 act. w. Julius Hopp & F. Zell (Camilio Walzel). Vienna (Carl) 8.3.1872. Paris (Gaité) 2.9.1873. Fr. w. Théodore Barrière. Vienna (Strampfert) 19.12.1873, rev. w. Anton Ascher.

Foire St. Laurent, La. Opéra-bouffe in 3 acts. w. Hector Crémieux & Albert de Saint-Albin. Paris (Folies-Dramatiques) 10.2.1877. Vienna (Theater an der Wien) 7.12.1877 as *Der Jahrmarkt von St. Laurent,* Ger. w. Julius Hopp.

Fortunios Liebeslied/Fortunios Lied see *La Chanson de Fortunio.*

Forty Winks see *La Nuit Blanche.*

Franzosen in Holland, Die see *La Fille du Tambour-Major.*

Friquette. Score sketched out for the Theater an der Wien in 1864 but not completed.

Fürst Acapulco see *Le Brésilien.*

Fürstin Tanagra. Opéra-comique in 3 acts. m. arr. Karl Lafite. w. Oskar Friedmann. Vienna (Volksoper) 1.2.1924.

Gascon, Le. Play in 3 acts by Théodore Barrière. Incidental music by Offenbach. Paris (Gaité) 2.9.1873.

Geneviève de Brabant. Opéra-bouffon in 2 acts. w. Adolphe Jaime & Etienne Tréfeu. Paris (Bouffes-Parisiens) 19.11.1859 (50). Revised in 3 acts, Paris (Ménus Plaisirs) 26.12.1867. new w. Hector Crémieux. Vienna (Theater an der Wien) 9.5.1868 as *Genovefa von Brabant.* Ger. w. Julius Hopp (12). New York (Francais) 22.10.1868. London (Philharmonic, Islington) 11.11.1871, in 2 acts. Eng. w. H. B. Farnie, London (Gaiety) 11.5.1872 and 6.11.1873. New York (Lyceum) 2.11.1874. Revised in 5 acts – Paris (Gaîté) 18.3.1875, w. Grangé, Buguet & Bernard. and m. Patusset. London (Philharmonic) 23.1.1878. London (Alhambra) 16.9.1878. p. Heugel, Paris. Vienna (Franz-Josef-Kaï) 6.4.1861 as *Die Schöner Magelone.*

Genovefa von Brabant see *Geneviève de Brabant.*

Géorgiennes, Les. Opéra-bouffe in 3 acts. w. Jules Moinaux. Paris (Palais-Royal) 16.3.1864. Vienna (Carl) 5.10.1864 as *Die Schönen Weiber von Georgien.* New York (Grand Opera House) 1870/1 season. London (Philharmonic, Islington) 2.10.1875, Eng. w. C. J. S. Wilson. Vienna (Theater an der Wien) 18.11.1877 (2).

Glückliche Insel, Die see *L'Île de Tulipatan.*

Goldschmied von Toledo, Der. Opéra-comique in 2 acts. m. arr. Julius Stern & Alfred Zamara. w. Karl George Zwerenz, based on Hoffmann's story 'Das Fräulein von Scuden'. Mannheim 7.2.1919. Vienna (Volksoper) 20.2.1920. Edinburgh 16.3.1922. London (Covent Garden) 4.5.1922 as *The Goldsmith of Toledo.*

Grand Duchess, The/Grand Duchess of Gerolstein, The see *La Grande-Duchesse de Gérolstein.*

Grande-Duchesse de Gérolstein, La. Opéra-bouffe in 3 acts. w. Henri Meilhac & Ludovic Halévy. Paris (Variétés) 12.4.1867. Vienna (Theater an der Wien) 13.5.1867 as *Die Grossherzögin von Gerolstein,* Ger. w. Julius Hopp. New York (Théâtre Français) 24.9.1867. London (Theatre Royal) 18.11.1867 as *The Grand Duchess of Gerolstein,* Eng. w. Charles Lamb Kenney. Birmingham

(Theatre Royal) 13.4.1868 as *The Grand Duchess*. London (St. James's) 5.5.1868, in French. New York (Pike's Theater) 24.9.1868 (156). Salt Lake City 1.6.1869 [1st opera to be performed there]. London (Astley's) 28.3.1870. London (St. James's) 1871/2. Vienna (Carl) 15.5.1886. New York (Casino) 1887 (145). London (Savoy) 4.12.1897 as *The Grand Duchess*, Eng. w. C. H. E. Brookfield. Vienna (Janschttheater) 17.1.1899. London (Daly's) 29.4.1937, Eng. w. C. P. Robinson, m. arr. Sydney Baynes. Paris (Marigny) 1966. Leipzig (Städtische) 21.2.1968. Ger. w. Otto Schneidereit, m. arr. Herbert Kawan. p. Brandus & Dufour, Paris.

Grossherzögin von Gerolstein, Die see *La Grande-Duchesse de Gérolstein*.

Guide to Paris, A see *La Vie Parisienne*.

Haine, La. Play with music in 5 acts. w. Victorien Sardou. Paris (Gaité) 3.12.1874.

Hannetons, Les. Revue in 3 acts. w. Eugène Grangé & Albert Millaud. Paris (Bouffes-Parisiens) 22.4.1875.

Hanni Weint – Der Hansi Lacht, Die see *Jeanne qui Pleure et Jean qui Rit*.

Happiest Girl in the World, The. Musical comedy. m. Offenbach. w. Fred Saidy, Henry Myers & E. Y. Harburg. New York (Martin Beck) 3.4.1961 (96).

Häuptling Abendwind see *Le Vent du Soir*.

Heimkehr des Odysseus, Die. Opéra-comique in 3 acts. m. arr. Leopold Schmiedt. w. Karl Ettlinger & E. Motz. Vienna (Carl) 23.3.1917.

Helen see *La Belle Hélène*.

Helen or *Taken from the Greek* see *La Belle Hélène*.

Helen goes to Troy see *La Belle Hélène*.

Herr und Madame Dennis see *Monsieur et Madame Denis*.

Herr von Zuckerl, Vater und Sohn see *Le Voyage de MM. Dunanan Père et Fils*.

Hidden Treasure, The see *Le Mariage aux Lanternes*.

Hochzeit bei Laternenschein, Die/Hochzeit unter der Laterne, Die see *Le Mariage aux Lanternes*.

Hoffmann Mesai see *Les Contes d'Hoffmann*.

Hoffmanns Erzählungen see *Les Contes d'Hoffmann*.

Howling Wind see *Vent du Soir*.

Île de Tulipatan, L'. Bouffonérie in 1 act. w. Henri Charles Chivot & Alfred Duru. Paris (Bouffes-Parisiens) 30.9.1868. London (Lyceum) May 1871, in French. London (Opéra Comique) 12.7.1873 as *Kissi-kissi* or *The Pa, the Ma, and the Padishah*, Eng. w. F. C. Burnand. Paris (Cluny) 22.9.1886. Vienna (Carl) 24.1.1889 as *Tulipatan*, Ger. w. Julius Hopp. Vienna (Volksoper) 8.6.1918 as *Die Glückliche Insel*, m. arr. Leopold Schmiedt, w. Oskar Blumthal. Vienna (Redoutensal) 28.9.1947 as *Die Insel Tulitapan*.

Jacqueline. Opérette in 1 act. w. Pol DArcy (Hector Crémieux & Ludovic Halévy). Paris (Bouffes-Parisiens) 14.10.1862. Vienna (Strampfertheater) 12.9.1871 as *Dorothéa*, Ger. w. Ferdinand Ernst. Berlin (Wallner) 1871. Vienna (Theater an der Wien) 28.11.1877.

Jahrmarkt von St. Laurent, Der see *La Foire St. Laurent*.

Jeanne qui Pleure et Jean qui Rit. Opérette in 1 act. w. Hector Crémieux & Phillippe Gille. Ems, 19.7.1864. Paris (Bouffes-Parisiens) 3.11.1865. Vienna (Carl) 4.2.1865 as *Di Hanni Weint – Der Hansi Lacht*, Ger. w. St. Remy (Nuitter & Tréfeu). London (Gaiety) 26.6.1871 (Nuitter & Tréfeu). Vienna (Varietetheater) 10.6.1869. Vienna (Fursttheater) 6.9.1884. Vienna (Theater an der Wien) 3.4.1892.

Jolie Parfumeuse, La. Opéra-comique in 3 acts. w. Hector Crémieux & Ernst Blum. Paris (Renaissance) 29.11.1873. London (Alhambra) 18.5.1874 as *The Pretty Perfumer*, Eng. w. Henry J. Byron. Vienna (Carl) 6.11.1874 as *Schönröschen*, Ger. w. Carl Treumann. London (Royalty) 3.10.1878, Eng. w. Charles Lamb Kenney. In Germany as *Pariser Parfüm*. p. Éditions Choudens, Paris.

Kakadu see *Vert-Vert*.

Kindergärtnerin, Die see *La Bonne d'Enfants*.

Kindsmädchen, Die. Opérette in 1 act. w. Karl Juin. Vienna (Harmonietheater) 2.11.1867.

Kissi-kissi see *L'Île de Tulipatan*.

Kleine Zauberflöte, Die see *Le Fifre Enchanté*.

König Carotte see *Le Roi Carotte*.

König ihres Herzens, Der. Opérette in 3 acts. m. arr. Karl Pauspertl von Drachenthal. w. Wilhelm Sterk. Vienna (Johann Strausstheater) 23.12.1930.

Kunstreiterin, Die see *Une Demoiselle en Loterie*.

Lawful Wife of Rustifum, The see *La Princesse de Trébizonde*.

Leçon de Chant, La. Bouffoniérie in 1 act. w. Ernest Bourget. Paris (Palais Royal) 28.6.1864 Ems, 20.7.1867. Paris (Folies-Marigny) 17.5.1873. London (Gaiety) 21.10.1873 as *Do-re-mi-fa*.

Lischen et Fritzchen. Conversation alsacienne in 1 act. w. Paul Dubois (Paul Boisselot & Charles Nuitter). Ems, 28.7.1863. Paris 15.7.1863. Paris (Bouffes- 2.6.1868, in French. London (Gaiety) 26.7.1869, Eng. w. W. Guernsey. London (Covent Garden) 4.1.1870. p. Brandus & Dufour, Paris.

Listigen Frau, Die see *Die Wilderer*.

Love Apple, The see *Pomme d'Api*.

Love by Lantern Light see *Le Marriage aux Lanternes*.

Luc et Lucette. Opérette in 1 act. w. Pittaud de Forges & Eugène-Germain Roche. Paris (Salle Herz) 2.5.1854.

Lurette see *La Belle Lurette*.

Madame Favart. Opéra-comique in 3 acts. w. Alfred Duru & Henri Chivot. Paris (Folies-Dramatiques) 28.12.1878. Vienna (Theater an der Wien) 7.2.1879, in French (23). London (Strand) 12.4.1879. Eng. w. H. B. Farnie (502). London (Avenue) 11.3.1882, ditto. New York (Fifth Avenue) 23.9.1881. Vienna (Theater an der Wien) 20.6.1883 as *Favartne* (1). London (Avenue) 18.4.1887. London (Criterion) 9.11.1893. Leipzig (Operettertheater) 15.10.1955, Ger. w. Heinrich Voigt, m. arr. Conny Odd. p. Éditions Choudens, Paris.

Madame Herzog see *Madame l'Archiduc*.

Madame l'Archiduc. Opéra-bouffe in 3 acts. w. Albert Millaud (Henri Meilhac) & Ludovic Halévy. Paris (Bouffes-Parisiens) 31.10.1874. New York (Français) 29.12.1874, in English. Vienna (Theater an der Wien) 16.1.1875 as *Madame Herzog (Die Verschwörung zu Montefiascone)*, Ger. w. Julius Hopp. London (Opéra-Comique) 13.1.1876, as *Marietta*, Eng. w. H. B. Farnie. Vienna (Redoutensaal), 21.3.1947. Ger. w. Karl Kraus, p. Éditions Choudens, Paris.

Madame Papillon. Bouffonniérie in 1 act. w. Servières (Ludovic Halévy) Paris. (Bouffes-Parisiens) 1.10.1855.

Madam vom Elixonzo (or *Elizondo*) see *Pépito*.

Mädchen von Elizondo, Das see *Pépito*.

Mademoiselle en Lotterie, Une see *Une Demoiselle en Loterie*.

Magic Fife, The see *Le Fifre Enchanté*.

Magic Melody, The see *La Chanson de Fortunio*.

Magic Violin, The see *Le Violoneux*.

Magpies, The see *Les Bavards*.

Maître Péronilla. Opéra-bouffe in 3 acts. w. MX. (Jacques Offenbach, Charles Nuitter & Paul Ferrier). Paris (Bouffes-Parisiens) 13.3.1878.

Malala! African Extravaganza in 2 acts. (Offenbach's music, arr.). London (Gaiety) 8.4.1871.

Mam'zelle Moucheron. Operette in 1 act. w. Eugène Leterrier & Albert Vanloo. m. ed. Léo Delibes. Paris (Renaissance) 10.5.1881.

Margot, Die Millionbackerin von Paris see *La Boulangère à des Ecus*.

Mari à la Porte, Un. Opérette in 1 act. w. Alfred Delacour (A.C. Lartigue) & Léon Morand. Paris (Bouffes-Parisiens) 22.6.1859. Vienna (Carl) 28.12.1859 as *Der Ehemann vor der Türe*, Ger. w. Carl Treumann. Vienna (Franz-Josefs-Kai) 8.11.1860. Vienna (Franz-Josefs-Kai) 21.6.1861, in French. Vienna (Harmonietheater) 20.5.1866 as *Ferj az Aito Elott* in Hungarian. Vienna (Varietetheater) 1.6.1869, in German. Vienna (Colosseum) 11.10.1871. London (Royalty) December 1872/January 1873, in French. Vienna (Ronachers) 26.6.1880. Vienna (Theater an der Wien) 13.11.1884. London (Fortune) 21.2.1950 as *A Husband on the Mat*, Eng. w. Geoffrey Dunn.

Mariage aux Lanternes, Le. Opérette in 1 act (revised version of *Le Trésor à Mathurin*). w. Jules Dubois (Michel Carré & Léon Battu). Paris (Bouffes-Parisiens) 10.11.1857. Vienna (Carl) 16.10.1858 as *Die Hochzeit bei*

Laternenschein, Ger. w. Carol Treumann. London (Lyceum) 9.5.1860, in French. Vienna (Franz-Josefs-Kai) 21.6.1861, in French. London (New Royalty) 18.1.1862 as *Love by Lantern Light.* London (St. George's Hall) 1.6.1869 as *The Treasure Found by Lantern Light,* Eng. w. Susan Pyne. London (St. James's) 16.10.1869 as *Treasure Trove.* Vienna (Varietetheater) 22.6.1870 as *Die Hochzeit bei Laternenschein.* London (Gaiety) 11.10.1871 as *Paquerette,* Eng. w. H. B. Farnie. Vienna (Ronachers) 12.6.1880. Vienna (Fursttheater) 26.4.1884. Vienna (Theater an der Wien) 18.2.1889 (6). London (Theatre Royal) 7.5.1902 as *Marriage by Lanterns,* Eng. w. Albert H. West. London (80, Paddington Street) 6.10.1915 and 19.10.1916 as *The Hidden Treasure.* Paris (Opéra-Comique) 4.12.1919. Vienna (Redoutensal) 28.9.1947. p. Heugel, Paris.

Marielle see *L'Alcôve.*

Marietta see *Madame l'Archiduc.*

Marocaine, La. Opéra-comique in 3 acts. w. Ernst Blum, Eduard Blau & Raoul Toche. Paris (Bouffes-Parisiens) 13.1.1879.

Martin der Geiger see *Le Violoneux.*

Meister Fortunio und sein Liebeslied see *La Chanson de Fortunio.*

Mere Blind, A see *Les Deux Aveugles.*

Mesdames de la Halle. Opérette-bouffe in 1 act. w. Armand Lapointe. Paris (Bouffes-Parisiens) 3.3.1858. Vienna (Franz-Josefs-Kai) 11.6.1861 as *Madames de la Halle.* Vienna (Franz-Josefs-Kai) 22.2.1862 as *Die Damen von Strand,* Ger. w. Alois Berla. Paris (Théâtre des Arts) 3.4.1913. Paris (Opéra-Comique) 4.5.1940.

Monsieur Choufleuri Restera chez lui. . . Opéra-bouffe in 1 act. w. Saint Remy (Auguste, Duc de Morny), Ernest Lépine, Hector Crémieux & Ludovic Halévy. Paris (Presidence du Corps Legislatif) 31.5.1861. Paris (Bouffes-Parisiens) 14.9.1861. Vienna (Franz-Josefs-Kai) 6.7.1861, in French. Vienna (Franz-Josefs-Kai) 17.10.1861 as *Salon Pitzelberger.* London (St. James's) 14.11.1871, in French. Berlin (Staatsoper) 19.10.1963, Ger. w. Horst Bonnet.

Monsieur et Madame Denis. Opérette in 1 act. w. M. Laurencin (Paul Aimé Chapelle) & Michel Delaporte. Paris (Bouffes-Parisiens) 11.1.1862. Vienna (Franz-Josefs-Kai) 26.4.1862 as *Monsieur und Madame Denis.* Vienna (Franz-Josefs-Kai) 5.6.1862. Vienna (K. K. Hoftheater) 1.1.1881. Vienna (Raimund) 20.3.1881. Vienna (Ronachers) 16.6.1883. Vienna (Theater an der Wien) 11.12.1904 as *Herr und Madame Denis.*

Moucheron see *Mam'zelle Moucheron.*

Nemesis or *Not Wisely, But Too Well.* Extravaganza w. H. B. Farnie. London (Strand) 17.4.1873. m. Offenbach, Hervé, Delibes, Vasseur, Lecocq, Roubillard and Jonas, arr. Fitzgerald.

Nesthäkchen see *Pomme d'Api.*

Nuit Blanche, Une. Opéra-comique in 1 act. w. Edouard Plouvier. Paris (Bouffes-Parisiens) 5.7.1855. London (St. James's) 30.5.1857, in French, Vienna (Stampfertheater) 19.2.1872 as *Der Schmuggler.* London (Haymarket) 2.11.1872 as *Forty Winks,* Eng. w. H. B. Farnie.

Nur ein Walzer see *Tarte à la Creme.*

Onkel Hat's Gesagt see *Pomme d'Api.*

Orphée aux Enfers. Opéra-bouffon in 2 acts. w. Hector Crémieux, based on a German play by Karl Cramer. add. w. Ludovic Halévy. Paris (Bouffes-Parisiens) 21.10.1858 (228). Breslau (Stadttheater) 17.11.1859. Ger. w. Ludovig Kalisch. Prague 31.12.1859 in German. Vienna (Carl) 17.3.1860 as *Orpheus in Der Unterwelt,* Ger. w. Johann Nestroy. Berlin 23.6.1860 in German. Brussels 28.6.1860 in French. Stockholm 13.9.1860 in Swedish. Copenhagen 11.10.1860 in Danish. Vienna (Franz-Josefs-Kai) 16.2.1861 in German. New York, March, 1861 in German. Vienna (Franz-Josefs-Kai) 8.6.1861 in French. Warsaw, 1861 in Polish. St. Petersburg, December 1861 in German. Budapest 28.12.1861 in German. Zurich, May 1862 in German. Amsterdam 1863 in German. Madrid 27.3.1864 in Spanish. Rio de Janeiro 3.2.1865 in French. London (Haymarket) 26.12.1865 as *Orpheus in The Haymarket,* Eng. w. J. R. Planché. Buenos Aires 30.11.1866 in French. Vienna (Theater an der Wien) 5.1.1867 as *Orpheus in der Unterwelt.* Milan, May 1867 in French. New York 17.1.1867 in French. Naples

23.10.1868 in French. Mexico 22.6.1869 in Spanish. London (St. James's) 12.7.1869 in French. Valparaiso 1869 in French. London (Princess's) 20.6.1870 in French. Sydney 1872 in English. London (Surrey Gardens) 3.5.1873 as *Eurydice* (burlesque version), Eng. w. W. F. Vandervell. London (National) 11.10.1873, ditto. Revised version in 4 acts – Paris (Gaîté) 7.2.1874. London (Royalty) 23.12.1876. Eng. w. Alfred Thompson. London (Alhambra) 30.4.1877, Eng. w. Henry S. Leigh (132). Paris (Gaîté) 4.8.1878. Vienna (Carl) 30.1.1892. Vienna (Colosseum) 30.4.1893 in German. Vienna (Carl) 2.12.1893 in French. London (His Majesty's) 20.12.1911 as *Orpheus in The Underground*, Eng. w. Alfred Noyes & Herbert Tree, m. arr. Frederic Norton. London (Sadler's Wells) 1960. p. Heugel et Cie.

Orpheus in Der Underwelt/Orpheus in Hades/Orpheus in The Haymarket/Orpheus in The Underground/Orpheus in the Underworld see *Orphée aux Enfers*.

Oyayayie ou La Reine des Îles. Anthropophagie musicale in 1 act. w. Jules Moinaux. Paris (Folies-Nouvelles) 4.8.1855.

Paimpol et Périnette. Saynète Lyrique in 1 act. w. Pittaud de Forges. Paris (Bouffes-Parisiens) 29.10.1855, originally billed as *Périnette* only. Vienna (Strampferttheater) 11.10.1871 as *Paimpol und Perinette*, Ger. w. Ferdinand Ernst.

Papillon, Le. Ballet in 3 acts. Paris (Opéra) 26.11.1860. London (Sadler's Wells) 19.2.1980.

Paquerette see *Le Mariage aux Lanternes*.

Pariser Leben see *La Vie Parisienne*.

Pariser Parfüm see *La Jolie Parfumeuse*.

Pascal et Chambord. Incidental music to a comedy in 2 acts (melée de chant) by Anicet Bourgeois & Eduard Brisebarre. Paris (Palais-Royal) 2.3.1839. London (St. James's) 26.12.1843.

Pépito. Opéra-comique in 1 act. w. Léon Battu & Jules Moinaux. Paris (Salle Herz) 27.2.1853 Paris (Variétés) 28.10.1853. Paris (Bouffes – Parisiens) 10.3.1856. London (St. James's) 7.5.1857 in French. Berlin 17.7.1858 as *Das Mädchen von Elizondo*, Ger. W. Carl Treumann. Vienna (Carl) 18.12.1859 as *Das Mädchen von Elisonzo*. Vienna (Franz-Josefs-Kai) 14.11.1860.

Périchole, La. Opéra-bouffe in 2 acts. w. Henri Meilhac & Ludovic Halévy. Paris (Variétés) 6.10.1868. New York (Français) 4.1.1869. Vienna (Theater an der Wien) 9.1.1969 as *Perichole, Die Strassensängerin*, Ger. w. Richard Genée. London (Princess's) 27.6.1870 in French. 3 act version – Paris (Variétés) 25.4.1874. London (Royalty) 30.1.1875, Eng. w. Frank Desprez. London (Alhambra) 9.11.1878, Eng. w. Alfred Murray. London (Garrick) 14.9.1897. Leipzig (Operetertheater) 23.2.1960, Ger. w. Henrich Voigt, m. arr. Conny Odd.

Périchole, Die Strassensängerin see *La Périchole*.

Périnette see Paimpol et Périnette.

Perle de l'Adriatique see *Le Voyage de MM. Dunanan Pere et Fils*.

Permission de Dix Heures, La. Opérette in 1 act. w. Mélesville (A. H. J. Duveyrier) & Pierre François Adrien Carmouche. Ems, 9.7.1867. Vienna (Carl) 7.3.1873 as *Urlaub nach Dem Zapfenstreich*. Paris (Renaissance) 4.9.1873.

Petits Prodiges, Les. Folie musicale in 1 act. m. Emil Jonas. Offenbach contributed 'Valse des animaux'. w. Adolphe Jaime & Etienne Tréfeu. Paris (Bouffes-Parisiens) 19.11.1857. Vienna (Franz-Josefs-Kai) 29.6.1861 in French.

Pierrette et Jacquot. Opérette in 1 act. w. Jules Noriac & Philippe Gille. Paris (Bouffes-Parisiens) 13.10.1876.

Pierrot Clown. Pantomime by M. Jackson. Paris (Bouffes-Parisiens) 30.7.1855.

Polichinelle dans Le Monde. Pantomime by Ludovic Halévy & William Busnach. Paris (Bouffes-Parisiens) 19.9.1855.

Pomme d'Api. Opérette in 1 act. w. Ludovic Halévy & William Busnach. Paris (Renaissance) 4.9.1873. London (Gaiety) 24.9.1874 as *The Love Apple*. Vienna (Theater an der Wien) 22.11.1877 as *Nesthäkchen* (3). London (Criterion) 2.8.1892 as *Poor Mignonette*, Eng. w. A. Schade. Lyrics P. Reeve. Produced in Germany as *Onkel Hat's Gesagt*, p. Éditions Choudens, Paris.

Pont des Soupirs, Le. Opéra-bouffe in 2 acts. w. Hector Crémieux & Ludovic Halévy. Paris (Bouffes-Parisiens) 23.3.1861. Vienna (Franz-Josefs-Kai) 15.6.1861 in French. Vienna (Franz-Josefs-Kai) 12.5.1862 as *Die Seufzerbrücke*. 4 act version – Paris (Variétés) 8.5.1868. New York (Edwin's) 1871/2 season. London (St. James's) 16.11.1872 as *The Bridge of Sighs* (3 acts), Eng. w. Henry S. Leigh. Vienna (Carl) 8.2.1873 as *Die Seufzerbrücke*. London (Alhambra) 5.5.1879 as *Venice*, Eng. w. H. B. Farnie. p. Gérard et Cie.

Poor Mignonette see *Pomme d'Api.*

Postillon en Gage, Un. Bouffonerie in 1 act. w. Edouard Plouvier & Jules Adenis, Paris (Bouffes-Parisiens) 9.2.1856.

Poule aux Oeufs d'Or, La. Musical Féerie in 3 acts. Music by Rossini, Hérold, Shield, Offenbach, Lecocq, Gevaert, Planquette, Sullivan, etc. & Jacobi (arr.). w. Dennery & Clairville. Eng. w. Frank Hall. London (Alhambra) 23.12.1878.

Pretty Perfumer, The see *La Jolie Parfumeuse.*

Princesse de Trébizonde, La. Opéra-bouffe in 3 acts. w. Charles Nuitter & Etienne Tréfeu. Baden-Baden 31.7.1869 (2 acts). Paris (Bouffes-Parisiens) 7.12.1869. London (Gaiety) 16.4.1870 as *The Princess of Trebizond*, Eng. w. Charles Lamb Kenney (rev. 1872). London (Lyceum) June 1871, in French. New York (Wallack's) 11.9.1871. Vienna (Carl) 1.2.1873 as *Die Prinzessin von Trapezunt*, Ger. w. Julius Hopp. London (Alhambra) 2.8.1879 as *The Princess of Trebizonde*. Vienna (Theater an der Wien) 17.1.1885. New York (Casino) 5.5.1883 (50) and 1887. Vienna (Jantschttheater) 20.1.1899 etc.

Princess of Trebizond, The see *La Princesse de Trébizonde.*

Prinzessin von Trapezunt, Die see *La Princesse de Trébizonde.*

Psychic Force. Musical sketch in 1 act. London (Gaiety) 2.5.1872 [Mr. J. L. Toole's benefit].

Refrains des Bouffes, Les. Revue in 1 act. Paris (Bouffes-Parisiens) 21.9.1865.

Regimentszauberer, Der see *Le Fifre Enchanté.*

Reise in den Mond, Die or *Die Reise zum Mond* see *Voyage dans la Lune.*

Rêve d'une Nuit d'Été, Le. Saynète in 1 act. w. Etienne Tréfeu. Paris (Bouffes-Parisiens) 30.7.1855.

Rheinnixen, Die. Opera in 3 acts. w. Charles Nuitter. Vienna (K. K. Hofoper) 8.2.1864, Ger. w. Alfred von Wolzogen (6).

Ritter Blaubart see *Barbe-bleue.*

Ritter Eisenfrass, Der. Letzte der Paladine see *Croquefer.*

Robinson Crusoé. Opéra-comique in 3 acts. w. Eugène Cormon & Hector Crémieux, based on Defoe. Paris (Opéra-Comique) 23.11.1867. London (Camden Festival) 1973. London. (Sadler's Wells) 27-31.7.1976. Eng. w. Don White.

Roi Carotte, Le. Opéra-bouffe-féerie in 4 acts. w. Victorien Sardou, based on Hoffmann. Paris (Gaîté) 15.1.1872. London (Alhambra) 3.6.1872, Eng. w. Henry S. Leigh, rev. 2.11.1874. New York (Grand Opera House) 26.8.1872. Vienna (Theater an der Wien) 23.12.1876 as *König Carotte*, Ger. w. Julius Hopp (37).

Roman Comique, Le. Opéra-bouffe in 3 acts. w. Hector Crémieux & Ludovic Halévy. Paris (Bouffes-Parisiens) 10.12.1861. London (Opera-Comique) 24.2.1873 as *The Bohemians: A Romance of Lorraine*, Eng. w. H. B. Farnie (music also drawn from other operettas).

Romance de la Rose, La. Opérette in 1 act. w. Etienne Tréfeu & Jules Prével. Paris (Bouffes-Parisiens) 11.12.1869.

Rose de Saint-Flour, La. Opérette in 1 act. w. Michel Carré. Paris (Bouffes-Parisiens) 12.6.1856. London (St. James's) 12.6.1857 in French. Vienna (Franz-Josefs-Kai) 6.7.1860 as *La Rose de Saint-Fleure* in French. London (Gallery of Illustration) 1.9.1864 as *Too Many Cooks*, Eng. w. Charles Furtado. London (Gaiety) 1.11.1869 as *The Rose of Auvergne* or *Spoiling the Broth*, Eng. w. H. B. Farnie. London (Alhambra) 13.11.1871 as *Spoiling the Broth*. Vienna (Strampfertheater) 19.2.1872. London (Covent Garden) 25.12.1873. London (Cremorne Gardens) 14.6.1875. London (Avenue) 24.12.1889. London (Royal Music Hall, Holborn) 6.7.1890. etc. p. G. Brandus, Dufour et Cie, Paris.

Rose de Saint-Fleure, La see *La Rose de Saint-Flour.*

Rose of Auvergne, The see *La Rose de Saint-Flour.*

Rouge et Noir see *La Bonne d'Enfants.*

Salon Pitzelberger see *Monsieur Choufleury Restera chez lui . . .*

Savetier et le Financier, Le see *Le Financier et le Savetier.*

Savoyarden, Die see *Le 66.*

Schäfer, Die see *Les Bergers.*

Schmuggler, Der see *La Nuit Blanche.*

Schneeball see *Boule de Neige.*

Schöne Helena, Die see *La Belle Hélène.*

Schöne Helena von Heute, Die see *La Belle Hélène.*

Schöne Lurette, Die see *La Belle Lurette.*

Schöne Magelone, Die, see *Geneviève de Brabant.*

Schönen Weiber von Georgien, Die see *Les Georgiennes.*

Schönröschen see *La Jolie Parfumeuse.*

Schuhflicker und Millionar see *Le Savetier et le Financier.*

Schwarze Korsar, Der. Opéra-comique in 3 acts. w. Jacques Offenbach & Richard
Genée. Vienna (Theater an der Wien) 21.9.1872. Rev. in Paris as *Le Corsaire
Noir.*

Schwätzerin von Saragossa, Die see *Les Bavards.*

Seufzerbrücke, Die see *Le Pont des Soupirs.*

Signor Fagotto, Il. Opérette in 1 act. w. Charles Nuitter & Etienne Tréfeu. Ems,
11.7.1863. Paris (Bouffes-Parisiens) 18.1.1864. Vienna (Carl) 11.2.1864 as
Signore Fagotto.

66, Le (Le Soixante-six). Opérette in 1 act. w. Pittaud de Forges & Aimé Laurencin
(Paul Aimé Chapelle). Paris (Bouffes-Parisiens) 31.7.1856. London (St. James's)
16.6.1857 as *Le 66! ou Les Savoyards,* in French. Vienna (Carltheater)
24.11.1859 as *Die Savoyarden,* Ger. w. Karl Treumann, m. arr. Bunder. Vienna
(Franz-Josefs-Kai) 5.12.1860 and 4.6.1862. London (Charing Cross) 1.7.1876 as
66, Eng. w. J. E. Wall. Vienna (Theater an der Wien) 25.11.1905. p. Heugel et
Cie (Ménestrel).

Soldat Magicien, Le see *Le Fifre Enchanté.*

Souper d'Amour – collective title of 3 Offenbach revivals (*Unter Einem Dach von
Paris; Souper bei Sacher; Salon Pitzelberger*) Vienna (Josefstadt) 2.6.1948.

Spoiling the Broth see *La Rose de Saint-Flour.*

Symphonie de l'Avenir, La. Part of *Carnaval des Revues.*

Tales of Hoffmann, The see *Les Contes d'Hoffmann.*

Tarte à la Crème. Valse in 1 act. w. Albert Millaud. Paris (Bouffes-Parisiens)
14.12.1875. In Germany as *Nur ein Walzer.*

Theaterprinzessin, Die see *La Diva.*

Tochter des Tambour-Majors, Die see *La Fille du Tambour-Major.*

Too Many Cooks see *La Rose de Saint-Flour.*

Toto see *Le Chateau à Toto.*

Treasure Found by Lantern Light see *Le Mariage aux Lanternes.*

Treasure Trove see *Le Mariage aux Lanternes.*

Trésor à Mathurin, Le. Opéra-comique in 1 act. w. Léon Battu. Paris (Salle Herz)
12.5.1853. Rewritten as *Le Mariage aux Lanternes.*

Trip to the Moon, A see *Le Voyage dans la Lune.*

Trois Baisers du Diable, Les. Opérette fantastique in 1 act. w. Eugène Mestépès.
Paris (Bouffes-Parisiens) 15.1.1857. Vienna (Harmonietheater) 26.10.1867 as
Die Drei Küsse des Teufels.

Tromb-al-Cazar (Kazar) ou Les Criminels Dramatiques. Bouffonerie musicale in 1
act. w. Charles Desiré Dupeuty & Ernest Bourget. Paris (Bouffes-Parisiens)
3.4.1856. London (Lyceum) May 1860, in French. Vienna (Franz-Josefs-Kai)
19.3.1862 as *Trombalcazar or Die Dramatische Verbrecher.* Vienna (Franz-Josefs-
Kai) 11.6.1862 in French. London (Gaiety) 22.8.1870 as *Trombalcazar* or *The
Adventures of an Operatic Troupe,* Eng. w. C. H. Stephenson. Vienna (Carl)
19.4.1873 etc.

Tschin-Tschin see *Ba-ta-clan.*

Tulipatan see *l'Île de Tulipatan.*

Tyrolienne de l'Avenir. Part of *Carnaval des Revues.*

Urlaub nach dem Zapfenstreich see *La Permission de Dix Heures.*

Venedig in Paris see *Le Voyage de MM. Dunanan Pere et Fils.*

Venice see *Le Pont des Soupirs.*

Vent-du-Soir, ou L'Horrible Festin. Opérette-bouffe in 1 act. w. Philippe Gille. Paris (Bouffes-Parisiens) 16.5.1857. Vienna (Franz-Josefs-Kai) 22.6.1861 as *Der Abendwind.* London (Crystal Palace) 22.9.1874 as *Howling Wind.*

Verlobung bei Laternenschein, Die/Verlobung bei der Laterne, Die see *Le Mariage aux Lanternes.*

Vert-Vert. Opéra-comique in 3 acts. w. Henri Meilhac & Charles Nuitter. Paris (Opéra-Comique) 10.3.1869. Vienna (Carl) 3.2.1870 as *Kakadu.* London (St. James's) 2.5.1874, Eng. w. Henry Herman & Richard Mansell. London (Globe) 26.9.1874, ditto.

Verwandelte Katze, Die (In Eine Frau) see *La Chatte Metamorphosée en Femme.*

Vie Parisienne, La. Opéra-bouffe in 5 acts. w. Henri Meilhac & Ludovic Halévy. Paris (Palais-Royal) 31.10.1866. Vienna (Franz-Josefs-Kai) 31.1.1867 as *Pariser Leben,* Ger. w. Karl Treumann. New York (Français) 29.3.1869. Vienna (Carl) 5.7.1871. London (Holborn) 30.3.1872, Eng. w. F. C. Burnand. Brighton (Royal) 17.9.1883 and London (Avenue) 3.10.1883 as *La Vie* (burlesque version, with music from other sources as well), Eng. w. H. B. Farnie. Vienna (Janscht) 3.12.1898 as *Pariser Leben.* Vienna (Theater an der Wien) 28.10.1911 (43). London (Alhambra) 27.5.1912 as *A Guide to Paris,* Eng. w. George Grossmith. London (Lyric, Hammersmith) 1929, Eng. w. A. P. Herbert m. arr. A. Davis Adams. London (Sadler's Wells) 1961. London (Coliseum) 1968 and 8.7.1974. Paris (Salle Favart) 5.11.1974, m. arr. François Rauber. p. Louis Gregh, Paris.

Violoneux, Le. Légende brétonne in 1 act. w. Eugene Mestêpès & Émile Chevalet. Paris (Bouffes-Parisiens) 30.8.1855. London (St. James's) 7.5.1857, in French. Vienna (Carl) 30.4.1859 as *Die Zaubergeige.* Vienna (Franz-Josefs-Kai) 16.11.1861, Ger. w. Carl Treumann. Vienna (Theater an der Wien) 5.11.1866. Vienna (Varietetheater) 23.5.1868. London (Lyceum) 2.5.1870 as *Breaking the Spell,* Eng. w. H. B. Farnie. London (Cremorne Gardens) 12.7.1875. Paris (Opéra-Comique) 14.12.1901. London (Garrick) 26.4.1904.

Vivandières de la Grande Armée, Les. Pièce d'occasion in 1 act. w. Adolphe Jaime & Pittaud de Forges. Paris (Bouffes-Parisiens) 6.7.1859.

Voyage dans la Lune, Le. Opéra-féerie in 4 acts. w. Albert Vanloo, Eugène Leterrier & Arnold Mortier. Paris (Gaîté) 28.10.1875. London (Alhambra) 15.4.1876, Eng. w. Henry S. Leigh. Vienna (Theater an der Wien) 16.4.1876 as *Die Reise in den Mond,* Ger. w. Julius Hopp. London (Her Majesty's) 26.3.1883 as *A Trip to the Moon,* Eng. w. Henry S. Leigh, [see 'The Theatre', May 1, 1883]. New York (Booth's) 14.3.1877 as *A Trip to the Moon.*

Voyage de MM. Dunanan Père et Fils, Le. Opéra-bouffe in 3 acts. w. Paul Diraudin & Jules Moinaux. Paris (Bouffes-Parisiens) 22.3.1862. Vienna (Franz-Josefs-Kai) 25.6.1862. Vienna (Franz-Josefs-Kai) 21.3.1863 as *Herr von Zuckerl, Vater und Sohn.* Vienna (Harmonietheater) 1.6.1866 in Hungarian as *Dunanan Apo es Fia ut Azasa.* Vienna (Theater an der Wien) 5.9.1903 as *Venedig in Paris.*

Wilderer, Die/Wilddiebe see *Les Braconniers.*

Zaubergeige, Die see *Le Violoneux.*

Zwei Arme Blinde see *Les Deux Aveugles.*

CHRONOLOGY OF STAGE WORKS

(First Paris performance, unless otherwise noted)

Pascal et Chambord (2.3.1839)
L'Alcove (24.4.1847)
Le Trésor à Mathurin (12.5.1853)
Pépito (27.2.1853)
Luc et Lucette (2.5.1854)
Oyayaie (4.8.1855)
Les Deux Aveugles (5.7.1855)
Une nuit blanche (5.7.1855)
Arlequin Barbier (5.7.1855)
Le Rêve d'une Nuit d'été (30.7.1855)

Pierrot Clown (30.7.1855)
Le Violoneux (30.8.1855)
Polichinelle dans le Mond (19.9.1855)
Madame Papillon (3.10.1855)
Paimpol et Périnette (29.10.1855)
Ba-ta-clan (29.12.1855)
Un Postillon en Gage (9.2.1856)
Tromb-al-Cazar (3.4.1856)
La Rose de Saint-Flour (12.6.1856)
Les Dragées du Baptême (15.6.1856)

Les Bergers de Watteau (24.6.1856)
Le 66 (31.7.1856)
Le Savetier et Le Financier (23.9.1856)
La Bonne d'Enfants (14.10.1856)
Les Trois Baisers du Diable (15.1.1857)
Croquefer (12.2.1857)
Dragonette (30.3.1857)
Vent du Soir, (16.5.1857)
Une Demoiselle en Loterie (27.7.1857)
Le Mariage aux Lanternes (10.10.1857)
Les Deux Pêcheurs (13.11.1857)
Mesdames de la Halle (3.3.1858)
La Chatte Metamorphosée (19.4.1858)
Orphée aux Enfers (2 acts) (21.10.1858)
Un Mari à la Porte (22.6.1859)
Les Vivandières de la Grand Armée
   (6.7.1859)
Geneviève de Brabant (2 acts)
   (19.11.1859)
Le Carnaval des Revues (10.2.1860)
Daphnis et Chloé (27.3.1860)
Le Papillon (26.11.1860)
Barkouf (24.12.1860)
La Chanson de Fortunio (5.1.1861)
Le Pont des Soupirs (23.3.1861)
M. Choufleuri Restera chez lui
   (14.9.1861) (private 31.5.1861)
Apothicaire et Perruquier (17.10.1861)
Le Roman Comique (10.12.1861)
M. et MM. Denis (11.1.1862)
Le Voyage de MM. Dunanan Père et Fils
   (22.3.1862)
Jacqueline (14.10.1862)
Les Bavards (20.2.1863)
   (Ems 11.7.1862)
Le Brésilien (9.5.1863)
Lischen et Fritzchen (5.1.1864)
   (Ems 21.7.1863)
L'Amour Chanteur (5.1.1864)
Il Signor Fagotto (18.1.1864)
   Ems 11.7.1863)
Rheinnixen, Die (8.2.1864)
Les Géorgiennes (16.3.1864)
La Belle Hélène (17.12.1864)
Les Refrains des Bouffes (21.9.1865)
Jeanne qui Pleure et Jean qui Rit
   (3.11.1865) (Ems July 1864)
Les Bergers (11.12.1865)
Coscoletto (11.7.1865) (Ems)
La Vie Parisienne (31.10.1866)
Barbe-bleue (5.2.1867)

La Grande-Duchesse de Gérolstein
   (12.4.1867)
Robinson Crusoé (23.11.1867)
Geneviève de Brabant (3 acts)
   (26.12.1867)
Le Chateau à Toto (6.5.1868)
L'Île de Tulipatan (30.9.1868)
Le Fifre Enchanté (30.9.1868)
   (Ems 9.7.1864)
La Périchole (6.10.1868)
Vert-Vert (10.3.1869)
La Diva (22.3.1869)
La Princesse de Trébizonde (7.12.1869)
   (Baden-Baden 31.7.1869)
Les Brigands (10.12.1869)
La Romance de la Rose (11.12.1869)
Boule-de-neige (14.12.1871)
Le Roi Carotte (15.1.1872)
Fantasio (18.1.1872)
Fleurette (8.3.1872)
Der Schwarze Korsar (21.9.1872)(Vienna)
Les Braconniers (29.1.1873)
La Leçon de Chant (17.6.1873)
   (Ems August 1867)
La Permission de 10 Heures (4.9.1873)
   (Ems 9.7.1867)
Pomme d'Api (4.9.1873)
La Jolie Parfumeuse (29.11.1873)
Orphée aux Enfers (4 acts) (7.2.1874)
La Périchole (3 acts) (25.4.1874)
Bagatelle (21.5.1874)
Madame l'Archiduc (31.10.1874)
La Haine (5.12.1874)
Dick Whittington (26.12.1874)(London)
Les Hannetons (22.4.1875)
La Boulangère à des Écus (19.10.1875)
Le Voyage dans la Lune (28.10.1875)
La Créole (3.11.1875)
Tarte à la Crème (14.12.1875)
Pierrette et Jacquot (13.10.1876)
La Boîte au Lait (3.11.1876)
Le Docteur Ox (26.1.1877)
La Foire Saint-Laurent (10.2.1877)
Maître Péronilla (13.3.1878)
Madame Favart (28.12.1878)
La Marocaine (13.1.1879)
La Fille du Tambour-Major
   (13.12.1879)
La Belle Lurette (30.10.1880)
Les Contes d'Hoffmann (10.2.1881)
Mam'zelle Moucheron (10.5.1881)

SONGS AND VOCAL WORKS

Le Sylphe – romance (w. Léon Laube), 1838.
Le Pauvre prisonnier – romance (w. Léon Laube), 1838.
Ronde tyrolienne (w. Charles Catelin), 1838.
Jalousie! – romance dramatique (w. Aimé Gourdin), 1839.
J'aime la rêverie – romance (w. Mme la Baronne de Vaux), 1839.
L'Attente – romance (w. ?), 1840.

L'aveu du Page – romance (w. Edouard Plouvier), 1842.

Six Fables (w. La Fontaine): *Le corbeau et le renard; Le rat de ville et le rat des champs; Le savetier et le financier; Le loup et l'agneau; La laitière et le pot au lait; Le berger et la mer.* 1842.

L'Arabe à son coursier – for bass (w. Reboul), 1843.

La croix de ma mère – chansonette (w. Numa Armand), 1843.

Dors mon enfant – mélodie (w. Numa Armand), 1843.

Doux ménestrel – romance (w. C. Saudeur), 1843.

Rends-moi mon âme – romance dramatique (w. Reboul), 1843.

Virginie au départ – romance dramatique (w. Edouard Plouvier), 1843.

A toi – romance (w. Numa Armand), 1843.

Meunière et fermière – duo bouffe (w. Edouard Plouvier), 1844.

Le Moine bourru ou les Deux poltrons – duo bouffe pour tenor et basse (w. Edouard Plouvier), 1846.

Le Sergent recrutateur (w. Edouard Plouvier), 1846.

La Sortie de bal – romance (w. ?), 1846 in *France musicale.*

Sarah la blonde – séguidille (w. ?), 1846 in *France musicale.*

Les Moissonneurs – choeur d'introduction et Ballade.

Le Langage des Fleurs – six romances (w. Edouard Plouvier), *La branche d'oranger; La rose; Ne m'oubliez pas; La marguerite; L'églantine; La pâquerette.* 1846.

Bürgerwehrlied mit Chorgesang, 1847.

Bleib bei mir – Lied (w. Sternau), 1848.

Im grünen Mai – Lied (w. Sternau), 1848.

Ständchen für Tenor und Männerchor (w. Sternau), 1848.

Leidvolle Liebe (tenor and male choir) (w. Sternau), 1848.

Lebe wohl (tenor and male choir) (w. Sternau), 1848.

Der deutsche Knabe/Das Vaterland – Zwei deutsche Lieder für eine Singstimme (w. H. Hersch), 1848.

Sérénade du torero (w. Theophile Gautier), 1850.

La chanson de Fortunio (w. Alfred de Musset) used in *Le Chandelier,* 1850.

Strophes de Lycisca (w. Auguste Maquet & Jules Lacroix) sung by Mlle. Rachel in *Valéria,* 1851.

Les Voix mystérieuses – six mélodies (à son Altesse Impériale la Princesse Mathilde) – *L'Hiver* (Armand Barthet): *La Chanson de Fortunio* (Alfred de Musset); *Les Saisons* (Jules Barbier); *Ma belle amie est morte* (Theophile Gautier); *La rose foulée* (Charles Poncy): *Barcarolle* (Theophile Gautier). 1852.

Lieder und Gesänge für eine Singstimme mit Begleitung des Pianofortes (Kölne, Schloss): Cathrein was willst du mehr. Frl. Cath. Weyden zugeeignet: *Meine Liebe gleicht dem Bächlein; Leb' wohl; Was fliesset auf dem Felde,* 1853.

Le Décaméron ou La Grotte d'azur – Légênde napolitaine (w. Méry), 1854.

INSTRUMENTAL
(Cello, Piano, etc.)

Divertimento über Schweizerlieder für das Violoncello and Quartet, Op. 1 1833.

Introduction et valse mélancolique pour Violoncelle, Op. 14, 1839.

Rêveries – six mélodies par F. de Flotow et J. Offenbach: *La Harpe Éolienne; Scherzo; Polka de Salon; Chanson d'autrefois; Les Larmes; Rédowa brillante.*

Chants du Soir – pour Piano and Violoncelle par. F. de Flotow & J. Offenbach: *Au bord de la Mer; Souvenir de Bal; La Prière du Soir; La Retraite; Ballade du Pâtre: Danse Norvégienne.* 1839.

Fantasie uber Themas polnischer Lieder fur Violoncelle. 1839.

Grosses Duo über Motive aus der Stummen von Auber (Jakob & Julius Offenbach), 1839.

École du Violoncelle (2 Cellos), Op. 19/21. 1839.

Le Cor des Alpes (Cello solo), Op. 15, 1841.

Caprice sur la Romance de Joseph en Egypte de Méhul (cello) Op. 27, 1843.

Elegie, pour Violoncelle, Op.25. 1844.

Danse bohémienne, pour Violoncelle. 1844.

Chants du Crépuscule, Op. 29 pour Violoncelle et Piano: *Souvenir du bal; Sérénade; le Sylphe, Op. 30.*

Prière et Boléro, Op. 22.

Quatrième mazurka, Op. 26.
    Ballade; Le Retour; L'Adieu: Pas villageois. 1845.
Adagio et Scherzo (4 cellos), 1845.
Le Rendez-vous (Trio), 1846
Sarah la Blonde. Seguidille. 1846.
Marche chinoise, pour le Violoncelle. 1846
Las Campanillas (cello), 1847.
Cours méthodique de Duos pour 2 Violoncelles, Op. 49/54. 1847/8.
Tarantelle – Lied ohne Worte für Violoncelle. 1848.
Militärkonzert für Violoncelle. 1848.
La Course au Traîneau, pour Violoncelle. 1849.
Arie aus 'Les Mariniers galants' (Rameau) for cello. 1851.
Harmonies du Soir, pour Violoncelle, Op. 68. 1852.
Fantaisies faciles Pour Violoncelle: on *'Richard Coeur de Lion'* (Gretry), Op. 69;
    'Richard de Paris' (Boieldieu), Op. 70; *'Le Barbier de Séville'* (Rossini), Op. 71;
    'Le Nozze di Figaro' (Mozart), Op. 72; *'Norma'* (Bellini), Op. 73; *Fantasie facile*
    sur différents motifs (Mompou, etc), Op. 74. 1853.
Mélodies pour Violoncelle seul aus den Opern: 'Parisina', 'Anna Bolena', 'L'Elisir
    d'Amore', 'Beatrice di Tenda'. 1853.
Gaîtés champêtres pour Violoncelle, Op. 75. 1853.
Harmonies des Bois pour Violoncelle, Op. 76; *Le Soir; La Chanson de Berthe; Les*
    Larmes de Jacqueline. 1853.
Oeuvres dansantes pour Piano: Rachel – valse; *Emilie* – polka-mazurka;
    Madeleine – polka-villageoise; *Delphine* – redowa; *Augustine* – schottische des
    Clochettes; *Louise* – valse; *Maria* – polka-mazurka; *Elisa* – polka-Trilby;
    Nathalie – schottische du Tambourin; *Clarisse* – Varsoviana. 1854.

(Orchestral)

Die Jungfrauen – suite de Valses. 1836.
Fleurs d'Hiver – suite de Valses. 1836.
Les Amazones – nouvelle suite de Valses. 1836.
Rebecca – valse sur des Motifs Israélites du XVme siècle. 1837.
Brunes et Blondes – valses. 1837.
Les trois Grâces – suite de Valses. 1838.
Grande Scène espagnole (Cello and String Sextet or Orchestra). 1840.
Hommage à Rossini, grosse Concert-Fantasie (Tell, Moses, etc.). 1843.
Musette, air de danse (Air de Ballet du 17me Siècle) (cello and orchestra) Op. 24 1843.
Grosse Concert-Phantasie. 1843.
Le Sylphe – grosse Konzert-Fantasie für Violoncelle. 1845.
Phantasie für Violoncelle über Themas aus der Nachtwandlerin. 1848.
Concertino pour Violoncelle. 1851.
Fantasie sur 'Robert le Diable' for 7 cellos. 1852.
Entr'actes et Mélodrame for *'Murillo'* (Langlé). 1853.
Zwischenakte for *'Romulus'* (Dumas). 1854.
Le Chanson de ceux qui n'aiment plus. 1859.
Abendblätter – Walzer. 1864.
Les belles Américaines – Valse. 1875.
Le Fleuve d'Or – Valse. 1875.
Pariser Mädchen – Valse. 1875.
Madeleine – Polka.
Postillon – Galop.

(Works planned but not completed)

Le Testament de Sganarelle – Opérette (Nérée-Desarbres & Nuitter).
Féodéa – opéra-comique (Meilhac & Halévy).
La Jeunesse de Don Juan – opérette (Crémieux & Gille).
La Belle Aurore – opérette (for the Viktoria Theater, Berlin).
Le Bourgeois Gentilhomme (for the Théâtre de Porte St. Martin).
Le Zéphir – opérette (Nuitter).
Don Quichotte – opéra-bouffe-féerie (Sardou).
Le Cabaret de Lilas – opérette (Blum & Toché).

159

Bibliography

BOOKS BY OFFENBACH

Offenbach en Amérique: notes d'un musicien en voyage; précédées d'une notice biographique par Albert Wolff. Paris: Calmann-Lévy, March 1877; as *Offenbach in America: Notes of a Travelling Musician with a Biographical Preface by Albert Wolff; translated from advance sheets of the Original Paris Edition.* New York: G. W. Carleton & Co., 1877; as *America and the Americans.* London: William Reeves, 1877: as *Offenbach in Amerika: Reisenotizen eines Musikers* translated Reinhold Scharnke. Berlin: M. Hesses, 1957; as *Orpheus in America: Offenbach's Diary of his Journey to the New World,* translated by Lander MacClintock. Bloomington: Indiana University Press, 1957. London: Hamish Hamilton, 1958.

ARTICLES BY OFFENBACH

'Letter to Hippolyte de Villemessant' in *Le Figaro*, 30.12.1860.

'Une Lettre à M. Bourdin' in *L'Autographe* No. 9, 1.4.1864. p. 75 (autobiographical).

'Giacomo Meyerbeer' in *L'Autographe*, 18.5.1864. p. 97-8.

'Foreword' to 'Les Soirées Parisiennes' by Arnold Mortier, Paris: Dentu 1875.

'Histoire d'une Valse', Paris 1872; *The Theatre* 1.10.1878; *Musical Courier XXXV*, 29.9.1897 (reprinted in *Jacques Offenbach* by Richard A. Northcott, 1917).

'Un Article Inédit: Richard Wagner' in *Paris-Musique,* special issue 1879.

BOOKS ON OFFENBACH AND HIS MUSIC

Les Contemporains: (No. 11) *Auber, Offenbach* by Eugène de Mirecourt. 64p. Paris: Fauré, 1869.

Richard Wagner und Jacob Offenbach: Ein Wort im Harnisch von einem Freunde der Tonkunst. Anonymous. Altona: 1871.

Célébrités dramatiques: Jacques Offenbach by Argus. Paris: Lachaud, 1872.

Offenbach: sa vie et son oeuvre by André Martinet. 299p. Paris: Dentu, 1887.

Jacques Offenbach by Paul Bekker. 224p. Berlin: Marquardt. 1909.

Jacques Offenbach: a Sketch of his Life and a Record of his Operas by Richard A. Northcott. 55p. London: Press Printers, 1917.

Jacques Offenbach edited by Henri de Curzon. Paris: Monde Musicale, 1919. Music.

Offenbach und seine Wiener Schule by Edwin Rieger. 84p. Vienna and Berlin: Wiener literarische Anstalt, 1920.

Offenbach (in the series *Les Maîtres de l'opérette française*) by Louis Schneider. 279 p. Paris: Perrin, 1923.

Jacques Offenbach: Beiträge zu seinem Leben und seinen Werken edited by Kurt Soldan. Berlin: F. A. Günther, 1924. Reprinted in *Die Szene*, XV:1, 1925.

Offenbach: Biographie critique (in the series *Les Musiciens Célèbres*) by René Brancour. 128p. Paris: Laurens, 1929.

Une Heure de Musique avec Offenbach ed. by Louis Schneider. 62p. (including 7 complete songs) Paris: Editions Cosmopolites, 1930.

Jakob Offenbach by Anton Henseler. 496p. Berlin and Schöneberg: Max Hesses, 1930.

Der junge Offenbach by Adolf Hanemann. Berlin: Heidelberg dissertation, 1930.

Der Aufstieg des Kölners Jacques Offenbach: Ein Musikerleben in Bildern by Hans Kristeller. 140 p. Berlin: Schultz. 1931.

La Vie Parisienne: a tribute to Offenbach by Sacheverell Sitwell. 108p. London: Faber & Faber, 1937.

Jacques Offenbach und das Paris seiner Zeit by Siegfried Kracauer. Amsterdam: A. deLange, 1937; as *Jacques Offenbach ou le secret du Second Empire* (translated by Lucienne Astruc) (Preface by Daniel Halévy), Paris: Grasset, 1937; as *Offenbach and the Paris of his Time* (translated by Gwenda David & Eric Mosbacher), 360 p. London: Constable, 1937; as *Orpheus in Paris*, New York, 1938; as *Pariser Leben: Jacques Offenbach und seine Zeit, eine Gesellschaftsbiographie*, Munich: B. List, 1962.

Offenbach, mon Grand-Père by Jacques Brindejont-Offenbach, 309p. Paris: Libraire Plon, 1940; as *Mein Grossvater Offenbach*, Berlin: Henschel, 1967.

Les Contes d'Hoffmann: Étude et Analyse by Raymond Lyon & Louis Saguer. 150p. Paris: Mellotée, 1948.

Cancan and Barcarolle: the Life and Times of Jacques Offenbach by Arthur Moss & Evalyn Marvel. New York: Exposition Press, 1954.

Die Musikalischt Parodie bei Offenbach by Dörffeldt. Frankfurt-am-Main: 1954.

Offenbach: Roi du Second Empire by Alain Decaux. 285p. Paris: Amiot, 1958; as *Offenbach: König des Zweiten Kaiserreichs* (translated by L. Nevinny). Munich: Nymphenburger, 1960; new French edition, Paris: Perin, 1966.

Das Imaginäre Tagebuch des Herrn Jacques Offenbachs by Alphons Silbermann. 456 p. Berlin & Wiesbaden: Bote & Bock, 1960.

Offenbach by Ivan Ivanovich Sollertinskii. Moscow: Gos. Muzykkalnoyeizd-vo, 1962.

Jacques Offenbach by Otto Schneidereit. 88 p. Leipzig: Bibliographisches Institut, 1966.

Jacques Offenbach (Catalogue of the Offenbach archives at the Koln Opernhaus) 36 p. Cologne: 1969.

Jacques Offenbach in Selbstzeugnissen und Bilddokumenten by P. Walter Jacob. 188 p. Hamburg: Rowohlt, 1969. pb.

Offenbach's Songs from the Great Operettas selected and introduced by Antonio de Almeida. 195 p. New York: Dover, 1976. 38 songs from 14 operettas.

Jacques Offenbach by Alexander Faris. 275p. London & Boston: Faber & Faber, 1980.

Jacques Offenbach: a Biography by James Harding. 274p. London: Calder, 1980: New York: Riverrun Press, 1980.

BOOKS WITH CHAPTERS, SECTIONS OR SUBSTANTIAL REFERENCES TO OFFENBACH

Allem, Maurice: *La vie quotidienne sous le Second Empire*. Paris: Hachette, 1948. p. 221-60.

Apthorp, William Foster: *Musicians and Music-Lovers, and Other Essays*. New York: Scribner, 1894. 'Jacques Offenbach', p. 179-99.

Barrault, Jean-Louis, and others: *Le Siècle d'Offenbach*. Paris: 'Cahier xxiv' Julliard, November, 1958.

Bauer, Anton: *150 Jahre Theater an der Wien*. Zurich, Leipzig and Vienna: Amalthea. 1952. Various references.

Bauer, Anton: *Opern und Operette in Wien*. Graz-Koln: Bohlaus, 1955. Listing of Viennese performances including Offenbach.

Bellaigue, Camille: *Études musicales et nouvelles silhouettes de musiciens*. Paris: Delagrave, 1898. p. 415-23.

Bethléem, Louis and others: *Les opéras, les opéras-comiques et le opérettes*. Paris: Revue des Lectures, 1926. p. 388-405.

Bisson, Alexandre Charles Auguste, and others: *Petite encyclopédie musicale*. 2 vols. Paris: Hennuyer, 1881/4. Vol. 2, p. 274-5.

Boas, Robert (ed): *The Decca Book of Opera*. London: Werner Laurie, 1956. p. 295-9.

Bruyas, Florian: *L'Histoire de l'Opérette en France, 1855-1965*. Lyons: Vitte, 1974.

Bruyr, José: *L'Opérette*. Paris: Presses Universitaires, 1962. p. 17-25.

Buguet, Henry: *Histoire Anecdotique des Théâtres de Paris: Bouffes-Parisiens*. Paris: Tresse (Foyers et Coulisses) 1873.

Buguet, Henry: *Gaité II*. Paris: Tresse, 1875.

Charnacé, Guy, Marquis de: *Musique et musiciens*. Paris: Lethielleux, 1874. 2 Vols.

Chouquet, Gustave: *Grove's Dictionary of Music and Musicians*. (ed. Eric Blom) 5th edition. London: Macmillan, 1954. Vol. VI, p. 176-80.

Commettant, Jean Pierre Oscar: *Musique et musiciens*. Paris: Pagnerre, 1862.

D'Almeras, Henri: *La Vie Parisienne sous le Second Empire*. Paris: Michel, 1933. ch. 'Offenbach'.

D'Ariste, Paul: *La Vie et le Monde du Boulevard (1830-1870)*. Paris: Tallandier, 1930. ch. 'Offenbach'.

D'Auriac, Philippe Eugène Jean Marie: *Le Théâtre de la Foire*. Paris: Garnier, 1878. ch. 'Offenbach'.

Davidson, Gladys: *The Barnes Book of the Opera*. New York: Barnes, 1962. p. 152-61 and 875-6.

Davidson, Gladys: *Stories from the Operas*. Philadelphia: Lippincott, 1931. p. 238-46, 714-26 and 1029-30.

De Lasalle, Albert: *Histoire des Bouffes-Parisiens*. Paris: Bourdilliat, 1860.

Dorn, Heinrich Ludwig: *Aus Meinem Leben*. Berlin: Liebelschen Buchhandlung, 1877. Vol. 5 *Ergebnisse aus Erlebnissen* – Jacques Offenbach, p. 80-7.

Drinkrow, John: *The Vintage Operetta Book*. Reading: Osprey, 1972. p. 73-86.

Ehlert, Louis: *Aus der Tonwelt*. Berlin: Behr, 1877. 'Offenbach und das zweite Kaiserreich', p. 37-51; as *From the Tone World* (trans. Helen D. Tretbar). New York: Tretbar, 1885 ('Offenbach and the Second Empire' p. 75-87).

Ewen, David: *The Lighter Classics in Music*. New York: Arco, 1961. 'Jacques Offenbach', p. 222-5.

Ewen, David: *European Light Opera*. New York: Holt, Rinehart & Winston, 1962. p. 14-5, 33-5, 113-5, 180-2, 188-9 and 242-3.

Ewen, David: *Encyclopedia of the Opera*. New York: Hill & Wang, 1963. p. 352-3, 372, 495-6 and 533.

Fabbro, Beniamino dal: *I bidelli del Walhalla. Ottocento maggiore e minore e altri saggi*. Vol. 6 of *Saggi di cultura moderna*. Florence: Parenti, 1954. p. 149-57.

Fétis, François Joseph: *Bibliographie universalle des musiciens et Bibliographie Génerale de la musique*. Paris: Firmin Didot, 1875. p. 354.

Frémiot, Marcel & Alphons Silbermann: *Die Musik in Geschichte und Gegenwart*. Kassel: Bärenreiter, 1961. 'Jacques Offenbach' Vol. IX. p. (columns) 1891-1902.

Gammond, Peter: *Music on Record*, Vol. 4. London: Hutchinson, 1963. 'Jacques Offenbach'. p. 259-62.

Gammond, Peter: *One Man's Music*. London: Wolfe, 1971. 'Jacques Offenbach'. p. 128-9.

Gammond, Peter & Peter Clayton: *A Guide to Popular Music*. London: Phoenix House, 1960. 'Jacques Offenbach. p. 158. As *Dictionary of Popular Music*. New York: Philosophical Library, 1961.

Gammond, Peter: *The Illustrated Encyclopedia of Recorded Opera*. London: Salamander, 1979. p. 140-3.

Gartenberg, Egon: *Johann Strauss*. Pennsylvania and London: Pennsylvania State University Press, 1974. 'French Soufflé'. p. 273-80, etc.

Grove, George: *Dictionary of Music and Musicians*. London: Macmillan 1878/89; 6th edition (ed. Stanley Sadie), 1981.

Grun, Bernard: *Die leichte Muse: Kulturgeschichte der Operette*. Munich: Langen/Muller, 1961. p. 105-34, 158-67, etc.

Halévy, Ludovic: *Notes et Souvenirs 1871-1872*. Paris: Calmann-Lévy, 1888.

Hanslick, Eduard: *Die moderne Oper: Kritiken und Studien*. Berlin: Allgemeiner

Verein für deutsche Literatur, 1889. Vol. III – *Aus dem Opernleben der Gegenwart*. p. 81-90 and 268-90.

Harding, James: *Folies de Paris: the Rise and Fall of French Operetta*. London: Chappell/Elm Tree, 1978. p. 37-86.

Helgar, James (ed.): *Gilbert and Sullivan*. Kansas: University Library, 1971. Meilhac and Halévy – and Gilbert: Comic Converses. p. 91-105.

Hibbert, H. G.: *A Playgoer's Memories*. London: Grant Richards, 1920. 'Opéra Bouffe'. p. 25-32.

Hughes, Gervase: *Composers of Operetta*. London: Macmillan, 1962. New York: St. Martin's Press, 1962. p. 19-56 and 64-82.

Imbert, Charles: *Histoire de la Chanson et de l'opérette*. Lausanne: Recontre, 1967.

Istel, Edgar: *Die Komische Oper*. Stuttgart: Gruniger, 1906. p. 23-6.

Jullien, Adolphe: *Airs variés*. Paris: Charpentier, 1877. 'M. Offenbach critique: sa profession de foi musicale'. p. 347-58.

Kalisch, Ludwig: *Pariser Leben*. Mainz: 1880. 'Jakob Offenbach'.

Kaubisch, Hermann: *Operette*. Berlin: Henschel, 1955. p. 7-27.

Kaufmann, Helen Loeb: *History's 100 Greatest Composers*. New York: Grosset & Dunlap, 1957. p. 97.

Keller, Otto: *Die Operette*. Leipzig, Vienna and New York: Stein, 1926. p. 89-106.

Kobbé, Gustave: *Complete Opera Book*. London: Putnam, 1922; rev. 1954. etc. p. 778-87.

Lubbock, Mark: *The Complete Book of Light Opera*. London: Putnam, 1962. p. 8-63 (synopses).

Mackinlay, Sterling: *Origin and Development of Light Opera*. London: Hutchinson, nd. p. 110-17, etc.

Marks, Edward B.: *They All Had Glamour*. New York: Messner, 1944. 'Jacques Offenbach: Revealing the Can-Can in Opéra-Bouffe'. p. 34-48.

Marsop, Paul: *Musikalische Essays*. Berlin: Hofmann, 1899. 'Offenbach und die wiener Operette'. p. 45-69.

Martin, Jules: *Nos Auteurs et Compositeurs Dramatiques*. Paris: Flammarion, 1897.

McSpadden, Joseph Walker: *Light Opera and Musical Comedy*. New York: Crowell, 1936; 2nd ed. as *Operas and Musical Comedies* 1946; new ed. 1951. p. 53-61.

Mortier, Arnold: *Les Soirées Parisiennes de 1874-1884* (11 Vols) (Foreword to Vol. 1 by Offenbach) Paris: Dentu 1875.

Newman, Ernest: *The Stories of Great Operas*. London: Newnes, issued in monthly parts, 1920s. Part 15 – 'The Tales of Hoffmann'. New York: Knopff, 1928-30 in 3 Vols. Vol. III, p. 236-57.

Northcott, Richard: *Opera Chatter*. London: Novello, 1921. p. 70-88.

Osborne, Charles (ed.): *The Dictionary of Composers*. London: Book Club Associates, 1977. p. 246-50.

Oster, Louis: *Les Opérettes du repertoire courant*. Paris: Editions du Conquistador, 1951. p. 145-7.

Page, Dudley & B. Richardson Billings: *Operas Old and New*. London: Simpkin Marshall, 1929. p. 125.

Parys, Henry-A.: *Histoire Anecdotique de l'Opérette*. Brussels: Editions L'Epoque, 1945. p. 70-7, etc.

Richardson, Joanna: *La Vie Parisienne 1852-1870*. London: Hamish Hamilton, 1971. p. 264-73, etc.

Riemann, Hugo: *Geschichte der Musik seit Beethoven (1800-1900)*. 2 Vols. Berlin and Stuttgart: Spemann, 1901. p. 550-3.

Rohozinski, L. (ed.): *Cinquante Ans de Musique française de 1874 à 1925*. 2 Vols. Paris: Les Editions musicale de la Libraire de France, 1925. 'Cinquante Ans d'Operette' by Jacques Brindejoint Offenbach. Vol 1, p. 199-322.

Saint-Saëns, Charles Camille: *Musical Memories* (Trans. Edwin Gile Rich). Boston: Small Maynard, 1919. p. 253-61.

Salter, Lionel: *The Gramophone Guide to Classical Composers and Recordings*. London: Salamander, 1978. p. 138-9.

Schneidereit, Otto: *Operette von Abraham bis Ziehrer*. Berlin: Henschel, 1969. p. 340-82.

163

Schonberg, Harold C.: *Lives of the Great Composers.* New York: 1970. London: Davis-Poynter, 1971. pb. 1978. p. 304-11, etc.

Scholes, Percy Alfred: *The Oxford Companion to Music.* 9th edition. London: Oxford University Press, 1955. p. 707.

Silbermann, Alphons; *Die Juden in Köln* Cologne; Bachern, 1959. 'Offenbach'. p. 218-236.

Speyer, Edward: *Wilhelm Speyer: der Liederkomponist 1790-1878.* Munich: Drei Masken, 1925. p. 404-6

Smith, Patrick J.: *The Tenth Muse.* London: Gollancz, 1971. p. 291-8, etc.

Vilhemer, Marquis de: *Nouveaux portraits parisiens.* Paris: Libraire Internationale, 1869. p. 93-100, etc.

Wagner, Richard: *Encyklopädie.* ed. Carl Friedrich Glasenapp. 2 Vols. Leipzig: Fri, 1891. Vol. 2, p. 71-1.

Wasielewski, Wilhelm Josef von: *Das Violoncelle und seine Geschichte.* Leipzig: Breitkopf und Härtel, 1911; 3rd ed. 1925. p. 195.

Weckerlin, Jean Baptiste Theodore: *La chanson populaire.* Paris: Firmin-Didot, 1886. p. 97.

Westermeyer, Karl: *Die Operette in Wandel des Zeitgeistes: von Offenbach bis Gegenwart.* Munich & Berlin: Dreimasken, 1931.

Williams, Roger Lawrence: *Gaslight and Shadows – the World of Napoleon III (1851-1870).* New York: Macmillan, 1957. p. 97-115.

Wolff, Albert; *Mémoires d'un parisien.* Paris: Victor-Havard, 1886. *La gloire à Paris*. p. 115-27.

Wolthens, Clemens: *Oper und Operette.* Vienna: Tosa, 1967. p. 179-81, 371-7.

Wurz, Anton: *Operettenführer.* Stuttgart: Reclam, 1952. p. 21-31.

OTHER ITEMS

'Jacques Offenbach d'après des documents inédits' by Martial Ténéo, in *S.I.M. Revue Musicale Mensuelle.* Vol. 7, No. 12, 1911.

'A Bibliography on Jacques Offenbach', by Robert L. Folstein, ed. Stephen Willis in *Current Musicology* No. 12, 1971.

'*Offenbach 1980 Centenary*' (contributions by James Harding, Nigel Gosling, Pierre Comte-Offenbach, Andrew Lamb, Robert Pourvoyeur & Richard Traubner). 48p. London: Offenbach 1980 Committee, 1980.

Index of persons
and productions

Illustrations are indicated in bold type

Printed and bound in Hungary at Kossuth Press
Contractors: I.P.V. Vue Touristique Publishing House Budapest